MEDIUMS, AND SPIRIT-RAPPERS, AND ROARING RADICALS

UNIVERSITY OF ILLINOIS PRESS / URBANA CHICAGO LONDON

Mediums, and Spirit-Rappers, and Roaring Radicals

SPIRITUALISM IN AMERICAN LITERATURE, 1850–1900

Howard Kerr

For Louise, Liz, Cathy, and Sarah, unflagging spirits

CONTENTS

ACKNOWLEDGMENTS

I wish to express my gratitude to those whose assistance made it possible to write this book. To Leon Howard, who thought it worth writing, I owe a lasting and more than scholarly debt for encouragement and counsel. Paul A. Newlin and Charles Vandersee suggested productive lines of investigation. Kermit Vanderbilt replied helpfully to questions about William Dean Howells, and Justin Kaplan supplied the clue which solved the mystery of Mark Twain's encounter with J. V. Mansfield. Mrs. Clinton Ober of Springfield, Massachusetts, tracked down and transcribed articles from the *Springfield Union*. Of special help in obtaining research materials were the staffs of the Harvard College, Princeton University, UCLA, University of Illinois at Chicago Circle, Buffalo and Erie County, Huntington, Watkinson, and Newberry libraries. Martha Banta read an early version of the manuscript and made a number of useful suggestions, and the last three chapters benefited greatly from the comments and queries of James Stronks. To the staff of the University of Illinois Press I am grateful for patience and good advice.

A Faculty Summer Fellowship and a grant from the University of Illinois at Chicago Circle aided the completion of my research, and the University's College of Liberal Arts and Sciences paid for the typing of the manuscript, a task ably performed by Mrs. Audrey Thiel.

A passage from an unpublished letter of William Dean Howells to

Francis Jackson Garrison appears by permission of Professor W. W. Howells, and may not be quoted again without his authorization.

Long ago I was introduced to the complexities of occult consciousness by my late aunt Elizabeth Senz, who was for many years a practicing medium. And to the indebtedness recorded in the dedication, I must add that it was my wife Louise who first detected spiritual mischief in *Huckleberry Finn*.

Howard Kerr

University of Illinois
Chicago Circle

MEDIUMS, AND SPIRIT-RAPPERS, AND ROARING RADICALS

I: "THE EPOCH OF THE RAPPING SPIRITS"[1]

American Spiritualism from 1848 to 1860

I | Spiritualism began in America in 1848. With the reality of reciprocal communication between the living and the spirits of the dead as its basic tenet and demonstration, it has always been a subject of occult curiosity and a steady source of consolation for the bereaved. But although historians have neglected it,[2] during its first three decades on the American scene spiritualism was also both a popular social fad and a vigorous and heterodox religious movement. At its peaks of popularity in the 1850's and 1870's its leaders were favored with celebrity or notoriety. During these periods it attracted national attention (much of it critical) as a nineteenth-century miracle promising religious and even social millennium, and as an empirical demonstration of the soul's immortality in an age of growing doubt. Eventually the movement's entranced mediums furnished

[1] Nathaniel Hawthorne, *The Blithedale Romance and Fanshawe*, Centenary edition, ed. William Charvat et al. (Columbus, Ohio, 1964), p. 198.

[2] An adequate historical treatment of American spiritualism as a religious and social institution remains to be written. A good analysis of twentieth-century spiritualism is George Lawton, *The Drama of Life after Death: A Study of the Spiritualist Religion* (New York, 1932). The best available history of spiritualism in general and of the early American years in particular is Frank Podmore, *Modern Spiritualism: A History and a Criticism* (London, 1902). A rather superficial and aggressively skeptical treatment is Joseph McCabe, *Spiritualism: A Popular History*

| 3

psychologists with dramatic glimpses of the workings of the unconscious mind. Against this background, from James Russell Lowell's
"Unhappy Lot of Mr. Knott" (1851) to Henry James's *Bostonians*
(1886), the spiritualistic movement exercised a distinct and fairly
unified influence on the American literary imagination.

Spiritualism had its obscure birth at Hydesville, in upstate New
York. On the night of March 31, 1848, the mysterious noises which
for some time had disturbed nocturnal peace in the farmhouse of John
D. Fox suddenly began responding to the commands of thirteen-year-
old Margaret Fox and her twelve-year-old sister Kate. When the girls'
distraught mother asked if a spirit were present, the knockings rang
out again. Mrs. Fox summoned the neighbors, who heard the mysterious intelligence affirm (by rapping) that it was the ghost of a
murdered peddler. Forty years later Margaret Fox was to confess that
she and Kate had meant only to tease their superstitious mother by
cracking their toe-joints against the bedstead.[3] But whatever the

---

from 1847 (London, 1920). A good but brief discussion of the movement's social
and religious significance during the 1850's is E. Douglas Branch, *The Sentimental
Years: 1836–1860* (New York, 1934), pp. 366–79. The same material is treated in
anecdotal fashion by Fred Lewis Pattee in *The Feminine Fifties* (New York,
1940). The first and perhaps the only scholarly treatment of spiritualism in the
life of a historically important American, and the only reliable guide to the movement's fortunes during the 1870's, is Richard W. Leopold, *Robert Dale Owen: A
Biography* (Cambridge, Mass., 1940). More recently the origins of spiritualism at
Hydesville and Rochester have been reliably summarized by Rossell Hope Robbins, "The Rochester Rappings," *Dalhousie Review* XLV (Summer 1965), 153–
64. The facts of Margaret Fox's life may be found in the first three and the last
of the fifteen chapters of Earl Wesley Fornell, *The Unhappy Medium: Spiritualism
and the Life of Margaret Fox* (Austin, Tex., 1964). The remainder of the work
is a collection of anecdotes about spiritualism with little attempt at historical
analysis or synthesis; the book is uncritical in its use of sources, and it is marked
by errors in fact and documentation. Whatever problems may arise in interpreting
their claims for the supernatural agencies of spiritualism, the spiritualistic historians
themselves are often better guides to the record of the movement as a human
institution than are McCabe, Pattee, and Fornell. The best of these spiritualistic
works are Eliab Wilkinson Capron, *Modern Spiritualism: Its Facts and Fanaticisms, Its Consistencies and Contradictions* (Boston, 1855), and Emma Hardinge
Britten, *Modern American Spiritualism: A Twenty Years' Record of the Communion between Earth and the World of Spirits* (New York, 1870).
[3] Reuben Briggs Davenport, *The Death-Blow to Spiritualism, Being the True
Story of the Fox Sisters as revealed by Authority of Margaret Fox Kane and Catherine Fox Jencken* (New York, 1897), pp. 84, 90.

causes of the Hydesville disturbances, within two weeks depositions testifying to their supernatural origin were recorded for inclusion in a pamphlet about the "Mysterious Noises."[4]

The noises might have remained a local curiosity had not an older sister, Leah Fox Fish, taken the girls to her home in Rochester. There the spirits began to communicate through a "spiritual telegraph" by rapping at appropriate intervals as the Foxes called out the letters of the alphabet. Soon the Rochester rappings took on a prophetic tone as the girls were instructed to announce to the world "the dawn of a new era"[5] of spirit communication. Attacks from press and clergy brought defenders to their side. By the end of 1848 all three Fox sisters were able to take up spirit-rapping as a profession, and the movement was underway.

During the following decade the spirits characteristically "manifested" themselves in the "séance" presided over by a "medium" whose "magnetism" elicited intelligible responses to questions asked of the spirits. These responses took either "physical" or "psychical" form. Physical phenomena included such palpable occurrences as alphabetical rappings, movements in the medium's table ("table-tipping"), and music played on accordion and guitar by unseen hands. Ostensibly the medium lent only her magnetic presence to the production of these manifestations. But the psychical phenomena were revealed directly through her "organism" while she was in a trance. They included clairvoyant visions, messages dictated by spirits controlling the medium's hand and pen ("spirit-writing"), and utterances by spirits utilizing her voice ("trance-speaking"). There were myriad other mediumistic gifts, but these were the standard modes of spirit communication during the 1850's.

Spiritualism thus united two previously separate strands of occult history. The physical phenomena made intelligible and benevolent the mischievous poltergeist who traditionally annoyed families by making noises and moving or breaking household objects. The psychical phenomena, on the other hand, were refinements of mesmerism, which

[4] E. E. Lewis, *A Report of the Mysterious Noises Heard in the House of Mr. John D. Fox* (Canandaigua, N.Y., 1848). This pamphlet is evidently no longer extant.
[5] William G. Langworthy Taylor, *Katie Fox, Epochmaking Medium, and the Making of the Fox-Taylor Record* (New York, 1933), p. 54.

had enjoyed some popularity during the 1830's and 1840's as a pseudo-science and parlor amusement. The early nineteenth-century's version of hypnosis, mesmerism was predicated on the existence of a universal magnetic fluid, which if activated by a "positive" mesmerist would induce trance in a "negative" clairvoyant. In public exhibitions the professional mesmerist magnetized his clairvoyant maiden, who then obeyed his unspoken will or, in the manner of Nathaniel Hawthorne's Veiled Lady, described trance journeys even to spiritland. Spiritualism incorporated the concepts and vocabulary of mesmerism as a scientific rationale for the medium's trance and for séance phenomena, the difference being that the spirits rather than the mesmerist now activated the magnetic fluid. Andrew Jackson Davis, the young Poughkeepsie seer whose clairvoyant prophecies had already generated a school of Harmonial Philosophy, was quick to see that the Foxes were fulfilling his recent prediction that communication between man and spirit would soon be dramatically demonstrated. Davis became an important theorist of spiritualism, and his followers edited its early journals.[6]

In the spring of 1850 residents of New York City were made curious by newspaper stories about the Rochester rappings and about alphabetical communications combined with spectacular poltergeist mischief in the house of Reverend Eliakim Phelps of Stratford, Connecticut (the "Stratford Rappings"), which Andrew Jackson Davis had pronounced spiritual in origin.[7] When Leah Fish brought her sisters to the city in June, therefore, crowds flocked to their thrice daily public séances at Barnum's Hotel. Never a believer himself, Horace Greeley entertained the sisters in his home, and he consistently defended their integrity in his *Tribune* while his wife tried to get in touch with her dead son, "Pickie."[8]

[6] Podmore, I, 25–43, 154–76, 202–4.
[7] Ibid., pp. 194–201; "Those Rochester 'Rappings,'" *New York Tribune*, March 6, 1850, p. 1; "The Rochester 'Rappings,'" *New York Tribune*, April 10, 1850, p. 3; "More 'Rappings'—in Connecticut," *New York Tribune*, April 22, 1850, p. 4; "The Rochester Rappings—Letter from Mr. Munn," *New York Tribune*, April 26, 1850, p. 6; "More about the 'Rapping,'" *New York Tribune*, April 27, 1850, p. 6.
[8] Fornell, p. 25; "An Hour with 'the Spirits,'" *New York Tribune*, June 5, 1850, p. 1; [George Ripley,] "An Evening with the Spirits," *New York Tribune*, June 8, 1850, p. 4; Horace Greeley, *Recollections of a Busy Life* (New York, 1868), pp. 234–41.

Soon private sittings for small parties were a fashionable amusement. Nathaniel Parker Willis wrote in his *Home Journal* of a "Post-Mortuum Soiree"[9] at the home of Rufus Griswold. Other guests included William Cullen Bryant, James Fenimore Cooper, George Bancroft, and George Ripley (once of Brook Farm and now Greeley's literary editor). After some false starts the spirit correctly knocked fifty times when asked how long ago Cooper's sister had died, and rightly guessed the cause of death as a fall from a horse. (Such "test questions" were typical.) Willis felt rappings jar the furniture. And although he jested that a Fulton or a Morse might put "ghost power into harness," he willingly conceded—perhaps in the punning manner of Mercutio—that the rappings warranted "grave attention."[10]

Others were less favorably impressed, finding their dead relatives forgetful of basic autobiographical data and observing that famous spirits often seemed to have changed their earthly views. One reporter noted, for instance, that John C. Calhoun rapped out an endorsement of abolition. The same skeptic thought that the rappings came from beneath the girls' feet.[11] But suspicions of fraud were not followed by proof, and when the Fox sisters left New York in August Greeley bade them farewell in the *Tribune*. Early the next year a committee of Buffalo physicians accused them more specifically of cracking their knee joints to produce the mysterious noises, and a relative of the Fox family said that Kate had taught her how to tell from the faces of her sitters which letter of the alphabet deserved a snap of the toe joints. But such charges did nothing to diminish the girls' popularity.[12]

When the Fox sisters returned to New York late in 1851, their prophetic mission was largely done. The new dispensation had spread from Maine to Washington, and through Ohio into the West. Rapping "epidemics" revealed mediumistic talents in young women throughout the land. William Dean Howells was to remember that in the Ohio town of his youth spiritualism was "rife in every second house in the village, with manifestations by rappings, table-tippings, and oral and written messages from another world through psychics

---

[9] N. P. Willis, *The Rag-Bag* (New York, 1855), pp. 185–94.
[10] Ibid., pp. 192–94.
[11] "To All Our Readers and Correspondents," *Holden's Dollar Magazine* VI (September 1850), 573.
[12] Podmore, I, 183–87.

of either sex, but oftenest the young girls one met in the dances and sleigh-rides."[13] Societies of believers sprang up in the cities, mediums and lecturers for the cause were soon traveling a regular circuit, and by 1855 a writer for the *North American Review* counted a new book every week dealing with the subject.[14] These developments were noted with humor or alarm in the secular press and reported at length in such spiritualist journals as the *Spiritual Telegraph, Light from the Spirit World,* and *Disclosures from the Interior and Superior Care for Mortals.*

The Fox girls suffered severe disappointments as the decade went by. Alphabetical rappings alone no longer interested the public after a time, and as mediums the girls were eventually forced to compete with others just as competent in eliciting marvelous phenomena. Both Margaret and Kate, moreover, chafed under Leah's strong managerial hand. And when Arctic explorer Elisha Kent Kane died in 1856 be-before he could marry Margaret after a half-secret courtship of almost three years, she abandoned her profession (which Kane had hated) and two years later became a Roman Catholic. Claiming to be "Margaret Fox Kane" by virtue of a common-law declaration by Kane, she thereafter drifted in and out of spiritualism, always resentful of Leah and suffering (with Kate) from chronic intemperance, until her death five years after her recantation of 1888.[15]

Throughout the 1850's, however, believers honored the girls as the founders of their movement and cited Hydesville and Rochester as the birthplace of a new religion. In addition, the girls and their séances were instrumental in making believers of such relatively eminent men as Judge John Worth Edmonds of the New York Supreme Court and elderly scientist and inventor Robert Hare. So well known were the sisters that Horace Greeley had to mention "Miss Fox" only once in an 1855 editorial admonishing the rest of the metropolitan press to

[13] William Dean Howells, *Years of My Youth* (New York, 1916), p. 106.
[14] [A. P. Peabody,] "Modern Necromancy," *North American Review* LXXX (April 1855), 512.
[15] [Margaret Fox,] *Memoir and the Love-Life of Doctor Kane: Containing the Correspondence, and a History of the Acquaintance, Engagement and Secret Marriage between Elisha K. Kane and Margaret Fox* (New York, 1866); Fornell, pp. 40–60, 174–81.

stop gossiping about Margaret and Elisha Kent Kane.[16] And journalistic humorists needed only to refer to "the three young sorceresses,"[17] or to "the Foxes" and "the Hares,"[18] or (in a stanza of doggerel) to "this wondrous farce of FOX and GOOSE."[19] Despite their vocational and personal problems the Fox sisters were for believer and critic alike the public symbols of the movement they had originated.

II | How large the movement was during these years cannot be precisely determined, nor can deeply committed believers be statistically separated from the merely curious. Undoubtedly the spiritualists exaggerated in claiming millions of adherents.[20] (They also erred in representing as converts men who had taken a passing interest in their manifestations. Conan Doyle revived an old legend when he wrote that James Fenimore Cooper had said on his deathbed, "Bless the Fox sisters for the peace which I now feel!")[21] Yet some of the movement's serious critics, alarmed at its growth, accepted such figures.[22] And historian E. Douglas Branch has estimated that in the 1850's one million of the nation's twenty-five million people owed "allegiance" to the spiritualistic "faith"[23]—a reasonable figure, so long as "allegiance" to the "faith" is taken simply to mean belief in the authenticity of séance communications.

The rise of this faith to such proportions was in part an extension into religious affairs of popular ideas of technological progress and "scientific" miracle. Thus it was that the mechanics of spirit communication were explained by the pseudoscientific concepts of mesmerism, that the innovation of alphabetical rappings was compared to the invention of the telegraph, and that the title of the movement's most important journal was the *Spiritual Telegraph*. Credit for orig-

[16] Ibid., pp. 53–54.
[17] "Modern Sorcerers," *Knickerbocker* XLIII (February 1854), 171.
[18] "Table-Turning in France," *Harper's* XIV (May 1857), 767–72.
[19] "An Apology for Vagrant Spirits," *Knickerbocker* XL (November 1852), 385.
[20] John Worth Edmonds and George T. Dexter, *Spiritualism*, I (New York, 1853), p. 37; "Modern Necromancy," p. 512; Robert Dale Owen, *Footfalls on the Boundary of Another World* (Philadelphia, 1860), p. 37n; Podmore, I, 303.
[21] Arthur Conan Doyle, *Our American Adventure* (New York, 1923), p. 143.
[22] "Modern Necromancy," p. 512; Podmore, I, 303.
[23] Branch, *The Sentimental Years*, p. 378.

inating the rappings was given to the most loquacious of famous spirits, Benjamin Franklin, who was still serving mankind as scientist and Postmaster General.[24] For some believers, moreover, the spirit world was merely a newly discovered and higher stage of evolution, the spirit body a form of matter too ethereal for living men to perceive.[25]

According to the spirits, man passed at death into a region of hierarchical spheres, his condition "superior" to its earthly state but his character and essential identity unchanged. Beginning in the lowest sphere, he "developed" or "progressed" upward on a spiral path toward a distant (usually seventh) sphere. There was neither redemption nor punishment in the spheres; "undeveloped" spirits simply took longer to ascend. This picture of immortality seems to have originated in the ideas of Emmanuel Swedenborg—not as they were interpreted by either the Swedenborgian cult or Ralph Waldo Emerson, but as they were popularized and democratized during the 1840's by the Universalist ministers and prophetic mesmerists and clairvoyants who furnished spiritualism with its first theologians.[26] No doubt John Humphrey Noyes was guilty of satiric exaggeration when he said that spiritualism was nothing but "Swedenborgianism Americanized."[27] But although the average professional medium or consolation-seeking believer may have had no direct knowledge of the Swedish seer's writings, the spirits they heard in their séances and the accounts of the afterlife they read in the spiritualist press often talked of the evolutionary progression through the spheres. And the preservation of the individual's identity was extended to take in his family relationships and friendships.[28]

Whether speaking of the progress of the soul or of the advance of science, spirits and spiritualists adopted the tone of millennial expectancy already familiar in the various apocalyptic and utopian move-

[24] Andrew Jackson Davis, *The Philosophy of Spiritual Intercourse: Being an Explanation of Modern Mysteries* (New York, 1851), pp. 78–81; "Literature and Logic of 'The Interior,'" *National Magazine* I (October 1852), 350.

[25] Capron, pp. 30–31; Podmore, I, 301–2.

[26] Podmore, I, 14–16, 166–67, 172, 225–26, 301.

[27] John Humphrey Noyes, *History of American Socialisms* (Philadelphia, 1870), p. 539.

[28] "Literature and Logic of 'The Interior,'" pp. 349–58; Edmonds and Dexter, *Spiritualism*, I, 46–47.

ments of the 1840's. The Fox sisters were instructed to awaken the world to "the dawn of a new era," and believers thought that the fact that their century had been singled out for enlightenment indicated that the material and spiritual realms were drawing ever closer together. Each new demonstration of this proximity was expected to be more dramatic than the last. (In the 1870's the demand for spirits one could see and talk to in the flesh was finally to be satisfied.)

The religious implication of this millennial impulse was that men no longer needed to depend on church and clergy and scripture for proof of the soul's immortality. For the social reformers who flocked to the new cause, spiritualism also seemed to indicate that the spirits wanted to make themselves felt in earthly affairs and would, in fact, lead mankind to social regeneration. Residents of some of the utopian communities of the time took up spiritualism; advocates of socialism, abolition, women's rights, and free love received angelic sanction for their programs; there were even a few plans for the reorganization of society along spirit-dictated lines.[29] Until it subsided in the 1870's this radical tendency was one of the features which distinguished American from British and Continental spiritualism. It also irritated many of the journalistic, clerical, and literary opponents of the movement. Probably it was more typical of lecturers and editors than of the ordinary medium or believer. Yet William Dean Howells was to note the connection between radicalism and spiritualism among the transplanted Yankees he remembered from his youth in the Western Reserve:

> They were radical in every way, and hospitable to novelty of all kinds. I imagine that they tested more new religions and new patents than have ever been heard of in less inquiring communities. When we first came among them they had lately been swept by the fires of spiritualism. . . . They were ready for any sort of millennium, religious or industrial, that should arrive.[30]

Whatever the social implications of spiritualism, so far as Christian orthodoxy was concerned even an undoctrinal belief that at a séance one could hear a dead relative rapping out words he might have spoken

---

[29] Podmore, I, 208–16, 229–30, 291–94.
[30] William Dean Howells, *Impressions and Experiences* (New York, 1896), p. 21.

in life was distinctly heretical. For through such palpable occurrences the movement's message of hope or consolation was that the pleasant immortality containing all the dead and awaiting all the living could be empirically verified. And whether it offered an alternative to the possible wrath of a Calvinistic God, or to loss of identity in the impersonal heaven of rationalistic faiths and in the transcendental Over-Soul, or to agonies of doubt in an age of increasing skepticism, this empirical demonstration was the substance of spiritualism's appeal as a religious faith.

The strength of this appeal was illustrated by the spiritualistic conversion and writings of Judge John Worth Edmonds of the Supreme Court of New York. Grieving over his wife's death, Edmonds was solaced in 1851 by the evidence of immortality he received from séances conducted by Margaret Fox and from spontaneous rappings in his own bedroom. An experienced politician as well as jurist, he now devoted his life to the leadership of Manhattan spiritualism. Resigning from his newly appointed seat on the New York Court of Appeals in 1853 because of newspaper attacks which suggested that his religious views might impair his judicial opinions, he published in the same year the first volume of *Spiritualism*,[31] a collection of the séance communications which he and a physician named George Dexter had received from such spirits as Bacon, Franklin, "Sweedenborg" [sic],[32] and Mrs. Edmonds. This and a second volume issued in 1855 were roundly denounced or humorously ridiculed by the movement's critics.

Yet *Spiritualism* was the decade's most popular treatise on the subject, providing the movement with the testimony of a relatively eminent and respectable citizen and enjoying a good sale with the general public. This popularity undoubtedly owed something to the optimistic doctrine—limited to no specific sect or social panacea—preached by the judge and his spiritual collaborators. Edmonds testified in an autobiographical preface that spiritualism could bring the growing multitudes of skeptics and materialists back to religion by illuminating the soul's destiny.[33] And one unnamed spirit commis-

[31] John Worth Edmonds and George T. Dexter, *Spiritualism* (New York, 1853, 1855).
[32] Ibid., I, 101.
[33] Ibid., pp. 7–10, 54–60, 71–72.

sioned him to liberate mankind from its pervasive fear of a wrathful God:

> Fear of God is a terrible fear. The soul shrinks within itself in contemplating the jealousy of an omnipotent God. Every nerve thrills with unutterable anguish at this anger, and many have wished that God had never existed, or had never caused them to exist.

> Your duty will be to lead the mind away from these theological errors; they have warped the soul too long already.[34]

Although Edmonds was rather easily hoaxed and vulnerable to ridicule, as the best-known spiritualist writer and believer of the 1850's he was not a complete failure in carrying out his mission.

The critical response to all this was variegated. Spiritualism was viewed as a swindle perpetrated by the Fox sisters, as an epidemic of hysterical delusion, and as mesmerism decked out with a specious theology.[35] But whether they took its phenomena to be fraudulent, delusive, or genuine, the most deeply concerned opponents of the movement were worried about its moral and religious consequences.[36] Sometimes the entire movement was blamed for the actions of the free-lovers among its members.[37] Spokesmen for orthodox Christian sects, moreover, regarded spiritualism as a species of infidelity which posed a serious threat to religion.[38] And some of them accepted the manifestations as genuine visitations of demonism.[39]

In a report he read to the Congregational Association of New York and Brooklyn in April, 1853, and later published as *A Review of the "Spiritual Manifestations,"*[40] Harriet Beecher Stowe's brother Charles

---

[34] Ibid., p. 56.

[35] Podmore, I, 283–90.

[36] "Editor's Table," *Harper's* IV (May 1852), 839–43; "Literature and Logic of 'The Interior,'" pp. 349–58; "Spiritual Materialism," *Putnam's* IV (August 1854), 158–72.

[37] Capron, pp. 380–81; Asa Mahan, *Modern Mysteries Explained and Exposed* (Boston, 1855), pp. 281–90; William H. Ferris, "Review of Modern Spiritualism," *Ladies Repository* XVI (January 1856), 46–52; Benjamin Hatch, *Spiritualists' Iniquities Unmasked, and the Hatch Divorce Case* (New York, 1859), pp. 5–23.

[38] Ferris; Capron, p. 176; C. L. Hequembourg, "The Necromancy of the Nineteenth Century," *New Englander* XII (February 1854), 33–44.

[39] Podmore, I, 291, 304.

[40] Charles Beecher, *A Review of the "Spiritual Manifestations"* (New York, 1853).

Beecher suggested quite seriously that demonic agency was responsible for the rappings.[41] (Admittedly reluctant to assent to any statement emanating from a relative of Mrs. Stowe, the reviewer for the *Southern Literary Messenger*, while rejecting the demonic theory, agreed with Beecher that mere collusion could not account for all the reported marvels.)[42] In addition, whatever the cause of the rappings, Beecher summarized the danger which spiritualism presented for Congregational orthodoxy. He called it a "subtle but genuine materialism" which rejected Biblical authority, found all men capable of divine inspiration equal to Christ's, regarded "sin" as mere lack of "development," and denied the doctrines of the Fall, "of total depravity, atonement, regeneration, pardon, etc. . . ."[43] Spiritualism, of course, was by no means the only target of such accusations in the last century. But with its spectacular demonstrations and its rapid rise to popularity, for a time the movement provided a dramatic focus for fears about the erosion of the doctrinal and institutional strength of the churches. Beecher himself was to undergo a heresy trial during the Civil War for accepting evolution and spiritualism,[44] and his curious *Spiritual Manifestations* (1879)[45] was to attempt the synthesis of spiritualism, the Bible, and liberal Christianity.

By the end of the decade the public furor over spiritualism had subsided. Probably the theological debate had left untroubled many people who saw no problem in adding the séance to their regular religious observances. Yet William Dean Howells was to remember that the mediumistic conflagration in the Western Reserve had "left behind a great deal of smoke and ashes where the inherited New England orthodoxy had been. . . ."[46] And in 1859, through his Professor, Oliver Wendell Holmes facetiously and hyperbolically described spiritualism as the "plague" which had destroyed orthodox notions of immortality "to a larger extent than most good people seem to be aware of":

[41] Podmore, I, 291.

[42] "Spiritual Manifestations," *Southern Literary Messenger* XIX (July 1853), 386.

[43] Quoted in Podmore, I, 301.

[44] Kenneth R. Andrews, *Nook Farm: Mark Twain's Hartford Circle* (Cambridge, Mass., 1950), pp. 33–34.

[45] Charles Beecher, *Spiritual Manifestations* (Boston, 1879).

[46] Howells, *Impressions and Experiences*, p. 21.

. . . you cannot have people of cultivation, of pure character, sensible enough in common things, large-hearted women, grave judges, shrewd businessmen, men of science, professing to be in communication with the spiritual world and keeping up constant intercourse with it, without its gradually reacting on the whole conception of that other life.[47]

Moreover, he indirectly laid the origin of this revolution at the feet of Margaret and Kate Fox when he said that the "Nemesis of the pulpit" had begun "with the snap of a toe-joint" and was ending "with such a crack of old beliefs that the roar of it is heard in all the ministers' studies of Christendom!"[48] Holmes was no more a friend to spiritualism than he was to Calvinism, and exaggerated though it was, few more disinterested tributes can ever have been paid to the influence of the Fox sisters.

III | The most immediate literary consequences of spiritualism were the writings of famous spirits. Most of these works were tracts for the times, and reviewers already hostile to their message rejected claims of spiritual authorship. A critic of Charles Hammond's transcription of *Light from the Spirit World: The Pilgrimage of Thomas Paine and Others to the Seventh Circle in the Spirit World* (1852),[49] by the spirit of Thomas Paine, felt called upon against his principles to defend Paine as a man who "knew how to write the English language. . . . A worthless, drunken scoundrel as he was, there was a time when Tom Paine would have blushed at the thought of being the author of such a farrago. . . ."[50] The same critic then offered a specimen of spiritual prose from Hammond's second work, *Light from the Spirit World: Comprising a Series of Articles on the Condition of Spirits and the Development of Mind in the Rudimental and*

[47] [Oliver Wendell Holmes,] "The Professor at the Breakfast-Table," *Atlantic Monthly* III (January 1859), 90.
[48] Ibid. The Professor said essentially the same thing in "The Professor at the Breakfast-Table," *Atlantic Monthly* III (May 1859), 611.
[49] Charles Hammond, *Light from the Spirit World: The Pilgrimage* (Rochester, 1852).
[50] "Literature and Logic of 'The Interior,'" p. 352.

Second Spheres (1852):[51] "Wisdom is wisdom. All is not wisdom. All is not folly. Wisdom wills good. Folly wills otherwise. One is right. One is wrong. Wisdom will do right. Folly will do wrong. He, that is wise, let him take heed. He that is unwise, let him get wisdom."[52] The messages from Bacon, Franklin, and "Sweedenborg" in Edmonds and Dexter's *Spiritualism* were better written than this. But one writer found them stylistically indistinguishable from the prose of Edmonds and Dexter,[53] and another suggested that the descendants of Bacon and Franklin sue for slander.[54] Before the decade was over, the spiritualists themselves were inclined to be skeptical about the authenticity of messages from spiritual celebrities.

A few mediums, however, claimed the power to elicit the creative energies of dead poets for literary purposes. Probably the most talented of these literary mediums was Thomas Lake Harris, once a clairvoyant associate of Andrew Jackson Davis, soon an apostate from "satanic" spiritualism, and eventually the founder of his own mystic cults. In the mid-1850's Harris turned out three spirit-dictated volumes: *An Epic of the Starry Heaven* (1854),[55] *A Lyric of the Morning Land* (1856),[56] and *A Lyric of the Golden Age* (1856).[57] A preface ("from the Lyrical Paradise of the Heaven of Spirits") to the first volume announced that the "Lyric Angels"[58] had decided to utilize Harris's poetic abilities. *An Epic* itself described in conventional Romantic diction a spiritual voyage throughout the solar system. And later the spirits of Rousseau, Byron, Coleridge, Keats, and especially Shelley rhymed through Harris in *A Lyric of the Golden Age*. Whatever their merits as poetry, Harris's works were impressive as feats of spoken trance-improvisation transcribed by others.

More closely dependent on specific earthly poems by her guiding spirits was Lizzie Doten, the Boston trance-poetess whose *Poems from*

[51] Charles Hammond, *Light from the Spirit World: Series of Articles* (Rochester, 1852).
[52] "Literature and Logic of 'The Interior,' " p. 352.
[53] *Graham's* XLVI (May 1855), 472.
[54] Mahan, pp. 161–62.
[55] Thomas Lake Harris, *An Epic of the Starry Heaven* (New York, 1854).
[56] Thomas Lake Harris, *A Lyric of the Morning Land* (New York, 1856).
[57] Thomas Lake Harris, *A Lyric of the Golden Age* (New York, 1856).
[58] Harris, *An Epic of the Starry Heaven*, p. xvi.

the Inner Life (1869)[59] collected the verses she had been speaking for years at spiritualist gatherings and funerals. Shakespeare, she said, was least able to utilize her "organism"[60] because her feeling of awe made her unable to sustain his power. This failure was perhaps evidenced by the opening lines of "Life":

> "To be, or not to be," is not "the question;"
> There is no choice of Life. Ay, mark it well—
> For Death is but another name for Change.
> The weary shuffle off their mortal coil,
> And think to slumber in eternal night.
> But lo! the man, though dead, is living still. . . .[61]

Robert Burns, on the other hand, "was pleasant, easy, and exhilarating,"[62] a mood reflected in his poetry:

> Is there a luckless wight on earth,
>   Oppressed wi' care and a' that,
> Who holds his life as little worth—
>   His home is Heaven for a' that. . . .[63]

Edgar Allan Poe had died just in time and in mysterious enough circumstances to be a favorite of the literary mediums, and Miss Doten's best work emanated from his spirit. His trance influence exhausted her physically, and his images were sometimes "dark and repulsive." But in the process of inspiring her, Poe realized the joyous meaning of spirit life, cast off his earthly imperfections, and struggled through to a manifestation of his "diviner self."[64] This new consciousness he expressed in the first stanza of "Resurrexion":

> From the throne of Life Eternal,
> From the home of love supernal,
> Where the angel feet make music over all the starry floor—
> Mortals, I have come to meet you,

59 Elizabeth Doten, *Poems from the Inner Life*, 7th ed. (Boston, 1869).
60 Ibid., pp. xix–xx.
61 Ibid., p. 86.
62 Ibid., p. xx.
63 Ibid., p. 97.
64 Ibid., pp. xxii–xxiii.

> Come with words of peace to greet you,
> And to tell you of the glory that is mine forevermore.[65]

"The Streets of Baltimore" told the story of Poe's last night of frenzied suffering and of his passage to bliss:

> For my soul from out that shadow
> Hath been lifted evermore—
> From that deep and dismal shadow
> In the streets of Baltimore.[66]

(Alfred Russel Wallace was to write that this and another of Poe's spirit poems were "finer and deeper and grander poems than any written by him in the earth-life, though, being given through *another* brain, they are deficient in the exquisite music and rhythm of his best known work.")[67] When Miss Doten last saw Poe in a vision, he was "radiant with victory,"[68] standing on a white crystalline mountainside and wearing a fiery olive-wreath on his brow.

A few near-believers and believers were serious writers whose works originated within their own imaginations. Thomas Holley Chivers thought that his own mystical experiences were confirmed by clairvoyant trance-excursions to spiritual realms, and he published a few verses in spiritualist journals. But he was contemptuous of physical manifestations and outraged by the attempt of Lydia Tenney, another literary medium, to add "Message from the Spirit of Edgar A. Poe" to the poet's works. Chivers objected that Poe could not have written such doggerel because he had done nothing like it while alive, and that his spirit would never stoop to plagiarizing such bad lines.[69]

Both spiritualism and Poe played important roles in the life and writings of the minor lyricist Sarah Helen Whitman. An early believer,

---

[65] Ibid., p. 104.

[66] Ibid., p. 133.

[67] Alfred Russel Wallace, *Edgar Allan Poe: A Series of Seventeen Letters Concerning Poe's Scientific Erudition in Eureka and the Authorship of Leonainie* (New York, n.d.), p. 9.

[68] Doten, *Poems from the Inner Life*, p. xxiii.

[69] S. Foster Damon, *Thomas Holley Chivers, Friend of Poe* (New York, 1930), pp. 175–77; Emma Lester Chase and Lora Ferry Parks, eds., *The Correspondence of Thomas Holley Chivers, 1838–58* (Providence, R.I., 1957), p. 141; Charles Henry Watts II, *Thomas Holley Chivers: His Literary Career and His Poetry* (Athens, Ga., 1956), p. 79.

Mrs. Whitman described séances in Providence, Rhode Island, for Greeley's *Tribune* in 1851,[70] and she apparently attempted to enlist John Hay, who as a college student frequented her literary salon later in the decade.[71] She was also Poe's second "Helen," and not long before his death had sadly broken their engagement because of his bad habits. But later she vigorously defended him against Rufus Griswold's calumnies by writing *Edgar Poe and His Critics* (1860).[72] In so doing she identified Poe as a prophet of spiritualism, saying that he had tried "to solve the problem of that phantasmal Shadow-Land, which, through a class of phenomena unprecedented in the world's history, was about to attest itself. . . ."[73]

Apparently Mrs. Whitman first turned to spiritualism while mourning Poe's death. She dealt with this experience in the title work of *Hours of Life and Other Poems* (1853).[74] *Putnam's* enthusiastic reviewer knew enough about her to say that the poem chronicled the journeys of a sensitive soul through some "bitterly actual experience" into a "sweet and simple faith" with the aid of "spiritual research."[75] But the poem itself presented this journey and research in terms of conventional allegory. The narrator suffered an unspecified but deep loss in the "Morning" hours, at "Noon" sought vainly from history and religion an answer to the riddle of immortality, and joyously heard a voice from heaven tell her at "Evening" that she should live on, secure in the belief that death would not be the end. The poem was an American *In Memoriam*, but one which used the cycle of the day rather than the year and offered the consolation of a perceptible voice of assurance.

The heavenly intelligence may well have been Poe's. Although he

[70] Caroline Ticknor, *Poe's Helen* (New York, 1916), p. 15.

[71] In 1859 Hay wrote Nora Perry from Springfield, Illinois, that he would "join a spiritual circle soon. I am, of course, an unbeliever, but Mrs. Whitman has taught me to respect the new revelation, if not to trust it" (John Hay, *A Poet in Exile: Early Letters of John Hay*, ed. Caroline Ticknor [Boston, 1935], p. 43). By 1883 respect had disappeared, for in that year he portrayed spiritualism as fraudulent, politically radical, and morally degenerate in *The Bread-Winners*, Biographical ed. (New York, 1899), pp. 99–114.

[72] Sarah Helen Whitman, *Edgar Poe and His Critics* (New York, 1860).

[73] Ibid., p. 72.

[74] Sarah Helen Whitman, *Hours of Life and Other Poems* (Providence, R.I., 1853), pp. 3–38.

[75] "Editorial Notes," *Putnam's* II (November 1853), 563.

was not identifiable beyond the allegorical veil, several shorter poems dedicated to him appeared in the same volume. And there was also a series of six sonnets addressed to an unidentified dead lover, one of which indicated that death had not severed communication:

> . . . oft thy spirit tells how souls, affied
> By sovran destinies, can no more part—
> How death and hell are powerless to divide
> Souls whose deep lives lie folded heart in heart.[76]

As for "sovran destinies," at one time or another Mrs. Whitman discovered that an old Irish spelling of her maiden name, Sarah Helen Poer, yielded the anagram "Ah, Seraph Lenore," while Edgar Poe was "A God Peer."[77]

Beyond these minor efforts, however, no writer of importance found affirmative inspiration in spiritualism—except, perhaps, for Walt Whitman, and then only once or twice. In 1867 Whitman retitled one of the earlier "Chants Democratic" as "Mediums,"[78] a term perhaps appropriate for his prophecy of bards who would "illustrate Democracy and the kosmos," and from whose lives and works would "emerge divine conveyers":

> Characters, events, retrospection, shall be convey'd
> in gospels, trees, animals, waters, shall be convey'd,
> Death, the future, the invisible faith, shall be
> convey'd.[79]

As for spirits, perhaps "The Mystic Trumpeter,"[80] that "ecstatic ghost" of a "dead composer," who hovered "unseen in air" and filled the night with "capricious tunes" recalling the past and predicting a joyous future, was related to the invisible musicians who offered testimony to the reality of immortality by playing celestial chords on the guitars, accordions, and occasional trumpets which floated in the air at dark séances. More generally, Whitman's own self-dramatization as inspired bard unconstrained by barriers of space or time resembled

[76] Whitman, *Hours of Life and Other Poems*, p. 195.
[77] Ticknor, *Poe's Helen*, p. 190.
[78] Walt Whitman, *Leaves of Grass*, ed. Harold E. Blodgett and Sculley Bradley (New York, 1968), pp. 480–81.
[79] Ibid., p. 481.
[80] Ibid., pp. 468–71.

in many ways the role of clairvoyant prophet played by Andrew Jackson Davis, Thomas Lake Harris, and others. But Whitman does not seem to have made much explicit use of spiritualism, which still awaited a Yeats for whom it could provide a unifying vision.

This is not to say that the literary reaction to spiritualism was negligible. It was significant both in extent and in the major figures—from Lowell, Melville, and Hawthorne to Howells, Twain, and James—who contributed to it. By and large, however, this reaction was critical. Through the 1850's and into the next decade, humorists made sport of the séance, mediums, believers, and spirits. Satirical novelists attacked the movement as a menace to religion and society, or as a curious excrescence of the national culture. A few writers made relatively neutral use of spiritual manifestations for occult atmosphere and supernatural fiction, but even in ghost stories there sometimes lurked amusement or hostility toward the movement. A generation later, Mark Twain would laugh at and denounce fraudulent mediums and credulous believers; William Dean Howells would examine the spiritualistic quest for assurance of immortality with critical compassion; and Henry James would view it ironically as a desiccated remnant of the reform impulse of the 1850's. For both Howells and James, moreover, as for their scientific contemporaries who were pioneering the investigation of the unconscious,[81] the entranced medium would present a psychological rather than a supernatural problem. But all three writers, whatever the nature of their sometimes painful personal encounters with the movement, would deal with it in ways growing out of the literary response to spiritualism during the 1850's and 1860's. Within broad and by no means mutually exclusive categories of humor, the occult, and satire, that response started to take shape about three years after "the epoch of the rapping spirits" had begun in the bedroom of Margaret and Kate Fox.

[81] Henri F. Ellenberger, *The Discovery of the Unconscious: The History and Evolution of Dynamic Psychiatry* (New York, 1970), pp. 85, 121.

II: "KNOCKS FOR THE KNOCKINGS" [1]

Humorous Literary Reactions to Spiritualism

I | It is not surprising that the first literary reactions to spiritual-
ism were comic. The movement's popularity and its more
obviously laughable features—silly and fraudulent mediums, uncritical
enthusiasts, bizarre séance phenomena, inane messages from famous
spirits—made it an easy target for topical ridicule. Two months after
the Fox sisters had scored such success with their "Post-Mortuum
Soiree" at his house, Rufus Griswold noted that "the journals have
been filled with jesting and speculation on the subject."[2] Sooner or
later most of the humorists of the 1850's took aim at the movement,
more amused or irritated than fascinated or deeply concerned. It was
in this vein that James Russell Lowell wrote the first significant literary
response to spiritualism, "The Unhappy Lot of Mr. Knott" (1851).[3]

Lowell was no stranger to supernatural phenomena. From boyhood

---

[1] *Knocks for the Knockings* was the title of a pamphlet in which Chauncey Burr
claimed to be able to produce rappings by seventeen fraudulent means (Frank
Podmore, *Modern Spiritualism: A History and a Criticism* [London, 1902], I,
189).

[2] "Authors and Books," *International Monthly Magazine of Literature, Science,
and Art* I (July 29, 1850), 138.

[3] James Russell Lowell, "The Unhappy Lot of Mr. Knott," *Graham's* XXXVIII
(April 1851), 281–87. Subsequent references are to *The Poetical Works of James
Russell Lowell* (Boston, 1858), II, 283–309.

onward he was subject throughout his life to occasional nocturnal visions of ghostly figures. He had already cited these visitations in describing one of his two selves as "clear mystic and enthusiast," and in so doing he had vouched for the sincerity of those often termed "religious imposters." But although always fascinated by his ghostly visitors, he never wholeheartedly granted them objective existence outside his own imagination, perhaps because of the skepticism of his other self, which he had identified as a "humorist."[4] And it was the humorous rather than the mystical Lowell who responded to the news that spirits were revealing themselves through the rappings of the Fox sisters.

In January, 1850, just as the fame of the Foxes was beginning to spread beyond Rochester, Lowell expressed toward them and their supporters an attitude indicative of satiric promise. His abolitionist friend Edward Davis had sent him a letter written by Oliver Johnson, an anti-slavery editor who had been associated with both William Lloyd Garrison and Horace Greeley, telling of an impressive séance conducted by Leah Fish and one of her sisters. Refusing to concede "that men are to be thumped into a conception of the spiritual world," Lowell was comprehensively and caustically skeptical in his reply to Davis. He attacked the alphabetical rappings as an inefficient code used only to communicate trivia; he claimed to have known people "who could make a 'mysterious knocking' by snapping one of their joints in and out"; perhaps with an eye to Johnson, who like many reformers was an enthusiastic supporter of the Foxes, he said that "only foolish little men . . . are fond of mysteries and fusses"; and he was confident that it would be easy to duplicate the messages reported by Johnson from Elias Hicks, George Fox, and St. Paul, and "to throw in a few more saints to boot."[5]

[4] *Letters of James Russell Lowell*, ed. Charles Eliot Norton (New York, 1894), I, 117; II, 370–71.
[5] Lowell, *Letters*, I, 174. As printed by Norton the letter mentioned only "O. J." but clearly referred to Johnson, who had also been associated with Edward Davis's *Pennsylvania Freeman*. E. W. Capron and H. D. Barron listed Johnson as a witness of the Rochester rappings in their pamphlet, *Singular Revelations: Explanation and History of the Mysterious Communion with the Spirits*, 2nd ed. (Auburn, N.Y., 1850), p. 95. In 1851 Johnson delivered to Garrison one of the many reconciliatory messages received through various mediums from the spirit of N. P. Rogers which finally convinced Garrison that Rogers was trying to make amends from the spirit

In these criticisms of clumsy fraud on the part of the Fox sisters, foolish credulity on the part of their patrons, and inanity on the part of their spirits, there was comic literary potential. It was natural, therefore, that when he needed a subject for a humorous poem commissioned for the 1850 Christmas issue of *Graham's,* Lowell turned to spiritualism and, taking so long that he missed his deadline, elaborated his remarks to Davis into almost nine-hundred lines of punning verse in "The Unhappy Lot of Mr. Knott." Saluted in advance of its appearance the next spring by Rufus Griswold as "a satire on 'the Rappers,'—a humorous and witty poem,"[6] Lowell's "Mr. Knott" burlesqued the Hydesville and Rochester rappings with a topicality which has never been recognized. Moreover, his approach to the subject was prescient, for it combined the two chief methods by which other writers were to poke fun at "the Rappers." By way of spoofing the birth of the Fox sisters' vogue, he adapted to a spiritualistic context the traditionally humorous plight of the credulously over-imaginative person frightened by what he thinks are ghosts—a pattern to be handled most creatively by Herman Melville in "The Apple-Tree Table" (1856). And Lowell's poem also marked the first literary appearance of the comic spirit-communications which Q. K. Philander Doesticks, Artemus Ward, and Petroleum V. Nasby were to record in their visits to the séance.

The plot of "The Unhappy Lot of Mr. Knott" was drawn from the humorous ghost-story tradition of "Tam O' Shanter" and "The Legend of Sleepy Hollow" and given a spiritualistic frame of reference. When A. Gordon Knott and his daughter Jenny—affianced against her will to rich but middle-aged Colonel Jones—moved into their vulgar new mansion, strange noises began at night. At first these sounds were caused by a combination of wind and bad construction. But news about the "raps that unwrapped mysteries" in Rochester soon led the

world for earthly hostility (Wendell Phillips Garrison and Francis Jackson Garrison, *William Lloyd Garrison, 1805–1879: The Story of His Life* [New York, 1889], III, 377). And according to Leah, the oldest of the Fox sisters, Johnson was to ask her to assist Horace Greeley in obtaining consolation after his wife's death in 1872 by eliciting a message from one of Mrs. Greeley's friends in the spirit world; Alice Cary's spirit answered the call (A. Leah Underhill, *The Missing Link in Modern Spiritualism* [New York, 1885], pp. 257–58).

6 "Authors and Books," *International Monthly Magazine* II (February 1851), 309.

superstitious Knott to believe that the noises were caused by his dead wife's ghost at her former daily tasks. Before long, alphabetical knockings began to spell out messages from an impressive list of famous spirits, and hordes of believers and curiosity-seekers came to witness the marvel. Finally the spirit of Eliab Snooks, a peddler, rapped out a message claiming that he had been murdered and buried by Colonel Jones. Snooks and his fellow spirits vowed that Knott would have no rest until Jenny was released from her betrothal to the guilty man and allowed to marry whom she pleased. Although the mechanism by which these intelligible rappings were produced was not made clear, a few skeptics realized that they came from Jenny and her lover, Dr. Slade. But Knott, terrified and exhausted, obeyed the ghostly instruction to let love take its course. After the wedding of Jenny and Slade, a jawbone of doubtful origin was exhumed from the alleged grave of the peddler Snooks, who then turned up alive and healthy. And although Parson Wilbur cautioned at the poem's end against belief in spirit-rappings, he was glad that "Miss Knott missed not her lover."[7]

Nowhere in the poem were mediums Lowell's explicit target. Gone was the animus he had shown toward the Fox sisters in his letter to Edward Davis. He neither mentioned them nor attempted the kind of play on names later used by Fitz-James O'Brien with "Madame Vulpes" in his best-known story, "The Diamond Lens" (1858). Yet it was news of the Rochester rappings which suggested to Knott that ghosts were responsible for the disturbances in his own house, and there were obvious parallels in the credulity of Knott and that for which Mrs. Fox was taken to task by her daughters' critics—parallels, too, in the lifelike spectral noises allegedly heard in both houses, in the overflowing throngs of curiosity-seekers who beleaguered both families, and in the Fox sisters' profitable tours and a circus operator's offer to take Knott's spirits in tow.[8] These and other similarities make it clear that the narrative was designed to burlesque the origins of spiritualism in Hydesville and Rochester.

The most convincing evidence of Lowell's intention was the ac-

---

[7] Lowell, *Poetical Works*, II, 288, 309.

[8] Ibid., 288, 297; Capron and Barron, pp. 15, 17; E. W. Capron, *Modern Spiritualism: Its Facts and Fanaticisms, Its Consistencies and Contradictions* (Boston, 1855), pp. 51, 66.

cusing ghost of Eliab Snooks, who was not a spectre merely of comic fiction. His name, in fact, may have been a gesture of derision toward Eliab W. Capron, the early spiritualist historian whom Lowell could easily have laid under obligation for some of the details of "Mr. Knott."[9] More importantly, Snooks's charge of murder against Colonel Jones, the inconclusive jawbone found in his supposed grave, and his reappearance in the flesh were synthesized from early incidents in the career of the Fox sisters. On the night of March 31, 1848, the first rapping spirit had identified himself as the ghost of a peddler who had been murdered and buried in the cellar of the Fox house by a former tenant. Some time later, according to spiritualistic accounts, his bones were found under the cellar floor, and the accusation of murder was revived by Leah Fish, now managing her sisters' affairs. Nothing came of it, however, for when the accused man returned in anger to Hydesville, his former neighbors gave him certificates of good character. But after Margaret and Kate had settled with Leah in Rochester, another peddler disappeared in that city. It was suggested that he, too, might have met with foul play, and one of the girls' growing band of imitators elicited raps instructing searchers to look for the corpse in a canal.[10] Like Eliab Snooks, however, the peddler reappeared, having gone to Canada to avoid creditors. It was not in a fanciful context, then, that Parson Wilbur advised caution in interpreting spirit-messages:

> . . . a charge by raps conveyed
> Should be most scrupulously weighed
>   And searched into, before it is
> Made public, since it may give pain
> That cannot be cured again.[11]

[9] Capron had done more than any other person to assist and publicize the Fox sisters before their departure from Rochester; he had spoken at the first public demonstrations of their rappings and had helped write a report on those meetings which was published in the *New York Tribune*. See Capron and Barron, pp. 46–48.
[10] Capron, pp. 60–62; Robert Dale Owen, *Footfalls on the Boundary of Another World* (Philadelphia, 1860), pp. 297–98. Tales of disappearing travelers and spirits haunting murder sites were frequent in Yankee folklore. See Richard M. Dorson, *Jonathan Draws the Long Bow* (Cambridge, Mass., 1946), pp. 56–68, 157–63.
[11] Lowell, *Poetical Works*, II, 308–9.

This attempt at a narrative *à clef* directed against the Fox sisters was not very effective. The poem's direct parallels to their experiences were obscured by its nonsensical love-story, its erudite punning, and its genuinely amusing burlesque of typical spirit-communications. And by substituting the unexplained machinations of Jenny and her lover for his original suggestion to Edward Davis that the rappings might emanate from the joints of the mediums themselves, Lowell lost the advantage of similar but more authoritative accusations made close to the time his poem was published. In February, 1851, a committee of skeptical Buffalo physicians, challenged by Leah Fish to a personal examination of her sisters, reported that no knockings took place so long as a firm grip was kept on the mediums' knees. Then in April a young relative of the girls said in a sworn statement printed in the *New York Herald* that Kate had shown her how to produce rappings with both knee and toe joints. Such charges did no more than Lowell's poem to dampen public interest in the Foxes. Horace Greeley had already pronounced them innocent of fraud after making a close inspection the preceding summer. And in Buffalo a committee of perfectly respectable citizens hastily assembled by Leah Fish contradicted the physicians in every detail.[12]

Whether or not Lowell's readers saw that he was following the tracks of the Foxes, they undoubtedly recognized the reference to "raps that unwrapped mysteries" in Rochester. Most of them probably also understood an explicit allusion to the Stratford rappings, the disturbances in the house of Reverend Eliakim Phelps which attracted almost as much public attention as the Fox girls' rappings. In describing such physical mischief perpetrated by Jenny and Slade as the snatching of Knott's hat from his head and the capricious slamming of doors, Lowell cited recent newspaper stories about Eliakim Phelps's poltergeist:

> . . . the tantrums of a ghost
> Not more than three weeks since, at most,
> Near Stratford in Connecticut.[13]

[12] Podmore, I, 183–87; Earl Wesley Fornell, *The Unhappy Medium: Spiritualism and the Life of Margaret Fox* (Austin, Tex., 1964), pp. 21–22.
[13] Lowell, *Poetical Works*, II, 295.

This was the first literary appearance of the Phelps's rappings, which were also to manifest themselves in works by Orestes Brownson, Elizabeth Stuart Phelps, and evidently even Mark Twain. For Lowell, however, the comparison was merely illustrative. However much he missed his quarry, he was hunting Foxes.

Lowell also looked to occult and demonological tradition as authority for Knott's poltergeist by citing such writers as Reginald Scot, John Webster, John Wesley, the Mathers of New England, and two recent historians of the supernatural, Catherine Crowe and Heinrich Jung-Stilling. Works by all of them, said the poet, were available in the Harvard College Library.[14] Skeptics sometimes cited such accounts as evidence that the rapping spirits were simply the sentimental figments of the same popular imagination which once had fearfully created witches and demons. Lowell was to take this view himself in "Witchcraft" (1868), a knowledgable discussion of some of the same authorities, by labeling all spiritualistic phenomena as "heirlooms"[15] left to the supposedly enlightened nineteenth century by its witch-fearing ancestors. And in one of the Lowell lectures of 1854–55 he was to illustrate the longevity of superstition with a reference to table-tipping: "Turning over the yellow leaves of the same copy of 'Webster on Witchcraft' which Cotton Mather studied, I thought, 'Well, that goblin is laid at last!'—and while I mused the tables were turning and the chairs beating the devil's tattoo all over Christendom."[16] Orestes Brownson (who thought the rapping spirits genuinely demonic) and Herman Melville were to make imaginative use of this presumed genealogy. Brownson gave the name "Increase Mather Cotton" to a character partially modeled on Eliakim Phelps in *The Spirit-Rapper: An Autobiography* (1854), and the narrator of Melville's "Apple-Tree Table; or, Original Spiritual Manifestations" (1856) discovered two Puritan heirlooms in his attic—a rapping table

[14] Ibid.

[15] [James Russell Lowell,] "Witchcraft," *North American Review* CVI (June 1868), 232. For similar views see "Modern Necromancy," *North American Review* LXXX (April 1855), 512–27, and "The Spirits in 1692 and What They Did at Salem," *Putnam's* VII (May 1856), 505–11.

[16] James Russell Lowell, *The Function of the Poet and Other Essays*, ed. Albert Mordell (Boston, 1920), p. 22.

and a copy of Mather's *Magnalia*, each a century and a half old. Beyond reciting his list of authorities in witty rhyme, however, Lowell made no attempt in "Mr. Knott" to relate spiritualism to the history of the occult.

Indeed, it was only in dealing with the messages rapped out by Knott's spirits, where Lowell was restricted neither by the details of supernatural tradition nor by the recent events at Hydesville, Rochester, and Stratford, that he was able to expand freely and inventively along the lines of his remarks to Edward Davis about spiritual inanity and human gullibility. To Davis, Lowell had likened alphabetical rappings to a clumsy "system of cryptography" used only to send messages taking half a day to decode and carrying only such news "as that my coat was brown, or that I ate an egg with my breakfast."[17] Now in verse he ridiculed the use of the same code by Knott's spirits to transmit messages equally trivial but requiring twice as long to make out:

> . . . just to ask *if two and two*
> *Really make four?* or, *How d'ye do?*
> And get the fit replies thereto
> In the tramundane rat-tat-too,
>   Might ask a whole day's patience.[18]

The eagerness to believe of "foolish little men" like Oliver Johnson, who had visited and endorsed the Fox sisters, was belittled by Lowell not only with the credulous Knott, but also with the throngs of "Seekers," who took their "strings of questions cut and dried" from the "Devout Inquirer's Guide." Lowell's rhyming version of such a "string" travestied the questions often asked at séances:

> Could matter ever suffer pain?
> What could take out a cherry-stain?
> Who picked the pocket of Seth Crane,

---

17 Lowell, *Letters*, I, 174.
18 Lowell, *Poetical Works*, II, 302–3. In the same month that "Mr. Knott" appeared, "E. L. B." published a doggerel appeal "To the Rapping Spirits," *Knickerbocker* XXXVII (April 1851), 311: "Why, then, so slow to tell/What you should know so well—/Making us guess and spell/Letter by letter?" Scientist Jacob Bigelow was to write an extended imitation of Lowell's parody of spirit communications in "The Spirit-Rappers to Their Mediums, by J. R. L.," *Eo-*

> Of Waldo precinct, State of Maine?
> Was Sir John Franklin sought in vain?[19]

The spirits were often asked the whereabouts of Franklin, the lost Arctic explorer. Eventually Asa Mahan was angrily to inquire, in *Modern Mysteries Explained and Exposed* (1855),[20] why no spirits had ever seen fit to make it unnecessary for Lady Franklin to wait years for confirmation of her husband's death. Evidently Mahan was unaware that through Lizzie Doten, the Boston trance-poetess, the spirits had announced Franklin's fate and foretold his wife's ordeal in "Song of the North" (1853):

> O, the sailor's wife, and the sailor's child
> They will weep, and watch, and pray,
> And the Lady Jane, she will hope in vain,
> As the long years pass away.[21]

For Lowell the inquiry about Franklin was an opportunity to make good his earlier boast to Edward Davis that he could equal the Fox sisters in the production of messages from Elias Hicks, George Fox, St. Paul, and "a few more saints to boot."[22] Here he assembled fifty-three diverse but rhyming spirits, including Mirabeau, Cicero, Rousseau, Defoe, Poe, James Crow, and "a disembodied Esquimaux"[23]—all of whom gave contradictory and nonsensical directions for finding Franklin.

Lowell's criticism of spiritual ignorance reflected in passing a personal feud which consumed a good deal more energy than did "Mr. Knott." He put the poem aside in December, 1850, to castigate publicly his old Harvard tutor Francis Bowen, who was engaged in a journalistic battle over Hungarian independence with Lowell's sister,

---

Iopoesis: American Rejected Addresses. Now First Published from the Original Manuscripts (New York, 1855), pp. 85–123.

[19] Lowell, *Poetical Works*, II, 297–98.

[20] Asa Mahan, *Modern Mysteries Explained and Exposed* (Boston, 1855), pp. 146–47.

[21] Elizabeth Doten, *Poems from the Inner Life*, 7th ed. (Boston, 1869), pp. xv, 21–25.

[22] Lowell, *Letters*, I, 174.

[23] Lowell, *Poetical Works*, II, 303.

Mary Putnam. Bowen had been provisionally appointed McLean Professor of History at Harvard, and Lowell wrote two long newspaper articles attacking him as an incompetent and dishonest historian.[24] The poet's anger against Bowen spilled over into the last section of "Mr. Knott" with a comparison of "bold and strong" rapping spirits, who "knew so little (and that wrong)," to "Professors of History."[25]

Even "shades august of eldest fame," who should have known better, were guilty of astonishing ignorance:

> One day, Ulysses happening down,
> A reader of Sir Thomas Browne
>   And who (with him) had wondered
> What song it was the Sirens sang,
>   Asked the shrewd Ithacan—bang! bang!
> With this response the chamber rang,
>   "I guess it was Old Hundred."
> And Franklin, being asked to name
> The reason why the lightning came
>   Replied, "Because it thundered."[26]

Such communications burlesqued the already pronounced tendency for famous spirits to speak out foolishly at séances—none more loquaciously than Benjamin Franklin, the inventor of the "spiritual telegraph." Frequent embarrassments of this sort led Franklin, at about the time Lowell was writing "Mr. Knott," to complain to Andrew Jackson Davis. According to the Poughkeepsie seer, Franklin told him that the "material instrumentality" of rappings, which he had devised to demonstrate the truth of the doctrine of immortality, was being misused by excited and ignorant mediums who failed to follow spiritual directions. As a result, said Franklin, "confusion has been 'rapped' out, and our characters for *good* and *evil* were . . . often at the mercy of our mediums and terrestrial audiences."[27] Lowell displayed

[24] Lowell, *Letters*, I, 189; Leon Howard, *Victorian Knight-Errant: A Study of the Early Literary Career of James Russell Lowell* (Berkeley, 1952), pp. 303–5, 310–11.
[25] Lowell, *Poetical Works*, II, 304.
[26] Ibid., p. 304.
[27] Andrew Jackson Davis, *The Philosophy of Spiritual Intercourse: Being an Explanation of Modern Mysteries* (New York, 1851), pp. 78, 80–81.

a nice sense of topicality by exploiting such "confusion" just as it was becoming a frequent subject for journalistic humor and invective.

But Lowell was no more able to ascend Parnassus by satirizing spiritualism than he had been with other "-isms" on his back. Despite the brief presence of Parson Wilbur at the end of the poem, Lowell's impulse toward allusive literary punning in the manner of A *Fable for Critics* overwhelmed any intention he may have had to write a satiric study of a Yankee enthusiasm on the model of *The Biglow Papers*. As Leon Howard has noted, moreover, Lowell could not function very effectively as a humorist without a "personal incentive to satire,"[28] yet he composed "Mr. Knott" more for the money than for emotional satisfaction. Promised for *Graham's* 1850 Christmas issue, the poem did not appear until the following April because its author interrupted it to take part in the more compelling controversy with Francis Bowen. The literary result of this combination of circumstances was that the trenchant analysis of the rappings in Lowell's letter to Edward Davis became diffuse and almost amiable when stretched out on the farcical framework of Knott's ordeal. Yet with its burlesque of the origins of spiritualism, and with its exploration of some of the humorous possibilities inherent in the subject, "The Unhappy Lot of Mr. Knott" remains of interest as the first significant literary manifestation elicited under the mediumship of the Fox sisters.

II | It was not long before the humorous journalists of the 1850's began to burlesque the séance in their sketches. As topical humorists they had the advantage over Lowell of writing about spiritualism after it had become quite familiar to their readers. Some of them were able to make use of firsthand experience with mediums and spirits. And by placing the spirit communication within the ordinary séance rather than in the historical context of Rochester and Hydesville, they simplified the narrative problem faced by Lowell. Their narrators—Uncle Toby, Q. K. Philander Doesticks, Artemus Ward, and later Petroleum V. Nasby—had only to tell of visits to the séance in which they whimsically cooperated with the medium

---

[28] Howard, pp. 310–11.

long enough for her to elicit ridiculous messages from the spirits of relatives, friends, and great men. Borrowing freely from one another, these "literary comedians" looked at the ludicrous aspects of spiritualism from an aggressively commonsensical point of view. And their séances, from Uncle Toby's visit to a session of "Spiritual Knockings" in the fall of 1851 to Artemus Ward's venture "Among the Spirits" late in 1858, were uniformly attended by wide-eyed dupes, presided over by silly or fraudulent "mejums," and addressed, usually through rappings, by "sperrits" either divinely ignorant or earthily humorous.

The Reverend Tobias Miller's "Uncle Toby" translated Lowell's contempt for clumsy rappings into the more realistic setting of the séance when he found himself among a dozen wildly staring seekers, "their hair on end, *a la* fretful porcupine." On Toby's behalf the medium asked "if the sperrit of Jedediah Snooks" was present, evoking a series of meaningless single raps in reply:

> "Has the spirit of my friend anything to communicate?"
> Rap!
> "What does he mean by that?"
> Rap!
> "Will he communicate anything further?"
> "Says he's busy—call again some other time. Says he wants you to hand over four-and-sixpence. Next gentleman in turn. Sperrits waitin' and very much drove."[29]

Jedediah Snooks was simply Eliab Snooks pressed into the service of a greedy medium.

Humorous anecdotes about "the Rappers" were favorite subjects during the 1850's for the fillers passed along the press exchanges. Young Sam Clemens borrowed two such items in the short-lived column he wrote for his brother's Hannibal newspaper.[30] In 1853 Lewis Gaylord Clark used half a dozen of these pieces in his "Editor's Drawer" in *Harper's*. Typical was an ancient joke, spiritualized, about a séance at which it was rapped out that a lady had four children, her

29 Tobias Miller [Uncle Toby,] "Spiritual Knockings," *Gleason's Pictorial Magazine* I (October 18, 1851), 247.
30 Minnie M. Brashear, *Mark Twain, Son of Missouri* (Chapel Hill, N.C., 1934), pp. 131, 133.

husband only two. The couple departed unbelievers: "There had been a mistake made *somewhere*."[31]

As editor of the *Knickerbocker*, Clark poked more extended fun at the "Rap-scallions." His first opportunity to do so came when Edward Fowler, a younger brother of the well-known phrenologists and himself a powerful medium of Judge John Edmonds's New York Circle of Spiritualists, found on his table a document bearing the legend, "Peace, but not without Freedom," with facsimile autographs of the signatories of the Declaration of Independence and a few of his own departed relatives. The message was thought to refer to the slavery controversy and was reproduced in the most important spiritualistic journal, the *Spiritual Telegraph*.[32] Clark wrote that after reading the *Telegraph* he had discovered on his own table the minutes of a recent "convention of spirits" in the "Third Sphere," called by Benjamin Franklin to protest (as, indeed, he had already done to Andrew Jackson Davis) this abuse of spiritual reputations. Holding up the reproduction of Fowler's manuscript, Franklin charged that "our signatures have been forged." Lacking only the vote of Edgar Allan Poe, who had fallen intoxicated through a window into the Milky Way, the convention resolved unanimously that the document was a fake perpetrated by the evil spirits of convicted forgers, and they delegated the ghost of the American humorist Robert Sands to warn mankind against such frauds through the pages of the *Knickerbocker*.[33]

More in the vein of Uncle Toby's attack on the séance was the letter intercepted by Clark in 1854 from "Wagstaff," a Nebraska pioneer who had become a "writing, tipping, knocking, rapping and speaking mejum." When a shower of knocks had threatened to shake his cabin apart, Wagstaff had simply proceeded to "knock off the alfabet":

"A?" "No." "B?" "No." "C?" "No." "D?" "No." "E, F, J?" Rap, rap, rap. "O?" Rap, rap, rap. "Well, let the *Seph* go. It's JOSEPH,

[31] "Editor's Drawer," *Harper's* VIII (December 1853), 136, was preceded by "Editor's Drawer," *Harper's* VI (March 1853), 567; (May 1853), 850–51; VII (June 1853), 133; (July 1853), 277; and (October 1853), 711.
[32] Emma Hardinge Britten, *Modern American Spiritualism: A Twenty Years' Record of the Communion between Earth and the World of Spirits* (New York, 1870), p. 84; Podmore, I, 236–39.
[33] [Lewis Gaylord Clark,] "A Visit from the Mysterious Knockers," *Knickerbocker* XL (August 1852), 176–78.

isn't it?" Rap rap, rap. "A, B, C, D, E, F, G, H, I, J, K, L, M, N, O, P"—Rap, rap, rap! "P," says I . . . . "What's the uset of wastin' time. It's JOSEPH PIPKINS, isn't it?" Rap, rap, rap!

But Pipkins turned out to move in a "low sphere" because he had died in a seizure of "delirian trimens." Wagstaff, like Franklin, decided that the spirits were imposters, and he vowed to abandon his mediumistic gifts. He hoped to keep spiritualistic schoolmasters and judges out of Nebraska, but he was upset by talk of forming a spiritual circle "almost before we have got a circle of acquaintance. When will commonsense grow and multiply?"[34]

Gradually the séance burlesque became formalized and conventional as the same jokes and patterns were handed down the line. The archetypal example was provided by Mortimer Thomson, as Q. K. Philander Doesticks, in "An Evening with the Spiritualists."[35] In collecting this and other sketches in *Doesticks What He Says* (1855), Doesticks claimed to have worked without assistance from spirits like Franklin, Byron, or Benedict Arnold, or from "the crack-brained masculine women or addle-headed feminine men"[36] who served them as mediums. Like most literary comedians, however, Doesticks did owe the spiritualists a debt for supplying him with humorous material and devices. For besides reporting his own visit to a séance in "An Evening with the Spiritualists," he also told in the same volume of receiving a message (clearly based on an experience of Judge John Edmonds) from the spirit of his pet dog.[37] And in *Plu-ri-bus-tah* (1856),[38] Doesticks's parody of *Hiawatha*, the Indian brave Plu-ri-bus-tah, once the paragon of American vitality, returned from the dead to prophesy through spirit-rappings that his dissolute son Yunga-merrakah would bring himself to an early ruin.[39]

Thomson was a reporter, and under his pseudonym he later collected

[34] [Lewis Gaylord Clark,] "Letter from the Late Editor of the 'Bunkum Flag Staff,' " *Knickerbocker* XLIV (August 1854), 190–91, 192.
[35] Mortimer Thomson, *Doesticks What He Says* (New York, 1855), pp. 253–61.
[36] Ibid., p. 13.
[37] "Special Express from Dog Paradise—A Canine Ghost," in Thomson, *Doesticks What He Says*, pp. 262–69.
[38] Mortimer Thomson, *Plu-ri-bus-tah: A Song That's By-No-Author* (New York, 1856).
[39] Ibid., pp. 210–18.

in *The Witches of New York* (1859)[40] a series of articles written for Greeley, providing sensational details on the city's occult underworld of abortionists, fortune-tellers, and clairvoyants—many of whom, he said, were capable of "more rappings than the Rochester Fox girls ever thought of."[41] It is possible that the same kind of firsthand experience went into the beginning of "An Evening with the Spiritualists," with its detailed description of a slatternly cut-rate medium, her cramped and shabby studio, and the "old foozles" and "old maids" gathered round her dinner table. But the events which followed the first spiritual agitations of the table immediately conformed to the conventions of the comic séance. First came a message from the spirit of a person who had never existed—Doesticks's uncle—demonstrating the medium's incompetent fraud and the triviality of afterlife in the "spheres." The alleged uncle said that he was happy fishing, hunting, chopping wood, and "making hickory whip stocks" in the second sphere. The liquor was good, his wife was *"Sober,* just at present," and he looked forward to apple dumplings in the third sphere. At this point exaggeration of the typical gave way to comic invention as famous ghosts began to rap out the news that "Tom Paine and Jack Sheppard keep a billiard table. Noah is running a canal boat. Xerxes and Othello are driving opposition stages. . . . Benedict Arnold has opened a Lagerbier saloon, and left a vacancy for S. A. Douglas (white man)." John Bunyan had become a circus clown; John Calvin, Dr. Johnson, and General Jackson were among those forming "a traveling theatre"; and Shakespeare was at work on a new play. The entire list of names and occupations resembled Lowell's rhyming strings in length if not wit. Finally the séance was brought to a violent end as all the spirits began to rap at once, causing the furniture to perform acrobatics, the rapping table itself turning somersaults and striking Doesticks's companion, Damphool. Doesticks's last thought was to denounce mediums as lazy liars who "sponge their bread and butter out of those weak enough to believe their idiotic ravings."[42]

With its movement from a reportorial opening through trivial and

---

[40] Mortimer Thomson, *The Witches of New York, as Encountered by Q. K. Philander Doesticks, P.B.* (New York, 1859).

[41] Ibid., p. 206.

[42] Thomson, *Doesticks What He Says,* pp. 256–57, 259, 261.

fantastic gossip from false and famous ghosts to an apocalypse of violent furniture and the narrator's denunciation of corrupt mediums and foolish believers, "An Evening with the Spiritualists" was a compendium of the methods used by the literary comedians in dealing with spiritualism. And it established a model for Charles Farrar Browne, who late in 1858 animated the example of Doesticks with the personality of Artemus Ward in "Among the Spirits."[43]

In his own voice Browne had already reported for the *Cleveland Plain-Dealer* a real séance with humorous possibilities. He had heard a young woman elicit conversation in the dark from a spirit named "George," who spoke through a floating tin trumpet and aroused the reporter's envy by audibly kissing some of the ladies in attendance. In a series of more strenuous accomplishments, each carried out in the dark and then revealed to the audience, "George" bound the medium to her chair, lifted her to the top of her table, and returned her to the floor, where a mischievous Irish spirit poured water over her feet. The young medium was the sister of the well-known Davenport brothers of Buffalo, whose search for a way of protecting the spirits against skeptical harassment (and themselves against exposure for fraud) during the performance of such physical feats was shortly to result in the "spirit cabinet," within which the brothers could safely sit, presumably tied to their chairs, while spirits played musical instruments and showed spectral faces at apertures in the cabinet, and from which fully visible and vocal spirits would eventually emerge in the "materialization" séances of the 1870's. Browne had not realized that he was witnessing a significant example of major change taking place in the style of the séance. But he had noted that the medium's father accompanied her, and that "George" demanded that the people in the front row of the audience be roped together.[44]

[43] Charles Farrar Browne, *The Complete Works of Artemus Ward* (London, 1884), pp. 48–51. "Among the Spirits" appeared in the *Cleveland Plain-Dealer*, December 13, 1858, according to Don C. Seitz, *Artemus Ward (Charles Farrar Browne): A Biography and Bibliography* (New York, 1919), p. 320.

[44] "Spirits," in Browne, pp. 488–90. For the history of the "spirit cabinet," see P. T. Barnum, *The Humbugs of the World* (London, 1866), pp. 49–55, and Podmore, II, 55–62. Edward Hingston, Ward's manager, wrote an amusing chapter about a cockney magician in San Francisco who showed the two of them how to fake clairvoyance and blood-writing. "Spiritualism and Conjuring," in Edward Hingston, *The Genial Showman, Being Reminiscences of the Life of Artemus*

That Browne did not exploit this firsthand material a year later for "Artemus Ward among the Spirits" perhaps suggests the degree to which the comic séance had become a standard formula for the literary comedian. This sketch was probably occasioned by newspaper stories from New York about scandals within the spiritualistic movement, including a report of a convention of "harmonial" spiritualists who listened to trance prophecies of a utopia based on free love; lurid charges of sexual and financial irregularity surrounding the separation of the beautiful young trance-lecturer, Cora Hatch, from her husband and magnetist, Dr. Benjamin Hatch; and the recantations of several professional mediums who warned the innocent believer against the misbehavior of their erstwhile colleagues.[45] In this light, Ward's reason for attending a "Sperretooal Sircle"—that his neighbors were "mourn harf crazy on the new fangled idear about Sperrets"—was not so anachronistic as it might appear to have been ten years after Hydesville. In reporting the messages received from the spirits, however, he simply adopted the conventions of Doesticks and his predecessors. Thus Ward's wish to speak with the spirit of his ex-partner, "Bill Tomkins," if Tomkins was present and sober, calls to mind both the temporarily sober wife of Doesticks's spurious uncle and the disorderly behavior of Wagstaff's old friend, "Joseph Pipkins." Similarly, when Tomkins said that "he & John Bunyan was travelin with a side show in connection with Shakespere, Jonson & Co.'s Circus," he was improving on Doesticks's disclosure that Bunyan had become a clown, that Shakespeare was writing a new play, and that Dr. Johnson was helping form "a traveling theatre."[46] Browne thus exploited Doesticks's formula so as to make fictional sense in terms of Artemus Ward's humorous character, dialect, and theatrical occupation. Indeed, the spirit of Ward's father chastised him for deserting his profession to write for the newspapers.

Reflected in Ward's contempt for the "4 or 5 long hared fellers"

Ward, and Pictures of a Showman's Career in the Western World (New York, 1870), pp. 106–11.

[45] *New York Times*, October 14, 1858, p. 4; November 29, 1858, p. 4; *New York Tribune*, November 25, 1858 p. 3; November 29, 1858, p. 7; December 2, 1858, p. 7; December 6, 1858, p. 5; *New York Weekly Tribune*, July 3, 1858, pp. 2–3; October 2, 1858, pp. 2, 7.

[46] Browne, pp. 48, 50.

who had set up in business as mediums were charges that recent scandals had proved spiritualism to be a menace to marriage and the family. To be sure, one of the seers honored the comic tradition by reducing Andrew Jackson Davis's "Harmonial Philosophy" to gibberish, declaring that "the ethereal essunce of the koordinate branchis of superhuman natur becum mettymorfussed as man progress in harmonial coexistunce." But Ward's wife had already driven one of the "long hared fellers" from her home for suggesting that she would make "a sweet mejium."[47] And Ward's own severest criticism was reserved for the morality rather than the philosophy of these itinerant seers:

> Just so soon as a man becums a reglar out & out Sperret rapper he leaves orf workin, lets his hare grow all over his face & commensis spungin his livin out of other peple. He eats all the dickshunaries he can find & goze round chock full of big words, scarein the wimmin folks & little children and destroyin the piece of mind of evry famerlee he enters. He don't do nobody no good & is a cuss to society & a pirit on honest peple's corn beef barrils. Admittin all you say abowt the doctrin to be troo, I must say the reglar perfessional Sperret rappers—tham as makes a bisnis on it—air abowt the most ornery set of cusses I ever enkountered in my life.[48]

Even here, Ward's objection to "spungin" mediums was that of Doesticks, expanded and adapted to his own dialect.

The attitude of the literary comedians at their most critical was crystallized in Ward's remarks about mediums. More serious writers would explore spiritualism's religious and psychological implications, treating its mediums not as mere parasitic sharpers but as enigmatic and complex personalities or demonically inspired radicals. For Ward, however, as for most of the humorists, spiritualism offered a topical focus for commonsensical ridicule of human foolishness, and the séance provided a convenient framework for recurrent comic patterns.

By the end of the 1850's the comic sketch of the rapping séance had almost exhausted itself as a humorous subtype, just as the rapping séance itself had gone out of style. But the spirits had always been

[47] Ibid., pp. 48, 49.
[48] Ibid., p. 50.

utilized to attack other things than spiritualism, and for David Ross Locke and James Russell Lowell the rappings were still available as a framing device for political satire. Locke used the "mejum" and the rappings of earlier humorists to allow the deceased giants of "Dimokrasy" to denounce the Copperhead sentiments of Petroleum V. Nasby. Asking whether the spirit of Thomas Jefferson supported a war in behalf of abolition, Nasby was embarrassed by raps of "awful distinknis" which answered, "We hold these trooths to be self-evident, that all men is creatid ekal."[49] At another séance, "Androo Jaxon" condemned Nasby and his fellow Cooperheads for having "strangled the Dimokrasy I left yoo, and . . . put Calhoon's into its close."[50] Such experiences led Nasby to repudiate the rappings as unreliable, the spirits as imposters. For Locke, of course, the séance was just one of several occult devices, such as the dream and the vision, for inflicting humiliation on Nasby.[51]

One of the last humorous invocations of the rapping muse was James Russell Lowell's prose introduction to "Kettelpotomachia" in *The Biglow Papers, Second Series* (1867).[52] Lowell was evidently much amused by the table-tipping and furniture-dancing séances of the 1850's, for sometime after publishing "The Unhappy Lot of Mr. Knott" in 1851 he had added to the poem some lines about talespinning tables, prophetic armchairs, a pedantic footstool, and a dancing teapoy[53]—perhaps around the time that he mentioned, in a letter of 1853, an eloquent teapoy, an "exhorting bootjack," and a Massachusetts judge whose mediumistic power required that he "drive back the furniture from following him . . . as one might a pack of too affectionate dogs."[54] There had also been "prophetic chairs" in "Fragments of an Unfinished Poem" (1853),[55] "chairs beating the devil's

[49] "Communes with Spirits," in David Ross Locke, *The Struggles (Social, Financial and Political) of Petroleum V. Nasby* (Boston, 1872), p. 102.
[50] "Consults the Spirits," ibid., p. 157.
[51] "Has a Dream," "Has a Frightful Dream," "Has a Vision," "Dreams a Dream," ibid., pp. 143–45, 152–53, 175–77, 183–85.
[52] James Russell Lowell, *The Biglow Papers, Second Series* (Boston, 1867), pp. 186–97.
[53] Lowell, *Poetical Works*, II, 295–96.
[54] Lowell, *Letters*, I, 198.
[55] James Russell Lowell, *The Complete Poetical Works of James Russell Lowell* (Boston, 1897), p. 159.

tattoo all over Christendom"[56] in one of his Lowell lectures, and Hosea Biglow's ghostly ancestor's remark that before discovering mediums to be liars he had "danced the tables till their legs wuz gone," in "Sunthin' in the Pastoral Line" (1862).[57] So taken was Lowell by the tables, in fact, that they were anachronistically still to be dancing "the Old One's own tattoo" in "Credidimus Jovem Regnare" (1887),[58] long after their popularity at séances had passed.

But for the present, faced with the problem of finding a place in *The Biglow Papers* for "Kettelpotomachia," his Latin verse satire on a journalistic dispute in Virginia, Lowell returned to the rappings he had begun with in "Mr. Knott." His expedient was to have the Reverend Mr. Hitchcock of Jalaam send the verses to the *Atlantic Monthly* (where they never appeared), along with a letter attributing them in good faith to the pedantic spirit of the recently departed Parson Wilbur, who had allegedly rapped them out in the presence of an adolescent medium. Pointing out that the young medium was a high-spirited sophomore who was familiar with other hexameters written by Wilbur before his death, a facetious editorial voice declared that the verses were being published despite their suspicious origin, "partly as a warning to their putative author which may keep him from such indecorous pranks for the future."[59]

Fittingly, Lowell was mining some of the last ore to be taken from the vein of comic material which he had discovered in "The Unhappy Lot of Mr. Knott." This material had not proved to be of the highest yield, but it had given the literary comedians one of their standard routines, the comic séance. Mark Twain had read some of these sketches, and he was already utilizing their techniques in his own pieces about spiritualism during the last days of his western apprenticeship. But aside from its appearance in these newspaper sketches by Twain, and its reappearance later in *Life on the Mississippi* (1883) and the unfinished Mysterious Stranger manuscript, "Schoolhouse Hill" (1898), this vein of material seems to have been played out by the end of the Civil War.

---

[56] Lowell, *The Function of the Poet and Other Essays*, p. 22.
[57] Lowell, *The Complete Poetical Works*, p. 264.
[58] Ibid., p. 423.
[59] Ibid., p. 270.

III | As with the comic séance, it took little time for writers to repeat Lowell's other discovery of the comic possibilities afforded by the union of spurious spiritual manifestations with the pattern of stories like Irving's "Legend of Sleepy Hollow." By 1853 an anti-spiritualistic *Harper's* editorial had prescribed the humorous supernatural tale as an antidote to popular superstition,[60] and humorists had begun to fill the prescription with tales of practical jokes and natural occurrences taken by the credulous as spontaneous spiritual manifestations. For the most part these pieces were ephemeral. But in "The Apple-Tree Table; or, Original Spiritual Manifestations" (1856), Herman Melville transcended the limitations of the type with an imaginative comic treatment of spontaneous rappings construed in terms of New England witchcraft and evoking a variety of attitudes toward spiritualism.

Spontaneous rappings and other phenomena easily lent themselves to tales of practical jokes. In "Mysterious Rappings Explained" (1853),[61] the humorous lecturer Ossian E. Dodge told of terrifying a believer in "the Rochester ladies"[62] by rapping and imitating the voice of his victim's dead wife. Rather improbably, spiritualism came to the old southwest in John B. Jones's *Life and Adventures of a Country Merchant* (ca. 1854),[63] when an exhorting revivalist, lying to a nocturnal camp-meeting about his séance experiences, was confounded by a sudden manifestation of hellfire as pranksters concealed above him in a tree poured brandy and sulphur on the flame of his torch. Benjamin P. Shillaber, editor of the *Carpet-Bag*, wrote about both deliberate and accidental pseudo-manifestations. His Mrs. Partington, although skeptical of "sperituous knockings," was nonetheless thrice bedeviled by her nephew Ike with spiritual trickery in sketches which Mark Twain read and perhaps remembered. Her skepticism about the spirits was shaken when Ike dressed up as his dead uncle in "Paul's

[60] [Tayler Lewis,] "Editor's Table," *Harper's* VI (April 1853), 699–703.
[61] Bob Lively [pseud.], "Mysterious Rappings Explained; or, An Artful Dodge," *Dodge's Sketches*, pp. 25–29, issued with Robert Morris, *The Faithful Slave* (Boston, 1853).
[62] Ibid., p. 26.
[63] John B. Jones, *Life and Adventures of a Country Merchant* (Philadelphia, 1875), pp. 90–94.

Ghost," and she was terrified when Ike made a teapot appear to float in air as if animated by spiritual power in "A Striking Manifestation." On a third occasion Ike hid in a chest and rapped out in his dead uncle's name a demand for "Sidur" in the spirit-world.[64]

As for accidental manifestations, the narrator of Shillaber's own version of "Mysterious Rappings" (1853)[65] parodied Poe in relating how incessant knockings from within a closet had driven him into a frenzy until he discovered leaking rainwater dripping on a hatbox and ruining the beauty of the hat "forevermore." Henry Bacon's tale of a servant girl frightened by a doorbell rung by kittens was entitled "The Mysterious Bell Ringing" (1853).[66] And in "Tolliwotte's Ghost" (1855),[67] thumping sounds made by an innocent intruder in the basement of a house stimulated a discussion by those above about the superiority of the aristocratic ghost of tradition to alphabetically rapping and table-tipping imposters.

The writers of such trifles used a common stock of devices. Like the humorists who visited séances, they ran to topical titles and often referred directly or indirectly to such personalities as the Fox sisters and Judge John Edmonds. But they were concerned with natural phenomena or practical jokes—with apparently spontaneous manifestations discovered (to the embarrassment of the credulous) to be false —rather than with mediums and séances. And they used these spurious manifestations as a way of providing a topical twist to familiar comic situations.

In much the same way Herman Melville fashioned "The Apple-Tree Table" for the May, 1856, issue of *Putnam's Monthly Magazine*.[68] Melville was evidently taken with an anecdote in a history of Berkshire County about insects which had noisily but beautifully emerged from a wooden tabletop many years after the eggs had been laid in the

---

[64] Benjamin P. Shillaber, *Life and Sayings of Mrs. Partington and Others of the Family* (New York, 1854), pp. 51–53, 83, 347–48.

[65] Benjamin P. Shillaber, *Rhymes, with Reason and Without* (Boston, 1853), pp. 43–46.

[66] Henry Bacon, "The Mysterious Bell Ringing," *Gleason's Pictorial Magazine* IV (June 25, 1853), 403.

[67] *Putnam's* V (April 1855), 421–26.

[68] [Herman Melville,] "The Apple-Tree Table," *Putnam's* VII (May 1856), 465–75. Subsequent references are to Melville, *The Complete Stories of Herman Melville*, ed. Jay Leyda (New York, 1949), pp. 409–35.

living tree.[69] And he seems to have been stimulated to write the story by Thoreau's use of the same incident at the end of *Walden* as a symbol of "resurrection and immortality."[70] For his own treatment of the table and its nascent bugs, Melville devised a comic framework of spurious, spontaneous rappings. Thus the subtitle, "Original Spiritual Manifestations"; the narrator's arch disclaimer that the events related in his tale "happened long before the time of the 'Fox Girls' "; and the astonishment and consternation caused in his household by the "unaccountable tickings" of insects eating their way out of a "mysterious table" which he had discovered in his long-locked attic.[71]

Within this rather conventional framework, however, Melville ingeniously juxtaposed several current responses to spiritualism in such a way as to suggest basically different attitudes toward the possibility of spiritual immortality in general. Although somewhat on the wane by the end of 1855, the spiritualistic movement was still newsworthy through the efforts of such enthusiasts as Judge John Edmonds, whose *Spiritualism* (1853, 1855) was the decade's most popular treatise on the subject, and Professor Robert Hare, a respected elderly scientist who in the fall of 1855 published his *Experimental Investigation of the Spirit Manifestations* and lectured on "Celestial Mechanics" before an audience of three thousand at Broadway Tabernacle.[72] Certainly the movement's opponents were disturbed by the persistent interest taken in spirits by such "conscientious, intelligent people." Some critics even saw a rekindling of the superstitious excitement which a century and a half before had led to the Salem witchcraft trials. Noting the "sad stuff" of Hare's lectures in his diary, George Templeton Strong, the New York lawyer who paid intermittent skeptical attention to spiritualism throughout the 1850's, was exasperated by the dual anomalies that in a supposedly enlightened age, "ex-judges of the Supreme Court" (Edmonds) and "professors of physical sciences" (Hare) should publicly testify to these "new

[69] See Jay Leyda's note to "The Apple-Tree Table," in Melville, *Complete Stories of Herman Melville*, pp. 470–71.

[70] Henry David Thoreau, *The Variorum Walden*, ed. Walter Harding (New York, 1962), p. 266.

[71] Melville, *Complete Stories of Herman Melville*, pp. 409–14, 419, 421.

[72] Edmonds and Dexter, *Spiritualism*, 2 vols. (New York, 1853, 1855); Hare, *Experimental Investigation* (New York, 1855); Fornell, pp. 76–77.

treasures," while others, with equal irrationality, should fear mediumistic phenomena "as a visible manifestation of demonic agency."[73] These attitudes—the faith of respectable and intelligent people in spirit communication, the fear of others that it was satanic in origin, and the suspicion of people like Strong that it was a new form of old superstition—formed the immediate topical background of "The Apple-Tree Table."

Melville treated these potentially serious matters in a thoroughly comic fashion. The table itself, with its "mysterious tickings," was the focal point of the attitudes he dramatized. His narrator's two daughters responded to the tickings in the manner of Strong's fearful acquaintances, hysterically convinced that the noises were caused by evil spirits. The narrator's termagant wife, however, was outraged both by the unexplained tickings and by her daughters' cries of "Spirits! Spirits!" Barely dissuaded from cutting into the table in her obsessive search for a natural solution, she exhibited the aggressive skepticism with which the claims of the spiritualists and their witch-fearing opponents alike were often greeted.[74] Her answer was eventually provided by the "lucid" but "prosy" naturalist, Professor Johnson, who explained how a beautiful insect captured by the narrator as it emerged from the wood had lain unhatched in its egg for one hundred and fifty years. With his sneer for any "crude, spiritual hypothesis,"[75] the professor displayed the general contempt of science (Robert Hare excepted) for spirit-rappings.

In the mind of the over-imaginative narrator these responses were polarized in the figures of Cotton Mather and Democritus. Along with the table the narrator had also reclaimed from his attic a tattered copy of Mather's *Magnalia,* and he had just frightened himself with its tales of witchcraft when the first tickings made his hair feel "like growing grass." The discovery that the sounds came from the cloven-footed little table sent him to bed in terror. In daylight, however, he

---

[73] George Templeton Strong, *The Diary of George Templeton Strong,* ed. Allan Nevins and Milton Halsey Thomas (New York, 1952), II, 133, 244–45.

[74] Melville, *Complete Stories of Herman Melville,* pp. 418–20. The wife's hostility toward spirits supports the view that she was of different biographical origin from her counterpart in "I and My Chimney," two of whose enthusiasms were Swedenborgianism and "the Spirit-Rapping Philosophy" (ibid., p. 386).

[75] Ibid., p. 434.

was "a jeerer at all tea-table spirits whatever," trying to imitate the complete skepticism of Democritus, who had ignored the attempts of little boys to frighten him with "spurious ghosts."[76] Indeed, the narrator's interpretation of Democritus' position to mean "that any possible investigation of any possible spiritual phenomena was absurd"[77] perhaps deliberately characterized the skeptical reaction to Robert Hare's *Experimental Investigation of the Spirit Manifestations*, which *Putnam's* reviewer had recently dismissed as unscientific theological speculation.[78] Similarly, Melville's subtitle, "Original Spiritual Manifestations," provided an ironic gloss for such titles as Adin Ballou's *Spirit Manifestations* (1852) and Charles Beecher's *Review of the "Spiritual Manifestations"* (1853).[79]

Melville's narrator was too susceptible to the uncanny to follow the advice of Democritus. He also felt the power of "doleful, ghostly, ghastly Cotton Mather," and he reverted after dark to his own apprehensive investigation of the mysterious tickings. Oscillating between the roles of Mather and Democritus and harassed by his daughters' hysteria and his wife's ill-tempered skepticism, the narrator underwent a comically exaggerated ordeal of fright and frustration for several nights before finally trapping an emergent bug for Professor Johnson's inspection. In the process he rid himself of his own fears of the demonic supernatural without falling into either the harsh materialism of his wife or the unimaginative scientism of the professor. Nor did he share the joy of his superstitious daughter, who insisted on drawing a "spiritual lesson" from the glowing insect even after its genesis had been explained: "Spirits! spirits! . . . I still believe in spirits, only now I believe in them with delight, when before I but thought of them with terror." Free by this time from Mather's grip and able to regard the table and its bugs with objective detachment, the narrator noted only that "the mysterious insect did not long enjoy its radiant life; it expired the next day."[80]

[76] Ibid., pp. 416, 430, 422.
[77] Ibid., p. 422.
[78] "Editorial Notes," *Putnam's* VII (January 1856), 103–4.
[79] Adin Ballou, *An Exposition of Views Regarding . . . Spirit Manifestations* (Boston, 1852); Charles Beecher, *A Review of the "Spiritual Manifestations"* (New York, 1853).
[80] Melville, *Complete Stories of Herman Melville*, pp. 416, 435.

Daniel G. Hoffman has written that Melville used the newly republished *Magnalia* as a "fearful emblem of spiritual life,"[81] and he has called attention to a short article about "The Spirits in 1692 and What They Did at Salem,"[82] published in the same issue of *Putnam's* as Melville's tale, as evidence of the topical currency of Salem witchcraft. Valid so far as it goes, Hoffman's view overlooks the anti-spiritualistic thrust of the *Putnam's* article and oversimplifies Melville's handling of the *Magnalia*. For just as Democritus stood in "The Apple-Tree Table" for skepticism toward the rappings, so Mather's book ironically represented the testimony of the spiritualists themselves.

Most obviously, of course, Mather's explanation of witchcraft was available to those who looked upon the rappings as a new outbreak of demonism. But it was not at all unusual for the spiritualists and their most skeptical critics alike to draw parallels between the spiritual manifestations of the 1850's and the events related in the *Magnalia*. Judge Edmonds, the leading spiritualistic writer of the day, wrote that "the history of Salem Witchcraft is but an account of spiritual manifestations, and of man's incapacity to understand them."[83] Scoffers, on the other hand, suggested that the testimony at Salem and Rochester sprang from the common root of superstitious credulity. The only difference between the two episodes, said the editor of the *North American Review* in "Modern Necromancy" (1855), was the difference between "infernal" and "celestial" spirits, and he predicted that spiritualism would eventually be remembered "with the same vague scepticism with which most persons regard the diabolical workings recorded in Mather's 'Magnalia.' "[84] As noted earlier, for James Russell Lowell table-tipping simply illustrated the hardihood of popular superstition: "Turning over the yellow leaves of the same copy of 'Webster on Witchcraft' which Cotton Mather studied, I thought, 'Well, that goblin is laid at last!'—and while I mused the tables were turning and the chairs beating the devil's tattoo all over Christen-

---

81 Daniel G. Hoffman, *Form and Fable in American Fiction* (New York, 1961), p. 291.
82 *Putnam's* VII (May 1856), 511.
83 Edmonds and Dexter, *Spiritualism*, I, 44.
84 [A. P. Peabody,] "Modern Necromancy," *North American Review* LXXX (April 1855), 523, 524.

dom."[85] And in criticizing Mather's tacit support of the Salem trials, the *Putnam's* article cited by Daniel Hoffman made the same connection more angrily, both in its title ("The Spirits in 1692 and What They Did at Salem") and in its conclusion:

> This misery it may be well to remember, for it grew out of an unwise and superstitious curiosity about devils and spirits, and became cruel and bloody through an epidemic fear—both of which may again recur; indeed, the former belief has been pressed upon us in our own day. . . . The belief out of which the Salem cruelties grew, is a proof that a false belief is sometimes deadly; and we are bound to protest against any theory of spirits presented on shallow proof.[86]

There was ample precedent, then, for Melville to look to the *Magnalia* for "Original Spiritual Manifestations."

Evidently more amused than disturbed by the notion that the spiritual rappings of the 1850's might be a rehatching of the Puritan witchcraft of the 1690's, Melville allowed his narrator to discover both the grotesque little table, with its hundred-and-fifty-year-old eggs, and the *Magnalia*, with its equally old demons, in the musty attic where they had long been locked away. He recapitulated the historical shift from the Puritan to the spiritualistic attitude with the elder daughter's conversion from a terrified to a delighted belief in spirits. And he brought his narrator from an equally frightened nighttime curiosity about devils and spirits to a position of noncommittal irony regarding both Mather's demonology and the "seraphical"[87] but short-lived bug of spiritualism.

It is quite possible, moreover, that Mather and his *Magnalia* represented more specifically for Melville's tale the example and testimony of Judge John Worth Edmonds. Just as Mather's was an authoritative account of demonic manifestations, so the two volumes of Edmonds

---

[85] Lowell, *The Function of the Poet and Other Essays*, p. 22.

[86] *Putnam's* VII (May 1856), 511. Edmund Wilson has pointed out that John W. De Forest's "Witching Times," which began to appear in *Putnam's* in December, 1856, was designed in part to "discourage that atmosphere of the supernatural" to which the Fox sisters had contributed (Edmund Wilson, *Patriotic Gore: Studies in the Literature of the American Civil War* [New York, 1962], p. 679).

[87] Melville, *Complete Stories of Herman Melville*, p. 433.

and Dr. George T. Dexter's *Spiritualism* (1853, 1855) constituted for the spiritualists of the 1850's a definitive record of celestial manifestations. Naturally enough, questions as to Edmonds's sanity, probity, and credibility had provoked a good deal of public discussion, the Judge and his defenders pointing to his reputation as a politician, lawyer, and jurist,[88] his critics often conceding his eminence and sincerity, and sometimes his intellect. Although remarking that such past examples of judicial fallibility as death sentences handed down for witchcraft made it impossible to rely altogether on Edmonds's professional stature, *Putnam's* unfavorable reviewer thought that the Judge's testimony in *Spiritualism* should command special respect:

> The reputation of such an indorser as Judge Edmonds too—a lawyer of great sagacity, accustomed to weighing evidence, and a man of the most exemplary integrity, whose words on a matter of fact cannot be doubted, ought to commend the subject to an impartial investigation, or at least shield it from the flippant commentaries of the lower order of journalists.[89]

Given the nature of his testimony, of course, nothing could have protected Edmonds from journalistic flippancy, and inevitably he had become a favorite target for topical humor. Dramatist John Brougham had caricatured him as "Smallbrain" in an 1855 skit.[90] After Edmonds claimed in the fall of 1854 that he had been informed of the sinking of the crack steamship *Arctic* by spirits of drowned passengers well before the news had reached New York, Q. K. Philander Doesticks detected in a message from the ghost of his drowned dog the influence of spiritual communications published in the newspapers by "a distinguished and formerly-supposed-sensible-and-sane Judge of the Superior Court of the Empire State."[91] Vexed that the spiritualists did think the Judge sensible and sane, George Templeton Strong observed

---

[88] Capron, pp. 197–203; Britten, *Modern American Spiritualism*, pp. 73–74, 94–102.
[89] "Editorial Notes," *Putnam's* II (December 1853), 680–81. For a sampling of other critical opinions, see *Knickerbocker* XLV (March 1855), 301–2; *Graham's* XLVI (May 1855), 472; Britten, *Modern American Spiritualism*, pp. 99–100.
[90] John Brougham, "Revenge; or, The Medium," *A Basket of Chips* (New York, 1855), pp. 191–99.
[91] Thomson, *Doesticks What He Says*, pp. 265–66; Fornell, p. 73.

of the *Arctic* disclosures that "Edmonds prints all this, and thousands of people, external to any lunatic asylum, believe it."[92]

Melville knew something of Edmonds's earlier experiences on the governing board of New York state prisons;[93] according to Jay Leyda, moreover, he was acquainted with the Judge's spiritualistic writings.[94] And it would appear that in his narrator's reflections on the power of Cotton Mather's tales of demonism, Melville utilized the idiom of the public debate over Edmonds to present a tongue-in-cheek version of the problem faced by readers of the Judge's reports of celestial spirits:

> Now, for the first time it struck me that this was no romantic Mrs. Radcliffe who had written the Magnalia, but a practical, hardworking, earnest man, a learned doctor, too, as well as a good Christian and orthodox clergyman. What possible motive could such a man have to deceive? . . . In the most straightforward way, he laid before me detailed accounts of New England witchcraft, each important item corroborated by respectable townfolk, and, of not a few the most surprising, he himself had been eyewitness. Cotton Mather testified whereof he had seen. But is it possible? I asked myself. Then I remembered that Dr. Johnson, the matter-of-fact compiler of a dictionary, had been a believer in ghosts, besides many other sound, worthy men.[95]

[92] Strong, *Diary*, II, 197–98.

[93] Jay Leyda, ed., *The Melville Log* (New York, 1951), II, 523. Leyda quoted a passage from Evert Duycinck's "Diary" (October 1, 1856): "Melville passed the evening with me—fresh from his mountain charged to the muzzle with his sailor metaphysics and jargon of things unknowable. . . . Melville instanced old Burton as atheistical—in the exquisite irony of his passage on some sacred matters; cited . . . a story from Judge Edmonds of a prayer meeting of female convicts at Sing Sing which the Judge was invited to witness and agreed to, provided he was introduced where he could not be seen. It was an orgie of indecency and blasphemy." This anecdote did not appear in Edmonds and Dexter's *Spiritualism*.

[94] Melville, *Complete Stories of Herman Melville*, p. 471. Leyda cited Melville's familiarity with "the literature of the craze—with the writings of Judge John W. Edmonds and Walter O. Dendy, with Horace Greeley's newspaper patronage of the Fox Girls." But the American edition of Dendy's *Philosophy of Mystery* appeared in 1845, when Allan Melville bought a copy—some two years before spiritualism began with the Hydesville disturbances. In 1850 Allan Melville pasted a clipping from Greeley's *Tribune* about the Rochester rappings into his copy of Dendy, thus providing a possible but hardly likely source for the narrator's reference to "the Fox Girls" (Leyda, ed., *The Melville Log*, I, 200, 362).

[95] Melville, *Complete Stories of Herman Melville*, p. 415.

For the spiritualists, at least—for those thousands of believers who were, in George Templeton Strong's words, "external to any lunatic asylum"—Judge John Worth Edmonds and Dr. George T. Dexter were "sound, worthy men" who believed in "ghosts" and, without apparent motive to deceive, laid before their readers detailed accounts of spiritual manifestations witnessed by themselves and other reputable members of the New York Circle of Spiritualists.

There was a pointedly skeptical irony in Melville's linking of Puritan and spiritualist. The spirits had told Edmonds that to believe in Christ meant to believe in the "doctrine" rather than the "person," and at the heart of the doctrine lay the proposition that all men, regardless of their earthly behavior and without undergoing much change at death, would enjoy an immortality of "progression onward, upward toward perfection forever." Such revelations, of course, ran counter to Calvinistic doctrine and orthodox Christian thought in general—in the case of Judge Edmonds, quite consciously so. For the spirits had commissioned him to publish their messages in order to offer mankind new hope by dispelling such "theological errors" as the belief in a wrathful God which had led too many men so to dread the afterlife as to wish for "annihilation"[96] instead. With the manifold masks of *The Confidence Man* (1856) not far ahead of him, Melville may have taken special enjoyment in disguising Edmonds, who had compared attacks against him to the Salem hangings, as the original Lightning Rod Man himself.

Whether Melville looked beyond Edmonds's public image to his book is open to conjecture. Elements common to both the narrator's tickings and the spontaneous rappings described by Edmonds as having surprised him in his bedchamber were perhaps inevitable in such experiences.[97] More suggestive is the narrator's declaration that when the insect thought by his daughters to be an evil spirit finally emerged in opalescent glory, it could not have charmed the girls more had it worn miniature sword, necklace, gun, and held "a tiny manuscript in its mouth—a Chaldee manuscript."[98] Spirits often manifested themselves in ancient or unknown tongues. Dr. Dexter had told in *Spir-*

[96] Edmonds and Dexter, I, 56, 65, 80.
[97] Ibid., p. 16; *Complete Stories of Herman Melville*, pp. 423, 431–32.
[98] Melville, *Complete Stories of Herman Melville*, p. 432.

itualism of hearing illiterate mechanics hold trance discourse in a number of exotic languages, among them Chaldaic. Edmonds himself had written of finding a piece of paper with undecipherable spiritual hieroglyphics under a séance table. And Edward Fowler, the young medium who had already received a letter from the spirits of '76, had said in an appendix to Edmonds and Dexter's first volume that ancient ghosts had twice visited him in costume to deliver messages inscribed in Hebrew and Sanskrit characters.[99] Such a document, perhaps, was Melville's imagined "Chaldee manuscript."

But for the source and ultimate irony of the spiritualistic context of "The Apple-Tree Table" we must look beyond the literature of the movement to the peroration of Thoreau's *Walden*:

> Everyone has heard the story which has gone the rounds of New England, of a strong and beautiful bug which came out of the dry leaf of an old table of apple-tree wood . . . from an egg deposited in the living tree many years earlier still . . . which was heard gnawing out for several weeks, hatched perchance by the heat of an urn. Who does not feel his faith in a resurrection and immortality strengthened by hearing of this? Who knows what beautiful and winged life, whose egg has been buried for ages under many concentric layers of woodenness in the dead dry life of society, deposited at first in the alburnum of the green and living tree, which has been gradually converted into the semblance of its well-seasoned tomb—heard perchance gnawing out now for years by the astonished family of man, as they sat round the festive board—may unexpectedly come forth from amidst society's most trivial and handselled furniture, to enjoy its perfect summer life at last![100]

Arguing that this passage suggested "The Apple-Tree Table" to Melville, Frank Davidson has pointed both to general similarities, such as the astonishment caused in the narrator's family by the ticking table, and to what appear to be distinct verbal echoes of Thoreau in the daughter's rhapsody over the beautiful and winged bug:[101]

[99] Edmonds and Dexter, I, 87, 25, 447–49.
[100] Thoreau, *The Variorum Walden*, p. 266.
[101] Frank Davidson, "Melville, Thoreau, and 'The Apple-Tree Table,'" *American Literature* XXV (January 1954), 479–88.

". . . if this beauteous creature be not a spirit, it yet teaches a spiritual lesson. For if, after one hundred and fifty years' entombment, a mere insect comes forth at last into light, itself an effulgence, shall there be no glorified resurrection for the spirit of man? Spirits! spirits! . . . I still believe in spirits, only now I believe in them with delight, when before I but thought of them with terror."

The mysterious insect [noted the narrator] did not long enjoy its radiant life; it expired the next day.[102]

Viewing the tale as spiritual autobiography rather than spirit-rapping comedy, Davidson has taken the narrator's ironic observation to express Melville's rejection of Thoreau's optimistic interpretation of the anecdote.[103] Although persuasive, this argument is incomplete. For it also seems clear that Thoreau's marvelous table, noisy bugs, domestic surprise, and the spiritual lesson he derived from them, must have appealed to Melville's sense of humor as resembling nothing so much, taken literally, as another ecstatic report of "Original Spiritual Manifestations." Thus the irony of the tale's criticism of Thoreau (who had written his sister that he would rather invest in an "Immediate Annihilation Company" than believe the Concord spiritualists)[104] lay in the daughter's use of his transcendental language to describe the happy significance of the emergence of the "seraphical" bug of spiritualism from a century and a half's entombment in the demonic furniture of Puritanism.

Melville erred in his narrator's prediction of a short life for spiritualism, although its radiance was soon to dim until the early 1870's. Yet in placing his narrator in the predicament of an over-imaginative reader of Judge Edmonds faced by spontaneous rappings in his own household, he maintained a sure-handed control which was unusual in his tales. And his discovery of complex spiritual ironies in the mysterious table showed that it was possible for a skeptical writer to deal with spiritualism on a level of philosophical comedy quite beyond the formulaic ridicule of Lowell and the humorists, while still working within the conventions of their tales of spurious rappings. Such objectivity perhaps bespoke the author's satisfaction at exploiting the

102 Melville, *Complete Stories of Herman Melville*, p. 435.
103 Davidson, pp. 484, 487.
104 Thoreau, *Letters to Various Persons* (Boston, 1865), p. 67.

table's potential as material for amusing magazine fiction while at the same time rejecting a variety of "-isms"—Puritan, transcendental, and spiritual. Although by the following autumn Melville was to have made up his own mind "to be annihilated,"[105] it was a thoroughly comic impulse which responded to Thoreau's spiritual optimism by equating Cotton Mather and Judge Edmonds to elicit the most imaginative literary rappings of the decade.

[105] Nathaniel Hawthorne, *The English Notebooks,* ed. Randall Stewart (New York, 1941), p. 432.

III: "GHOSTS AND GHOST-SEEING" [1]

Spiritualism in Occult Fiction

I | While Lowell and the literary comedians were laughing at
spiritualism during its early years, other writers found its
mediums, manifestations, and doctrines suitable for serious literary
treatment. With its millennial tone and its attraction for reformers
and community men of all sorts, and with its susceptibility to charges
of demonism and infidelity, the movement became the object of serious social and religious satire. Questions of belief aside, it also
offered a topical frame of reference for supernatural fiction, and
its phenomena—rappings, spirit-writing, materialized hands, spectral
guitar music—offered specific occult devices. Exploitation along these
lines was perhaps limited by the polemical furor which accompanied
the movement, and by the inanities which drew the ridicule of humorists. Yet by repeatedly bringing ghosts to public attention, spiritualism
probably helped stimulate the general appetite for supernatural fiction
(as would the work of the Society for Psychical Research toward the
end of the century). The mediums themselves, especially attractive
young seeresses like the Fox sisters and Cora Hatch, fit neatly into
established patterns of Gothic romance simply by virtue of their hu-

1 [Tayler Lewis,] "Editor's Table," Harper's VI (April 1853), 699. Lewis's editorial (ibid., pp. 699–703) distinguished between traditional "ghost stories" and
spiritualistic "ghost-seeing."

man situation and puzzling talent, and as time passed they came to provide a focus for writers interested in exploring unusual states of consciousness. Even in the work of the most serious writer, however, there was always the possibility that spiritualism might provoke laughter.

Nathaniel Hawthorne was the first writer of note to make serious literary use of such material. Hawthorne's attitude toward spiritualism grew out of his feelings about the "strange science" of mesmerism. Accepting mesmeric clairvoyance as physiological fact, he distrusted its use as ethically dangerous and denied that it was in any way super-natural. He was especially repelled by mesmeric claims of spirit com-munication. In 1841 he warned his fiancée, Sophia Peabody, whose interest in the occult was always to trouble him, against "magnetic miracles" which promised glimpses of the afterlife. Whatever hap-pened, he told her, was "the result of a material and physical, not of a spiritual influence. . . . I should as soon think of seeking revelations of the future state in the rottenness of the grave."[2]

Despite his dislike of mesmerism, Hawthorne employed it profitably in *The House of the Seven Gables* (1851)[3] and *The Blithedale Ro-mance* (1852)[4] as a source of the marvelous with both supernatural ambience and potentially rational explanation, and as one version of the unpardonable sin.[5] The magnetic trances of Alice Pyncheon and Priscilla in these romances were of the very spirit-seeking sort against which he had cautioned Sophia.[6] But though he often commented on

[2] Nathaniel Hawthorne, *Passages from the American Note-Books* (Boston, 1891), pp. 244–45.
[3] (Boston, 1851); subsequent citations are to Nathaniel Hawthorne, *The House of the Seven Gables*, Centenary edition, ed. William Charvat et al. (Columbus, Ohio, 1965).
[4] (Boston, 1852); subsequent citations are to Nathaniel Hawthorne, *The Blithe-dale Romance and Fanshawe*, Centenary edition, ed. William Charvat et al. (Columbus, Ohio, 1964).
[5] Randall Stewart, ed., *American Notebooks*, by Nathaniel Hawthorne (New Haven, 1932), pp. lxxiv–lxxvi.
[6] At almost the same time that Lowell was writing about the requests addressed to Mr. Knott's spirits to identify the culprit "Who picked the pocket of Seth Crane, / of Waldo precinct, State of Maine," Hawthorne described Matthew Maule's attempt to convert Alice Pyncheon's mind "into a kind of telescopic medium" through which he could "obtain a glimpse into the spiritual world" and thereby find out who had stolen the entire Waldo precinct from the Pyncheon

spiritualism itself in his journals, he never dealt with it very extensively in his fiction.[7] Nonetheless his early rejection of the American "epoch of the rapping spirits" in *The House of the Seven Gables* and *The Blithedale Romance* anticipated the lengthier attacks soon to follow from religious and social satirists, and perhaps indicated some of the problems which the phenomena of spiritualism posed for the writer of occult fiction. Later, in Italy, he discovered spiritualistic materials which he could adapt to his own habitual literary patterns. These materials he transformed into appropriate Gothic decor in *The Marble Faun* (1860)[8] and drew upon for central character relationships in two of his unfinished romances, *Doctor Grimshawe's Secret* (1882)[9] and *The Dolliver Romance* (1876).[10] At no time, however, was he anything but skeptical of the spirits.

Hawthorne's skepticism took almost humorous initial form in *The House of the Seven Gables*. It is possible that the subject came to his attention as he worked on the book in the fall and winter of 1850–51. Late in the narrative Clifford Pyncheon insisted to a fellow railroad-passenger that spirit-rappings, along with mesmerism and electricity, were "harbingers of a better era" of spirituality in human life: "These rapping spirits that little Phoebe told us of, the other day. . . . What are these but the messengers of the spiritual world, knocking at the door of substance? And it shall be flung wide open!"[11] In Clifford's words Hawthorne accurately caught the millennial tone of mesmeric and spiritualistic prophets like Andrew Jackson Davis, the Pough-

---

family. It is clear from the internal evidence, however, that Alice's trance was mesmeric and not at all spiritualistic; Hawthorne made no effort to connect it with the rappings which Clifford Pyncheon mentioned as a novelty (James Russell Lowell, *The Poetical Works of James Russell Lowell* [Boston, 1858], II, 297–98; Nathaniel Hawthorne, *The House of the Seven Gables*, pp. 206, 263–64).

7 The most complete record of Hawthorne's attitudes toward spiritualism will be found in Elizabeth Ruth Hosmer, "Science and Pseudo-Science in the Writings of Nathaniel Hawthorne" (Ph.D. diss.: University of Illinois, 1948), pp. 274–303. Under the heading of "spiritualism," however, the author included any kind of communication with spirits, such as those practiced by the Shakers and the mesmerists well before the coming of the Fox sisters and the spiritualistic movement.

8 Nathaniel Hawthorne, *The Marble Faun* (Boston, 1860).

9 Nathaniel Hawthorne, *Dr. Grimshawe's Secret*, ed. Julian Hawthorne (Boston, 1882).

10 Nathaniel Hawthorne, *The Dolliver Romance* (Boston, 1876).

11 Hawthorne, *The House of the Seven Gables*, pp. 263–64.

keepsie seer, who had predicted even before the first rappings of the Fox sisters that "the world will hail with delight the ushering in of that era when the interiors of men will be opened, and the spiritual communion will be established such as is now being enjoyed by the inhabitants of Mars, Jupiter, and Saturn."[12] Clifford's vision and the bracketing of spiritualism with mesmerism (itself already established in the person of Holgrave as a characteristic enthusiasm of reformers) suggest that Hawthorne first viewed the rappings as a foolish addition to the pattern of contemporary utopianisms criticized in the book.[13] But the reply of Clifford's commonsensical listener, that he would "love to rap, with a good stick, on the empty pates of the dolts who circulate such nonsense,"[14] indicated that the movement did not yet disturb the author very deeply.

A year later, however, *The Blithedale Romance* made it clear that Hawthorne had grown disgusted with spiritualism and mesmerism alike. Clifford's millennial rhetoric became sinister (and more like that of the Poughkeepsie seer) when assigned to the evil mesmerist, Westervelt, who spoke "of a new era . . . that would link soul to soul, and the present life to what we call futurity, with a closeness that should finally convert both worlds into one great, mutually conscious brotherhood."[15] And while setting the scene for the Veiled Lady's final trance, Hawthorne's narrator Coverdale suddenly launched into a harangue on the evils of the "epoch of the rapping spirits" which had since succeeded mesmerism:

> Alas, my countrymen, methinks we have fallen on an evil age! If these phenomena have not humbug at the bottom, so much the worse for us. What can they indicate, in a spiritual way, except that the soul of man is descending to a lower point than it has ever before reached while incarnate? We are pursuing a downward course in the eternal march, and thus bring ourselves into the same range

[12] Andrew Jackson Davis, *The Principles of Nature, Her Divine Revelations, and a Voice to Mankind*, 3rd ed. (New York, 1847), pp. 675–76; Frank Podmore, *Modern Spiritualism: A History and a Criticism* (London, 1902), I, 163.

[13] Like Clifford, Holgrave sensed "harbingers abroad of a golden era, to be accomplished in his own lifetime" (Hawthorne, *The House of the Seven Gables*, pp. 179, 84, 176).

[14] Ibid., p. 264.

[15] Hawthorne, *The Blithedale Romance*, p. 200.

with beings whom death, in requital of their gross and evil lives, has degraded below humanity! To hold intercourse with spirits of this order, we must stoop and grovel in some element more vile than earthly dust. These goblins, if they exist at all, are but the shadows of past mortality, outcasts, mere refuse-stuff, adjudged unworthy of the eternal world, and, on the most favorable supposition, dwindling gradually into nothingness. The less we have to say to them the better, lest we share their fate![16]

Perhaps this passage was included to point out the contemporary relevance of the novel's mesmeric background. But Coverdale's alternative explanations of the spirits as either fraudulent or "mere refuse-stuff," to communicate with whom "we must stoop and grovel in some element more vile than earthly dust," suggest that Hawthorne was lecturing his readers in the same way that he had warned Sophia a decade earlier against mesmerism. Probably, therefore, Coverdale's harangue resulted from an associative overflow of Hawthorne's own irritated and fearful feelings about trafficking with spirits, whether mesmeric or spiritualistic.

Among these feelings was probably a dislike of the earthly company kept by spirits who endorsed the abolitionist, dietary, and free-love ideas of millenarian reformers. Hawthorne did not violate reality, after all, by giving first Holgrave and then Westervelt both utopian and occult interests; such combinations were characteristic of all sorts of reformers, from the bizarre Andrew Jackson Davis and John Murray Spear to the more respectable Albert Brisbane and even William Lloyd Garrison. But perhaps there was also the writer's resentment at seeing his stock of supernatural and Gothic effects trivialized by the deluge of reported spiritual manifestations. Hawthorne was later to remark in his English journal that the spiritualists suffered less from an excess of imagination than from a lack of it.[17] Similarly, at the very beginning of *The Blithedale Romance*, his narrator noted the contrast between the artfully designed mystification of the Veiled Lady's appearances a decade earlier, and the mundane "simplicity and openness of scientific experiment" which nowadays marked the public performances of

[16] Ibid., pp. 198–99.
[17] Nathaniel Hawthorne, *The English Notebooks*, ed. Randall Stewart (New York, 1941), p. 154.

spiritualistic mediums. And whereas the harpsichord music played by Alice Pyncheon's ghost had been a major Gothic motif in *The House of the Seven Gables,* Coverdale now denounced "bells self-tolled at funerals, and ghostly music performed on jewsharps. . . ."[18]

At this point in the early 1850's Hawthorne's literary response to spiritualism had been altogether negative. He was also innocent, it would seem, of direct contact with the séance and spirits. It was not until the summer of 1858 in Florence that he finally obtained first-hand knowledge of the subject by witnessing the spiritual excitement among his new friends in the Browning Circle and by discovering a medium in his own household. In no way diminishing his basic skepticism, these Italian experiences forced him to consider the subject anew, and a few of them so appealed to his imagination that they found a place in his last writings.

The Anglo-American community in Florence was intensely interested in spiritualism. Its séances were private and respectable in the English style, rather than public and prophetic like those which Hawthorne had scorned in America. Intelligent people whom he respected, including Mrs. Browning and Hiram Powers, were regular participants in these spiritual circles, and evidently only Robert Browning was thoroughly skeptical. In Florence, moreover, séances took place in a romantic setting of storied buildings fit for haunting by a cast of suitably Gothic ghosts.[19]

Under these circumstances Hawthorne began to pay closer attention. Despite repeated protestations of boredom and disbelief, he carefully recorded in his notebook the stories told by the Browning and Powers families about the messages and invisible handshakes they had received in dark séances with the famous young medium, Daniel Dunglas Home. From the same sources he also heard other tales about spirits condemned to inhabit Florentine palaces. An English lady supplied him with a written account of Home's exorcism of the spirit of "Giannana," a murderous monk who had haunted a staircase and chamber in her residence. But Hawthorne noted that except for the

[18] Hawthorne, *The Blithedale Romance*, pp. 5, 199.
[19] There is little about Hawthorne and nothing about any literary consequences of his introduction to Florentine spiritualism in Katherine H. Porter's treatment of the occult interests of the Anglo-Florentines, *Through a Glass Darkly: Spiritualism in the Browning Circle* (Lawrence, Kans., 1958), pp. 54, 73, 76, 91, 99.

touch of invisible hands, all of these phenomena were like those of mesmeric clairvoyance, "returning the inquirer's thoughts and veiled recollections to himself, as answers to his queries." Nor was he willing to think the hands spiritual in origin, and he enjoyed Browning's insistence that those which Home had once made to materialize so as to put a laurel wreath on Mrs. Browning's head "were affixed to the feet of Mr. Home, who lay extended in his chair, with his legs stretched far under the table." As for Mrs. Hiram Powers's claim that she had touched her dead son's invisibly materialized spirit, he wrote that "these soberly attested incredibilities are so numerous that I forget nine tenths of them, and judge the others too cheap to be written down."[20] Yet he continued to write them down.

Hawthorne became an "investigator" himself for a short time when Ada Shepard, his children's governess, suddenly discovered that she was a writing medium. But he analyzed Ada's powers, too, as mesmeric rather than spiritual, just as he had the accomplishments of the magnetic maidens of the early 1840's. Thus he suspected that the messages received from the spirit of his mother-in-law were innocently transcribed by Ada's pencil at the unconscious direction of his wife. And in comparing the séance to a waking dream in which "the whole material is . . . in the dreamer's mind, though concealed at various depths below the surface,"[21] Hawthorne anticipated both psychologists and storytellers of psychological bent who later in the century were to study the medium's trance and the believer's perception of ghosts as abnormal states of consciousness.

Neither familial manifestations nor his analysis of them struck Hawthorne as literary material. For that he drew chiefly on the domestic situation of Seymour Kirkup, the elderly English artist, antiquarian, and spiritualist who had witnessed the funerals of Keats and Shelley. Hawthorne called on Kirkup at his Florentine house, which had once been occupied by Knights Templar and was now filled with the painter's collection of antiquities, including books on the occult. Kirkup was

20 Nathaniel Hawthorne, *Passages from the French and Italian Note-Books* (Boston, 1893), pp. 393, 412, 396, 296, 392–94, 411–14, 427.
21 Ibid., p. 393. Having always "kept aloof in mind, because Mr. Hawthorne has such repugnance to the whole thing," Sophia was quite upset by the messages from her mother's spirit (Rose Hawthorne Lathrop, *Memories of Hawthorne* [Boston, 1897], p. 397).

known as a "necromancer" because he talked through a medium with "dead poets and emperors," Dante being his favorite. For Hawthorne, "the greatest curiosity of all" was Imogen, the four-year-old daughter of Kirkup's former medium-in-residence, who on her deathbed had persuaded the painter that he was the child's father. Despite her youth Imogen was also a medium, and Kirkup, who doted on her, was still able to talk to Dante.[22]

Hawthorne noted that a romance might be built around the contrast between the "white-bearded old man, thinking all the time of ghosts, and looking into the child's eyes to seek them," and "the child herself, springing so freshly out of the soil, so pretty, so intelligent, so playful." Later in England, working directly from his notebook, Hawthorne did put Kirkup into his Italian romance, *The Marble Faun* (1860), as the white-bearded English "necromancer" who lived with "ghostly books, pictures, and antiquities . . . and one bright-eyed little girl," and who had told Donatello the legend of Monte Beni's fountain maiden.

With his record of Kirkup and Imogen, Hawthorne combined another notebook entry about Florentine spiritualism: the account of Daniel Dunglas Home's conversation with the spirit of Giannana, the unquiet monk. The necromantic Englishman modeled on Kirkup had also told Donatello about a medieval monk who had been confined in "The Owl Tower" before being burned at the stake. Donatello's butler, moreover, remembered stories "of a hooded monk creeping up and down these stairs, or standing in the doorway of this chamber." Donatello, himself guilty of murdering a monk, speculated that the reported apparition, if genuine, must have been the ghost of the martyred holy man.[23]

---

[22] Hawthorne, *Passages from the French and Italian Note-Books*, pp. 386–89. For Kirkup's eccentric role in Florentine spiritual circles (but not his influence on Hawthorne), see Porter, pp. 44, 53–54, 87, 104. James Martin Peebles later wrote that Kirkup had told him that Longfellow was a spiritualist and had "enjoyed a séance with the medium then residing" with the old artist (James Martin Peebles, *What Is Spiritualism? Who Are the Spiritualists? And What Can Spiritualism Do for the World?* 5th ed. [Battle Creek, Mich., 1910], pp. 94–103). By no means a spiritualist, Longfellow did attend a few séances and no doubt heard his brother-in-law, Tom Appleton, hold forth on the subject many times.

[23] Hawthorne, *Passages from the French and Italian Note-Books*, pp. 389, 413–14, and *The Marble Faun*, II, 34–35. Among Hawthorne's commentators, his use of

Thus Hawthorne drew on the spiritualistic experiences of his friends and acquaintances in Florence to provide Monte Beni with Gothic atmosphere appropriate to Donatello's development of a consciousness of human evil. But perhaps the novelist was at the same time providing himself with an opportunity for a last denial of the spiritual hopes of those friends. For when Donatello, having spoken of the necromancer and the monk, asked Kenyon if he believed in "ghosts," the sculptor replied in words Hawthorne himself might have used to express his doubts: "I can hardly tell. . . . on the whole I think not." Because he had not been visited by the ghost of his own victim, Donatello agreed authoritatively: "Ghosts never rise! so much I know, and am glad to know it!"[24]

Apparently Hawthorne had been too impatient with the American rappers to see the literary possibilities of their "child mediums." But in Kirkup and Imogen, Florentine spiritualism gave him a usable version of the fairytale relationship between wizard and maiden which had proved fruitful in "Rappaccini's Daughter" and in the mesmeric contexts of *The House of the Seven Gables* and *The Blithedale Romance*. Kirkup's situation, merely suggested in *The Marble Faun*, took powerful hold in Hawthorne's imagination. As George Parsons Lathrop first pointed out, Kirkup was recast as the old apothecaries Grimshawe and Dolliver, and Imogen as Elsie and Pansie, in two of Hawthorne's unfinished romances, *Doctor Grimshawe's Secret* (1882) and *The Dolliver Romance* (1876).[25] In the first work they were lifted out of the

---

Florentine spiritualism in *The Marble Faun* was evidently noticed only (and that imprecisely) by Van Wyck Brooks in *The Dream of Arcadia: American Writers and Artists in Italy, 1760–1915* (New York, 1958), p. 143.

24 Hawthorne, *The Marble Faun*, II, 35–36.

25 Hawthorne, *Doctor Grimshawe's Secret*, pp. 8, 13–14, *The Dolliver Romance*, pp. 21–22, and *Passages from the French and Italian Note-Books*, pp. 386–89; George Parsons Lathrop, *A Study of Hawthorne* (Boston, 1876), pp. 278–79. Julian Hawthorne discussed the circumstances behind Kirkup's recognition of the child as his daughter, saying of the pair's appearance in the last two romances, "*mutatis mutandis*" (Julian Hawthorne, *Hawthorne and His Circle* [New York, 1903], p. 348). Edward Davidson has shown that Hawthorne did not bring his abstraction of the quirky old apothecary to life with details from his notes on the appearance and personality of Kirkup until he wrote the last two of the manuscript studies from which Julian Hawthorne assembled the first published version of *Doctor Grimshawe's Secret*. But Davidson has exaggerated Kirkup's leadership of Florentine spiritual circles and ambiguously identified the child Imogen as "Kirk-

mediumistic context altogether. But the use of Kirkup, a believer in spiritualistic immortality, as a model for Dolliver, the discoverer of a chemical elixir of everlasting life, was not at all inappropriate. Indeed, it is not out of the question that Hawthorne's encounters with spiritualism in Italy had something to do with his return to the theme of immortality in some of his last works.

Hawthorne's unfinished romances were failures for many other reasons than their partial dependence on spiritualistic sources. But it is fair to say that a deep-seated aversion to the movement—to its religious, social, psychological, and literary implications—kept him from ever turning the subject to more than momentary account in occult fiction. This attitude was consistent throughout the 1850's, whether expressed ironically in *The House of the Seven Gables*, angrily in *The Blithedale Romance*, or more dispassionately through Kenyon in *The Marble Faun*. And when he did borrow spiritualists as models for central characters in *Doctor Grimshawe's Secret* and *The Dolliver Romance*, he left séance and spirits far behind.

At the same time, however, Hawthorne's treatment of the subject in all these works was at least indicative of its serious literary potential. Spiritualism was to be subjected to extended satirical attack by Orestes Brownson and Bayard Taylor as a symbol of demonic or immoral radicalism. And the figures of the deluded or evil wizard and his innocent young spirit-medium were to attract the attention of melodramatic romancers (including Hawthorne's son Julian)[26] and social and

---

up's daughter by a late marriage." Kirkup had not married Imogen's mediumistic mother, and there was great doubt as to whether he was the father. These complications struck Hawthorne as adding "to the romance of the affair,—the idea that this pretty little elf has no right whatever to the asylum which she has found." Neither Lathrop, Julian Hawthorne, nor Davidson mentioned Hawthorne's use of Kirkup for the necromancer of *The Marble Faun* (Edward Hutchins Davidson, *Hawthorne's Last Phase* [New Haven, 1949], pp. 65–66, 139; Hawthorne, *Passages from the French and Italian Note-Books*, pp. 388–91; Lionel Henry Cust in DNB. s.v. "Kirkup, Seymour Stocker [1788–1880]").

[26] Julian Hawthorne, *A Messenger from the Unknown* (New York, 1892). Others of the type included Allan Pinkerton, *The Spiritualists and the Detectives* (New York, 1876); Edward Bellamy, *Miss Ludington's Sister: A Romance of Immortality* (Boston, 1884); Hamlin Garland, *The Tyranny of the Dark* (New York, 1905); Gelett Burgess, *The Heart-Line: A Drama of San Francisco* (Indianapolis, 1907); Richard Harding Davis, *Vera, the Medium* (New York, 1908).

psychological realists alike. "Rappaccini's Daughter," *The House of the Seven Gables*, and *The Blithedale Romance* have properly been identified among the literary prototypes for William Dean Howells and Henry James's explorations of the wizard-medium relationship in terms of spiritualism in *The Undiscovered Country* (1880) and *The Bostonians* (1886). In these two novels Howells and James, more objectively critical of the spiritualistic movement than Hawthorne was ever able to be, were successfully to translate the occult ambience of magnetic wizard and trance maiden into thoroughgoing studies of prophetic and mediumistic personality. But even here Hawthorne had preceded them with his own faltering attempts to explore the same relationship, recalling the necromantic Kirkup and the mediumistic Imogen, in his last unfinished romances.

II | Hawthorne's unwillingness or inability to utilize spiritualism as an important frame of reference for supernatural fiction appears to have been the rule rather than the exception among the writers of the 1850's. Although Orestes Brownson's *Spirit-Rapper* (1854) and Bayard Taylor's "Confessions of a Medium" (1860) presented supernatural interpretations of spiritualism as demonic in origin, they were largely polemical in intention. No doubt there were more Gothic thrillers in the rationalistic tradition of *The Mysteries of Udolpho* than Arthur Hastings's "Birchknoll: A New Ghost Story of Old Virginia" (1856)[27] or Mrs. Southworth's "Haunted Homestead" (1860),[28] in which frightening phenomena were discovered to result from human villainy or natural accident. Such tales were merely the melodramatic counterparts of Benjamin Shillaber and Herman Melville's comic records of spurious manifestations. But of the serious ghost-story, that branch of supernatural fiction dealing with the mysterious or terrifying return of the dead to the land of the living, there were fewer examples involving spiritual manifestations and mediums than one might expect.

This failure to exploit probably owed a great deal to the public im-

[27] [Arthur Hastings,] "Birchknoll," *Harper's* XII (February 1856), 336–40.
[28] E.D.E.N. Southworth, *The Haunted Homestead and Other Nouvellettes, with an Autobiography of the Author* (Philadelphia, 1860), pp. 45–110.

age of spiritualism. Because of the polemical furor over the movement, few writers responded to it in a neutral enough way to use it for mystification and terror. The mood and doctrine of the séance also mitigated against such effects. The sessions presided over by the Fox sisters, for instance, seem to have been altogether mundane in atmosphere. Rather than trying to baffle or frighten their clients, the girls emphasized the wonderful naturalness of communication with the departed, annoying one observer by eating peanuts and whispering to the young men in attendance. Especially did the inanity which so often subjected spiritual manifestations to the ridicule of humorists render them unlikely as dramatic material for supernatural fiction. Leah Fish closed her sisters' public séances by singing "Hail, Columbia" to the rhythmic accompaniment of rappings.[29] There was "no poetry," said the *Knickerbocker,* in these "Modern Sorcerers" whose bewitched table danced out replies to questions "of such popular interest as the number of teeth at present tenanting the interior of Mrs. Hobbs's mother's head."[30] The theology of the rappers had the same effect: the essence of Judge Edmonds's revelation was that death was no longer a terrifying mystery; rather, it was every man's promotion to a higher stage of existence not unlike the earthly one. Discussing "ghosts and ghost-seeing" in *Harper's,* Tayler Lewis charged the movement with "naturalizing" rather than "cultivating the imagination, or enhancing its religious awe, which was always more or less the effect of the old ghostly tales. . . ."[31] It was in this critical vein that Hawthorne, who had relied on Alice Pyncheon's ghostly harpsichord music as an occult motif in *The House of the Seven Gables* (1851), soon denounced "tables upset by invisible agencies . . . and ghostly music performed on jewsharps"[32] as trivial demonism or humbug in *The Blithedale Romance* (1852).

Inevitably, of course, some writers did exploit spiritualism for supernatural effects, though not always successfully. For instance, at about the same time that Hawthorne was rejecting both magnetic trance and séance music, Herman Melville, in *Pierre; or, The Ambiguities*

[29] "To All Our Readers and Correspondents," *Holden's Dollar Magazine* VI (September 1850), 573–74.
[30] "Modern Sorcerers," *Knickerbocker* XLIII (February 1854), 171.
[31] [Tayler Lewis,] "Editor's Table," *Harper's* VI (April 1853), 699.
[32] Hawthorne, *The Blithedale Romance,* p. 199.

(1852),[33] was dramatizing Isabel Banford's revelation of secret kinship to Pierre Glendinning in terms of mesmeric electricity and spiritual guitar music. Just as Phoebe Pyncheon had responded to "a certain magnetic element" in Holgrave's nature, so Isabel felt Pierre's "glance of magnetic meaning."[34] Likewise, after singing her chant of "Mystery! Mystery!" Isabel appeared to Pierre "to swim in an electric fluid; the vivid buckler of her brow seemed as a magnetic plate."[35] Such mesmeric metaphors for emotional and sexual attraction were commonplace in fiction. Indeed, while Melville was writing *Pierre*, the mesmeric and potentially incestuous affinity between a betrothed couple unaware that they were brother and sister was treated so as to satisfy the *Knickerbocker's* standards of propriety in Caroline Cheesebrough's "Magnetic Influences" (1851).[36]

But Isabel was more than magnetic. Singing her wild chant to the accompaniment of a guitar played by the ghost of her wronged mother, while lightning flashed outside the window, she became a spiritual medium:

> "Hark now; thou shalt hear my mother's spirit". . . . the magical untouched guitar responded with a quick spark of melody. . . . Again, after a preluding silence, the guitar as magically responded as before. . . . and again Pierre felt as in the immediate presence of the spirit. . . . Pierre felt himself surrounded by ten thousand sprites and gnomes, and his whole soul was swayed and tossed by supernatural tides.[37]

Isabel's mediumship added her mother's testimony to the story of her mysterious origin, and it spiritualized her hold on Pierre, defining her at first glance as possessing magical power. (Newton Arvin called her guitar a "Magical Instrument"[38] borrowed by the novelist from

[33] Herman Melville, *Pierre; or, The Ambiguities* (New York, 1852); subsequent citations are to *Pierre; or, The Ambiguities* (New York, 1963).
[34] Hawthorne, *The House of the Seven Gables*, p. 222; Melville, *Pierre*, p. 222.
[35] Ibid., p. 212.
[36] Herbert Ross Brown, *The Sentimental Novel in America, 1789–1860* (Durham, N.C., 1940), pp. 184–91; Caroline Cheesebrough, "Magnetic Influences," *Knickerbocker* XXXVII (May 1851), 430–41.
[37] This passage has been synthesized from Melville, *Pierre*, pp. 209–11.
[38] Newton Arvin, *Herman Melville* (New York, 1950), p. 235.

Gothic tradition.) Melville qualified this power, however, by observing that the "all but intelligent responsiveness of the guitar" seemed inexplicable "at the time."[39] And by noting that "sparks quivered" on the metallic strings of the instrument as its chords sounded near an open window outside of which "heat-lightnings and ground-lightnings wove their wonderfulness,"[40] he suggested, with a less explicit ambiguity than Hawthorne might have employed, a natural electrical explanation as an alternative to the spiritual one. (The father of Egeria Boynton, the medium of Howells's *Undiscovered Country,* was sadly to conclude that static electricity was the source of his daughter's powers.)

What Melville did, then, was to extend Hawthorne's treatment of mesmerism within a Gothic framework to include spiritualism. Whether he was wise in selecting a musical manifestation to enhance the "Mystery of Isabel" is another matter. Since the early days of the séance, the guitar had been the spirits' favorite instrument. E. W. Capron had told of exquisite guitar music "played by unseen hands" in *Singular Revelations* (1850), a work which reached a much wider audience than did *Pierre.* And any reader who recognized the spiritualistic nature of Isabel's mysterious chords might well have been inappropriately reminded of Capron's enthusiastic but hardly Gothic report that "on one occasion we were getting the guitar played by these unseen musicians, and were asked to sing several tunes, among which were 'Get Off the Track,' and 'The Old Granite State!' "[41] Not until he directed ironic laughter at rappers and demons alike four years later did Melville successfully control spiritualistic material by concentrating on the psychology of his narrator's response to the mysterious tickings in "The Apple-Tree Table."

More in the manner of Edgar Allan Poe was Ferdinand C. Ewer's "Eventful Nights of August 20th and 21st, 1854" (1854).[42] As he later

---

[39] Melville, *Pierre,* p. 212.
[40] Ibid., p. 211.
[41] E. W. Capron and H. D. Barron, *Singular Revelations: Explanation and History of the Mysterious Communion with Spirits,* 2nd ed. (Auburn, N.Y., 1850), p. 73.
[42] The story was reprinted as part of F. C. Ewer, *The Eventful Nights of August 20th and 21st, 1854; and How Judge Edmonds Was Hocussed; or, Fallibility of "Spiritualism" Exposed* (New York, 1855), pp. 19–58.

explained in an analysis admittedly inspired by Poe's "Philosophy of Composition," Ewer selected the device of spiritual manifestations to lend topical interest to the narrative of a soul's passage "through the gates of death and into the regions beyond."[43] Ewer's narrator told of having been summoned to the deathbed of John F. Lane, a spiritualist who before dying was told by the spirits that as a supreme test he himself would communicate with the narrator from the next world. Following Lane's agonized passing, the clammy fingers of his corpse seized the narrator's hand and pencil to describe spiritland as "a long grand, misty, undulating arch-way towards a *harmony*, as it were, of far-off music." After two nights of such written communications, Lane's body suddenly came awake to cry out loud, in horror, that his spirit was being transported into another realm beyond the spirit world, and that further communication would be impossible. "A whole universe was between us," said the narrator. Aware that he would be attacked as "one of the insane dupes of the spiritual rappers," he made the incident public out of a sense of duty.[44]

With the ghastly writing and speaking of Lane's corpse, Ewer's tale reflected the interest taken by writers of sensational thrillers and speculative science-fiction alike in the possibility of postmortem revivification (a possibility perhaps realized by the spiritualists themselves with the "materializations" of the 1870's). Indeed, with its charnel-house horror and pseudoscientific circumstantiality, "The Eventful Nights" evidently reminded some readers that Poe had drawn a grisly picture of the results of mesmeric interference with the physical processes of death in "The Facts in the Case of M. Valdemar" (1844), for Ewer was later at some pains to deny any such indebtedness.[45] His tale also bore some resemblance to William North's imitation of Poe, "The Living Corpse" (1853).[46] Most such fiction, of course, bobbed somewhere in the wake of *Frankenstein*. Although the anonymous author of *Zillah, the Child Medium* (1857)[47] said that his aim was simply to report his own observations of spiritualism "in the form of a

---

[43] Ibid., pp. 80, 77.
[44] Ibid., pp. 35–36, 57, 21.
[45] Ibid., pp. 74–75.
[46] [William North,] "The Living Corpse," *Putnam's* I (January 1853), 32–39.
[47] *Zillah, the Child Medium: A Tale of Spiritualism* (New York, 1857).

domestic story," his climax was the satanic attempt of an insane scientific medium to recall life to the naked limbs of the dead Zillah by means of the magnetic touch of his hand.[48]

Questions about the nature of consciousness were sometimes raised by such stories. The lapse of Ewer's John F. Lane into eternal silence two nights after his death, for instance, may have reflected the physiological problem of how long, if at all, the brain goes on functioning after death. Ambrose Bierce's ironic hypothesis of a hanged man's fleeting illusion of continued life in "An Occurrence at Owl Creek Bridge" (1891)[49] would considerably shorten this period of "postmortem consciousness." S. Weir Mitchell treated the ethical complications of restoring consciousness to a dead murderer with a quite unspiritualistic blood-pump in "Was He Dead?" (1870),[50] one of the more thoughtful tales of the kind. Mitchell had already dealt humorously with a similar theme in "The Case of George Dedlow" (1866),[51] using a spiritualistic hyperbole to explore one aspect of the human nervous system's subjectivity. As a medical man Mitchell had been intrigued during the Civil War by amputees' claims that they retained the sensations of their lost limbs. When his George Dedlow asked at a séance if his amputated legs were present in spirit, so lifelike a feeling of their existence came over him that he astonished the medium's other customers by walking about the room for a moment on his invisible limbs. The psychological point of the tale was evidently missed by the spiritualists, however, for according to Mitchell they were happy to accept George Dedlow's case as a real one when they read about it in the *Atlantic*.[52]

Even more Poe-like than Ewer's "Eventful Nights" itself was its success as a literary hoax.[53] Neither Lane's experiences in the spirit world

[48] Ibid., pp. iii, 223–35.
[49] Ambrose Bierce, *Tales of Soldiers and Civilians* (New York, 1891), pp. 21–39.
[50] [S. Weir Mitchell,] "Was He Dead?" *Atlantic Monthly* XXV (January 1870), 86–102. See H. Bruce Franklin's introduction to the story in *Future Perfect: American Science Fiction of the Nineteenth Century* (New York, 1966), pp. 218–220.
[51] [S. Weir Mitchell,] "The Case of George Dedlow," *Atlantic Monthly* XVIII (July 1866), 1–11.
[52] S. Weir Mitchell, *The Autobiography of a Quack and The Case of George Dedlow* (New York, 1900), p. x.
[53] Ewer, pp. 63–106.

nor his revivified body owed anything to orthodox spiritualism. Indeed, for spirits to vanish so quickly into a realm of silence was inconsistent with the possibility of continued séance communication. Nonetheless Ewer's imitation of sincere accounts of spiritual manifestations was authentic enough to fool Judge John W. Edmonds. For when Ewer disingenuously sent the Judge a copy of the first part of the story in his San Francisco magazine, *The Pioneer*, Edmonds reprinted it in *The Christian Spiritualist* as a genuine report of spiritual intercourse. To Edmonds's inquiry about further communications from Lane's spirit, Ewer responded only with the issue of *The Pioneer* containing the second half of the story. But in reprinting this second part, Edmonds appended additional messages which he, too, had received from the spirit of John F. Lane. Ewer's ironic disclosure of Edmonds's mistake embarrassed the spiritualists when it appeared in the *New York Herald*. The Judge replied publicly, admitting that he had been "fool enough to receive as true" a narrative signed by Ewer, and stating that long experience as a criminal judge had taught him "something of the degradation to which the influence of evil passions, and a perverted education, may sink the fairest-seeming among us." A letter to the *New York Daily Chronicle* came to his rescue by pointing out that a military officer named John F. Lane had committed suicide in 1836: "*There*, Messrs. Editors, is a verifiable, genuine 'John F. Lane,' and no mistake. When Judge Edmonds summoned the spirit of 'J. F. L.,' who is authorized to say that the genuine John did not respond?" Ewer had the last word, however, in a volume entitled *The Eventful Nights of August 20th and 21st, 1854; and How Judge Edmonds Was Hocussed; or, Fallibility of "Spiritualism" Exposed* (1855).[54] From his discussion of the tale's composition it seems clear that Ewer's first thought was to write a topically interesting ghost story, and that not until it had been printed did he see its humorous possibilities. But nowhere better illustrated was the thin line separating the supernatural from the ludicrous potential of spiritualistic literary materials.

III | The most successful adaptation of spiritualism to supernatural fiction during the 1850's was that of Fitz-James O'Brien, the decade's most accomplished writer of science fiction, fantasy, and

---

[54] Ibid., pp. 95, 97, 106.

ghost stories. Thoroughly dependent on topical inspiration, O'Brien found it several times in spiritualism and related occult interests. At the beginning of his American career in 1852 he looked upon the movement as a subject for conventional humorous satire: "When a table follows a man about a room like a pet spaniel, who can doubt the existence of a spiritual presence among the company assembled?"[55] But O'Brien's attitudes were dictated by the literary task at hand, and he later drew upon spiritualistic theory and phenomena to lend topical and pseudoscientific plausibility to two ghost-stories, "The Pot of Tulips" (1855)[56] and "What Was It?" (1859).[57] And in his best-known story, "The Diamond Lens" (1858),[58] he used a séance conducted by a Fox sister as both a supernatural narrative device and a way of dramatizing his narrator's madness.

Turning first to mesmerism, O'Brien dealt with the possibility of using clairvoyance to find buried treasure in "The Bohemian" (1855).[59] Actual attempts to do so had been mentioned by John Greenleaf Whittier in his studies of New England superstition,[60] and the legendary attempt to locate the title to the Pyncheon lands had been framed in terms of magnetic trance in *The House of the Seven Gables*. Like Hawthorne, O'Brien wrote of the exploitation of a trance maiden by a ruthless mesmerist: the beautiful clairvoyant was able to direct the wizard to a treasure hoard on Coney Island, but she died of the strain she underwent in trance. The story was a routine thriller; Hawthorne had dealt with the dangers of the trance state much more effectively.

"The Bohemian" was quickly followed in *Harper's* by "The Pot of Tulips" (1855). Here O'Brien ingeniously cited the findings of Ger-

[55] [Fitz-James O'Brien,] "Fragments from an Unpublished Magazine," *American Whig Review* XVI (September 1852), 269.
[56] Fitz-James O'Brien, *The Poems and Stories of Fitz-James O'Brien*, ed. William Winter (Boston, 1881), pp. 332–54.
[57] Ibid., pp. 390–407.
[58] Franklin, pp. 328–51.
[59] [Fitz-James O'Brien,] "The Bohemian," *Harper's* XI (July 1855), 233–42.
[60] Whittier had treated three such efforts humorously in "New England Super-naturalism," *United States Magazine and Democratic Review* XIII (November 1843), 515–16, and in the book he later assembled from his various magazine treatments of the same subject, *The Supernaturalism of New England* (Boston, 1847), pp. 57–59.

man spiritual science to rationalize the hackneyed return of a conscience-stricken ghost bent on righting a wrong he had committed before death. First perceived by O'Brien's narrator, Harry Escott, as a stream of cold air, the ghost then took human form in a "luminous cloud," with "tongues of fire" streaming from his fingers. Convinced that all "mysterious phenomena" depended on "certain natural laws," Escott referred in passing to similar visitations recorded in the works of Baron von Reichenbach, Heinrich Jung-Stilling, and Justinius Kerner,[61] all of whose explanations of apparitions as compatible with "natural laws" were familiar in the arguments about spiritualism. Von Reichenbach, whose mesmeric researches were well known in England and America, claimed to have discovered a form of energy called "odic" or "odylic" force, emanating as heat, cold, or luminosity from all things; the human fingertips and new graves were strong sources of "odyle."[62] Jung-Stilling had been cited in Lowell's "The Unhappy Lot of Mr. Knott" as one of the occult authorities whose work was available in the Harvard College Library.[63] He and Kerner were the most important of the German magnetists who, before the rise of spiritualism, had explained the presence of ghosts in mesmeric terms. According to Frank Podmore, the magnetists theorized that the newly dead soul was clad in an ethereal substance called *"Nervengeist,"* which attracted "grosser particles" of matter to it, becoming "visible even to the fleshly eye" in the case of low, earthbound spirits (perhaps such as the guilty one of whom O'Brien wrote).[64]

Similar analyses, probably derived ultimately from mesmerism, were offered by scientifically inclined spiritualists. Professor Robert Hare was instructed by the spirits that the spiritual body was built along principles "analogous to, but not identical with, material elements." Adin Ballou, the patriarch of the Hopedale Community, spoke in *Spirit Manifestations* (1852) of a "subtle ethereo-spiritual substance"

61 O'Brien, *The Poems and Stories of Fitz-James O'Brien*, pp. 344, 345, 347–48.
62 Podmore, I, 118.
63 Lowell, *Poetical Works of James Russell Lowell*, II, 295. Jung-Stilling's *Theorie der Geister-Kunde* (Berlin, 1827) had been translated in America as *Theory of Pneumatology* (New York, 1851) by George Bush. Bush's translation and Lowell's "Mr. Knott" had both been noticed as effective attacks on spiritualism in Rufus Griswold's *International Monthly Magazine of Literature, Science, and Art* II (February 1851), 309.
64 Podmore, I, 107, 95–104.

called "spiricity."[65] And Capron and Barron's *Singular Revelations* (1850) mentioned "the more refined substance to which we give the name of spirit."[66]

O'Brien gave credit to Reichenbach and the magnetists only for specific physical resemblances between his ghost and theirs. But Escott's concluding remarks show that some such theory as "odic force" or "*Nervengeist*" underlay the entire tale: "I myself believe in ghosts. ... and if it suited me to do so I could overwhelm you with a scientific theory of my own on the subject, reconciling ghosts and natural phenomena."[67] In "The Pot of Tulips," then, O'Brien animated a perfunctory ghost-story plot, of the traditional moralizing sort praised by Tayler Lewis's anti-spiritualistic *Harper's* editorial about "ghosts" and "ghost-seeing,"[68] with a pseudoscientific speculation which owed its topicality to spiritualism. Perhaps that topicality had something to do with the many inquiries elicited by a postscript inviting readers interested in further investigation to write the author in care of *Harper's*.[69] Like Ewer's "Eventful Nights," "The Pot of Tulips" was part hoax.

A similar speculation provided the pseudoscientific basis for "What Was It? A Mystery" (1859). Indeed, Harry Escott was again the narrator, and he rested his claim to expertise in occult matters on his authorship of "The Pot of Tulips." One night, after discussing the idea of "terror" over an opium pipe with his friend Doctor Hammond, Escott awoke in the dark to find himself in danger of being strangled by a fierce assailant. Subduing the attacker with difficulty, Escott tied him to the bed. But when the lamp was lit, nothing was to be seen but the taut, straining bonds. This was not the luminous ghost of "The Pot of Tulips." Rather, it was both corporeal and invisible. These qualities and its insensate rage made the strange being the "King of Terrors" which Escott and Hammond had been unable to define in the abstract. Before the creature died of starvation, having refused all conventional nourishment, a plaster cast had revealed its dwarfish

[65] Ibid., pp. 301–2.
[66] Capron and Barron, p. 8.
[67] O'Brien, *The Poems and Stories of Fitz-James O'Brien*, p. 354.
[68] [Tayler Lewis,] "Editor's Table," *Harper's* VI (April 1853), 699.
[69] Francis Wolle, *Fitz-James O'Brien: A Literary Bohemian of the Eighteen-Fifties* (Boulder, Colo., 1944), p. 107.

body and ghoulish countenance. But the puzzle posed in the story's title remained unsolved. This mystery, of course, was essential to the effect which O'Brien so well achieved—the terror inherent in the idea of the inimical unknown.

Yet O'Brien did allow the narrator's friend, Doctor Hammond, to theorize possible solutions to the problem of invisible flesh. And in so doing the writer would seem to have had in mind a "scientific theory" similar to that announced by the narrator of "The Pot of Tulips" as "reconciling ghosts and natural phenomena":

> Here is a solid body which we touch but which we cannot see. The fact is so unusual that it strikes us with terror. Is there no parallel, though, for such a phenomenon? Take a piece of pure glass. It is tangible and transparent. A certain chemical coarseness is all that prevents its being so entirely transparent as to be totally invisible. It is not *theoretically impossible*, mind you, to make a glass . . . so pure and homogenous in its atoms that the rays from the sun will pass through it as they do through the air. . . . We do not see the air, and yet we feel it.[70]

Given "The Pot of Tulips," it appears likely that these remarks were extrapolated either from the spiritual chemistry of the German magnetists, whose *"Nervengeist"* was invisible except when it attracted gross material particles, or from the materialistic theories of such spiritualists as E. W. Capron and H. D. Barron, who wrote of "the more refined substance to which we give the name of spirit."

A spiritualistic explanation seems especially probable in view of Hammond's direct reference to the séance in answering Escott's objection that the glass analogy failed to account for the monster's animation: " 'You forget the strange phenomena of which we have so often heard of late,' answered the doctor gravely. 'At the meetings called "spirit circles," invisible hands have been thrust into the hands of those persons around the table—warm, fleshly hands that seem to pulsate with mortal life.' "[71] A standard feature of the "dark" séance, such invisibly materialized hands had been felt in the presence of the Fox sisters as early as 1852, when one of their patrons reported to the

[70] O'Brien, *The Poems and Stories of Fitz-James O'Brien*, p. 403.
[71] Ibid., pp. 403–4.

Tribune that he was able to distinguish strong masculine hands from gentler feminine ones and "the soft hands of children petting us on the head and face. . . ."[72] Such were the hands of which Hawthorne had heard with bored incredulity in Florence. Some unbelievers maintained that these mysterious hands belonged to the mediums or their accomplices moving about in the dark, and perhaps there was a certain amount of irony in Doctor Hammond's gravity. Perhaps, too, O'Brien may have enjoyed the irony implicit in his use of the theory and manifestation of benevolent ghosts to rationalize a monster. But as in "The Pot of Tulips," he seems primarily to have been interested in the dramatic value of such materials. Here the experiences of the spiritualists provided him with a reported reality—invisible hands—clarifying the quasi-spiritualistic hypothesis of invisible matter with which he lent an air of speculative plausibility to his fictional experiment in terror.

Between "The Pot of Tulips" and "What Was It?" O'Brien had already developed his most complex treatment of spiritualism in his finest story, "The Diamond Lens" (1858). Here O'Brien's goal was not the embodiment of terror, but the simultaneous dramatization of scientific wonder and scientific madness. Similarly, his narrator, Linley, was not a rational observer of the marvelous like Escott, but an obsessed microscopist whose experience of the marvelous, whether genuine or hallucinatory, left him insane. Devoted since boyhood to microscopy, Linley relied on spirit direction to construct a "perfect lens" out of a rare diamond which he committed murder to obtain. He then fell in love with the tiny feminine animalcule revealed to him by his lens in a drop of water, only to see her disappear in agony when her environment evaporated. Mentally broken, he was left to give incoherent lectures on optics to amused young men's groups as "Linley, the mad microscopist."[73] Never explicitly resolving the question as to whether "Animula" really existed outside his narrator's imagination, O'Brien achieved with science the ambiguously supernatural tone attained by Poe with Gothic materials in "Ligeia."

Linley's conversation with "The Spirit of Leeuwenhoek" at the studio of Madame Vulpes, the spirit medium, was brief but impor-

[72] Earl Wesley Fornell, *The Unhappy Medium: Spiritualism and the Life of Margaret Fox* (Austin, Tex., 1964), p. 31.
[73] Franklin, ed., pp. 333, 351.

tant.[74] Despairing of ever finding the perfect lens, Linley was told by Jules Simon, a shady Frenchman, that Madame Vulpes's spirits could read one's inmost secrets. Immediately Linley consulted her secretly in the hope of obtaining spiritual guidance. When he sat down at the séance table, a shower of rappings prompted the medium to observe that "they" were "very strong" that evening. Further rappings instructed Linley to write down the name of the spirit he wished to consult. He wrote the name of Leeuwenhoek, the founder of microscopy, on a piece of paper which he concealed under the table. Shortly thereafter the medium's own hand was seized and made to write: "I am here. Question me. Leeuwenhoek."[75] Astounded, Linley wrote a series of inquiries about the perfect lens, to which the Dutch scientist responded through the medium's hand:

> A diamond of one hundred and forty carats, submitted to electromagnetic currents for a long period, will experience a rearrangement of its atoms *inter se*, and from that stone you will form the universal lens. . . . Pierce the lens through its axis. . . . The image will be formed in the pierced space, which will itself serve as a tube to look through. Now I am called. Good night.[76]

Linley left the medium's chambers a convert to spiritualism, but entirely at a loss as to how to obtain the requisite diamond. Mention of such a stone, however, elicited consternation from Jules Simon. Plied with liquor, Simon eventually showed Linley a 140-carat diamond which he had stolen in Brazil. Recognizing the "hand of Destiny,"[77] Linley murdered Simon and worked the spirit-dictated changes in the gem which led him to the discovery of his beloved Animula.

As a plot device the séance prepared for that discovery by providing Linley with the formula for the lens. It also provided an implicit precedent: Leeuwenhoek was thought to have been the first man to catch sight of human spermatazoa through the microscope. As a scientist Linley thought of the spirits in terms of the spiritual hypothoses of "What Was It?" and "The Pot of Tulips," as "subtiler organisms"[78]

[74] Ibid., pp. 335–38.
[75] Ibid., pp. 336–37.
[76] Ibid., p. 337.
[77] Ibid., p. 341.
[78] Ibid., p. 335.

than his own. And that the existence of spirits like Leeuwenhoek had been proclaimed as a reality for almost a decade by the spiritualists, whose reports of séances O'Brien carefully imitated, perhaps made Linley's further testimony about microscopic wonders appear less singular. Indeed, the spiritualist trance-poet and preacher Thomas Lake Harris had seen Leeuwenhoek, "a man of the eighteenth century in appearance, and surrounded by a shining sphere, in the midst of which appeared continuous gleamings, as of the eyes and wings of brilliant insects," during a clairvoyant journey to heaven recorded in *The Wisdom of Angels* (1857).[79] Here as elsewhere, spiritualism served O'Brien as a means of naturalizing and domesticating the marvelous.

At the same time, however, Linley's ready acceptance of Leeuwenhoek's spiritual authority suggested that he was deluded from the beginning. It is clear, for instance, that the formula for the lens was composed not by a spirit but by Madame Vulpes, with the aid of mesmeric clairvoyance. Linley himself dismissed that possibility, claiming that while the medium "might, by means of biological *rapport* with my own mind, have gone so far as to read my questions and reply to them coherently,"[80] she could not have thus discovered the secret of the diamond lens. Yet he had spoken earlier of experimenting with a small diamond, and he admitted here that the possibility of electromagnetic conversion might previously have occurred to him. Moreover, Jules Simon insisted that the medium was merely clairvoyant, and he feared her because she had divined his secret—the stolen diamond. It would seem, therefore, that Madame Vulpes simply combined her knowledge of Simon's gem with her clairvoyant perception of Linley's preoccupation with the lens. And thus she led Linley to believe in false spiritual sanction for his own unconscious invention, for the sake of which he then committed murder.

Linley was not the first man of science to be misled by spiritualism. Robert Hare's long and productive career had closed with lectures on "Celestial Mechanics." Converted to spiritualism by Margaret Fox's séances, John Fairbanks, the editor of *Scientific American*, had leapt from a fifth-story window under spirit direction.[81] And in 1854 the de-

[79] Thomas Lake Harris, *The Wisdom of Angels* (New York, 1857), p. 41.
[80] Franklin, ed., pp. 337–38.
[81] Fornell, p. 79.

sign for an engine constructed along the lines of the human body and operated by a "New Motive Power" had been presented to humanity, through the mediumship of John Murray Spear, by a group of scientific spirits calling themselves the "Association of Electricizers." Despite the vicarious pangs of parturition suffered by a lady spiritualist in bringing the organic machine to life, it had failed to perform and had been smashed by intolerant unbelievers.[82]

Nor was Linley the last fictional scientist to be so misled. A year after the appearance of "The Diamond Lens," the lunacy of an evil inventor was to be explicitly defined at the outset of J. D. Whelpley's "Atoms of Chladni" (1859)[83] by his claim that spirits designed his inventions, one of which was an unsuccessful "new motive power."[84] Taking into account O'Brien's public acknowledgment that Whelpley had assisted him with "the scientific mechanism" of "The Diamond Lens" and had witnessed "the gradual development of the story,"[85] it is plausible that Linley's delusion as to the source of the message from Leeuwenhoek characterized him as simply another "mad" scientist even before his discovery of Animula. It therefore helped to define that discovery as hallucinatory, an example of what Linley himself referred to in another context as the propensity of microscopists to "supply the defects of their instruments with the creations of their brains."[86]

But perhaps the strongest evidence that O'Brien used the séance to point to Linley's madness was a topical joke quite as pointed as Whelpley's reference to John Murray Spear's "new motive power." Linley's visit to Madame Vulpes was a séance *à clef*, suggesting nothing so much as the sessions presided over by the Fox sisters. Once the girls had mastered spirit-writing in the early 1850's, their séances for single customers often followed the same sequence of manifestations as Madame Vulpes's: rappings indicating the presence of spirits, then pointed rappings spelling out instructions as to procedure, and finally written answers through the medium's hand to questions asked by the

---

82 Podmore, I, 298–99.
83 [J. D. Whelpley,] "The Atoms of Chladni," *Harper's* XX (January 1860), 195–206; reprinted in Franklin, ed., pp. 189–217.
84 Ibid., p. 190.
85 Ibid., p 322.
86 Ibid., pp. 332–33.

sitters. Like some customers of the Foxes, Linley noted that the proceedings were businesslike and without any attempt to mystify: "This intercourse with the spiritual world was evidently as familiar an occupation with Mrs. Vulpes as eating her dinner or riding in an omnibus."[87] And the question as to whether the medium's power was genuinely spiritual or merely clairvoyant was exactly that which had often been posed about the Foxes. The careers of other seeresses were characterized, of course, by some of the same features. But lest his readers fail to recognize the composite identity of his medium, O'Brien gave her the Latin name for Fox—"Vulpes"—and almost facetiously allowed the Frenchman Jules Simon, trying to remember her name, to refer to "*le renard*."[88]

Only six months before "The Diamond Lens" appeared in the *Atlantic Monthly*, Leah and Katie Fox had been the most prominent of a group of mediums tested and denounced, under the auspices of the *Boston Courier*, by a committee which included Professors Peirce, Agassiz, and Horsford of Harvard. The committee had decided that "any connection with Spiritualistic Circles, so-called, corrupts the morals and degrades the intellect," and they had consequently felt it "their solemn duty to warn the community against this contaminating influence, which surely tends to lessen the truth of man and the purity of women."[89] Perhaps James Russell Lowell, the *Atlantic*'s editor, enjoyed O'Brien's satirical allusion to the Fox sisters almost seven years after his own "Mr. Knott." Certainly it is less likely that he and other critics of the sisters read O'Brien's tale as a compound of ghostly and scientific wonders than as a study of scientific obsession, one of the dangers of which was susceptibility to mediumistic imposition.[90]

[87] Ibid., p. 335.

[88] Ibid., p. 334.

[89] "The Spiritualists Checkmated," *Harper's Weekly* I (July 11, 1857), 438. The *Courier* had offered $500 for any concrete proof of spiritual presence which would satisfy the committee. In addition to Leah and Kate, the mediums participating had included the Davenport brothers and J. V. Mansfield, the "spirit postmaster." For a spiritualistic analysis of the episode, see Emma Hardinge Britten, *Modern American Spiritualism: A Twenty Years' Record of the Communion between Earth and the World of Spirits* (New York, 1870), pp. 185–94.

[90] [Fitz-James O'Brien,] "The Diamond Lens," *Atlantic Monthly* I (January 1858), 354–67. A "scientific" imitation of O'Brien's story was T. Hill's "Were They Crickets?" *Atlantic Monthly* XVII (April 1866), 397–406.

Yet by vividly telling the story from the point of view of the deluded scientist, O'Brien left it open to both interpretations. The same ambiguity was sometimes to mark the exploitation of spiritualistic and psychic materials by later writers using the supernatural tale to dramatize the subjectivity of human consciousness. S. Weir Mitchell was to write about the return in spirit of missing limbs in "The Case of George Dedlow," and the spiritualists were to fail to distinguish fiction from their own accounts of spiritual manifestations, receiving the story, according to Mitchell, "as a valuable proof of the truths of their beliefs."[91] And in "The Turn of the Screw" (1898) Henry James was to draw on apparitions reported by the Society for Psychical Research,[92] in order to explore a young woman's consciousness of evil spirits whose status as genuine ghosts or hallucinations was to be debated by critics with a vigor approaching that of the controversy over the reality of the spirits summoned by the Fox sisters. In any event, whether designed by its author as science fiction or psychological fiction, or both, "The Diamond Lens" provided further testimony, with Madame Vulpes, to the literary impact of the Fox sisters during the decade in which they were the public symbols of spiritualistic mediumship.

[91] S. Weir Mitchell, *The Autobiography of a Quack and The Case of George Dedlow*, p. x.
[92] Francis X. Roellinger, "Psychical Research and 'The Turn of the Screw,'" in Henry James, *The Turn of the Screw*, ed. Robert Kimbrough (New York, 1966), pp. 132–42.

IV: "FOLLIES AND DELUSIONS OF THE NINETEENTH CENTURY"[1]

Satiric Attacks on Spiritualism and Reform

I | The most thorough literary treatments of spiritualism during the 1850's were neither humorous sketches nor ghost stories, although at times they displayed elements of both. Instead they were satiric and melodramatic attacks on the movement from one or both of two points of view. Some writers, taking the spirits seriously or professing to do so, adopted the theory of demonic causation advanced by many clergymen (and playfully traced to Cotton Mather by Herman Melville) in order to warn the public against contamination. Another major source of criticism was the view which saw spiritualism as a vulnerable symbol of the various radical and millenarian impulses of the time. Both attitudes were combined by Orestes Brownson in *The Spirit-Rapper: An Autobiography* (1854)[2] to show that the Devil was the prime mover in spiritualism, Fourierism, women's rights, and reform in general. Later, in Bayard Taylor's dealings with the subject in "Confessions of a Medium" (1860)[3] and *Hannah Thurston: A Story*

[1] Part of the subtitle of the pseudonymous Fred Folio's *Lucy Boston; or, Women's Rights and Spiritualism, Illustrating the Follies and Delusions of the Nineteenth Century* (Auburn, N.Y., 1855).
[2] Orestes Brownson, *The Spirit-Rapper: An Autobiography* (Detroit, 1884).
[3] [Bayard Taylor,] "Confessions of a Medium," *Atlantic Monthly* VI (December 1860), 699–715.

of American Life (1863),[4] there was a shift away from the emphasis on demonism and toward a concern with spiritualism as a characteristic but purely human enthusiasm of the times.

The demonic explanation of the spirits was utilized by Jedediah Vincent Huntington, a Catholic journalist, in the first novel to deal extensively with spiritualism, *Alban: A Tale of the New World* (1851).[5] A former Protestant minister who had been converted to Catholicism, Huntington told of the similar experience of his hero, Alban Atherton. Sent down from Yale because of his Romish sympathies to study with Doctor Cone, an elderly Presbyterian minister, Alban decided his course when he witnessed a Catholic priest exorcising demonic poltergeists from Cone's house after Presbyterian and Episcopalian efforts had embarrassingly failed. Huntington drew the details of the disturbances caused by these poltergeists from accounts of the Stratford rappings which had upset the household of Reverend Eliakim Phelps, himself an elderly Presbyterian minister, in the spring and summer of 1850. (Already, in "The Unhappy Lot of Mr. Knott," Lowell had referred in passing to "the tantrums of a ghost"[6] at Stratford.) Both Phelps and Cone's spirits broke dishes and windows, moved furniture, rapped out messages, dropped notes out of the air, and erected dramatic tableaux of mannequins made of stuffed clothing. Although identifying the spirits as demonic in origin and explaining that Cone had invited his affliction by experimenting at an earlier date with mesmerism (as had Eliakim Phelps), Huntington was humorous in demonstrating Protestant ineffectuality. The spirits left Cone's Bible open to passages capable of salacious interpretation, and when Soapstone, the Episcopal cleric, attempted to drive them out they upset his Bible and holy water and set fire to his surplice.[7] One reviewer was annoyed by Huntington's use of the Stratford rappings, saying that it was not funny if meant as a joke, and undignified if meant as a serious argument for Catholicism.[8]

---

[4] Bayard Taylor, *Hannah Thurston: A Story of American Life* (London, 1863).

[5] J. V. Huntington, *Alban: A Tale of the New World* (New York, 1851).

[6] J. R. Lowell, *The Poetical Works of James Russell Lowell* (Boston, 1858), II, 295.

[7] Huntington, pp. 421–77; Frank Podmore, *Modern Spiritualism: A History and a Criticism* (London, 1902), I, 194–201.

[8] *American Whig Review* XIV (December 1851), 491–93.

But Orestes Brownson, by this time a Catholic editor sometimes at odds with Huntington,[9] made use of *Alban* in his own curious romance of ideas, *The Spirit-Rapper: An Autobiography* (1854). Like Doctor Cone, Brownson's narrator slipped from mesmeric trifling into spiritualistic demonism, and like Alban he finally embraced Catholicism, though only on his deathbed. But Brownson's was a far wider focus. He borrowed from the Stratford rappings, but he also dealt with the Fox sisters, Andrew Jackson Davis, and Judge Edmonds in attacking spiritualism, with tongue only half in cheek, as a sinister epidemic of Satanism. And his purpose, stated in his own review of the work, was to warn the public, under "a slight veil of fiction," against infection.[10]

As much as spiritualism, however, Brownson's target was the millennial radicalism which had increasingly vexed him since his own conversion to Catholicism in 1844. He had already written in 1845 that the devil's most successful disguise was his modern one of "LIBERAL PHILANTHROPIST, AND REFORMER."[11] Now from the ranks of reform came spiritualism's early spokesmen, whose writings, Brownson claimed, affirmed the link between "modern philanthropy, visionary reforms, socialism . . . revolutionism,"[12] and the new movement. The demonic explanation of spiritualism, therefore, allowed him to implicate reformers and rappers alike as servants of the Devil.

The "slight veil of fiction" under which he did so was the deathbed autobiography in which his narrator confessed to having been the human agent secretly responsible for the outbreak of spiritualism. A speculative graduate of Union College, he had first become a powerful mesmerist, able to make tables dance to his magnetic whim. Sensing that reform—with its "seers and seeresses, enthusiasts and fanatics, socialists and communists, abolitionists and anti-hangmen, radicals and women's-rights men of both sexes"[13]—was the "spirit of the age,"[14] he quietly placed his mesmeric gifts at its disposal with the aid of Pris-

[9] Theodore Maynard, *Orestes Brownson: Yankee, Radical, Catholic* (New York, 1943), pp. 220–21, 234.
[10] *Brownson's Quarterly Review*, 3rd ser., II (October 1854), 531.
[11] Orestes Brownson, *The Works of Orestes A. Brownson*, ed. Henry F. Brownson (Detroit, 1884), XIX, 117.
[12] Brownson, *The Spirit-Rapper*, p. 1.
[13] Ibid., p. 29.
[14] Ibid., p. 67.

cilla, a married feminist with whom he formed an intellectual liaison. Their aim was to establish chains of human magnetism throughout the world, all directed toward reform and revolution.

Once this step was taken, the magnetic forces within the narrator's table began to express themselves independently with a trivial written message from Benjamin Franklin, wild dancing to dissonant guitar music, and the disclosure, by means of rappings, that they were intelligent spirits. Immediately they demanded another medium to speak through, on the grounds that the narrator's awe hampered communication. The Rapper therefore gave a magnetized bunch of flowers to two sisters who lived nearby. And shortly thereafter these girls, "the since world-renowned Misses Fox,"[15] began to be troubled by the "strange, mysterious knockings" which announced the birth of spiritualism to the world.

With his repentant yet arrogant claims that the Foxes had been his unwitting dupes rather than fraudulent cheats, and that to him alone was due the damage caused by "the Rapping-Mania," Brownson's magnetic Rapper was modeled on the archcriminal of sensational fiction. Especially belittling was his boast of power over the Poughkeepsie seer: ". . . nobody has suspected Andrew Jackson Davis, the most distinguished of the American *mediums*, of having any relations with me. He does not suspect it himself, yet he has been more than once magnetized by me, and it has been in obedience to my will that he has made his revelations."[16] Davis's *Revelations*, of course, had supported Fourierism, criticized the Bible, and attacked priestcraft.[17]

Brownson's narrator realized that he was serving Satan, but for him Satan was "the natural" and "benevolent" spirit of reform. Christianity was man's real foe, and spiritualism would dilute Christian resurrection to a Swedenborgian progress through the spheres while adulterating Christian morality with sentimental philanthropy. It would succeed where like attempts had failed because men would regard the direct communication of its doctrines from such spirits as Penn, Washington, Franklin, Jefferson, and Paine "as overriding Moses and the prophets, our Lord and his apostles." When the rap-

[15] Ibid., p. 81.
[16] Ibid., p. 83.
[17] Podmore, I, 164.

pings quickly spread through America and Europe the narrator was sat-isfied that he had successfully "set afloat a system which . . . would supplant Christianity," and he retired to observe his handiwork.[18]

Unfortunately, just as he was led to doubt the benevolence of diabolical power, the Rapper was mistakenly but fatally stabbed by Priscilla's husband, who with his wife had become Catholic. Dying lingeringly, the Rapper devoted the last third of his account to bedside debates on the nature of spiritualism. All points of view were heard— that it was fraudulent, that it was mesmeric, that it was hallucinatory, and that it was genuine and angelic. But each argument was easily won by Mr. Merton, a learned and reverent young Catholic who argued that mesmeric magnetism was utilized by evil spirits to agitate furni-ture and to counterfeit convincing messages supposedly from the spir-its of great men. Finally the Rapper himself became a Catholic and ended his narrative assured that "good is greater than evil, and love stronger than hell."[19]

Brownson's leading biographers, Arthur Schlesinger and Theodore Maynard, have pointed out that this curious work was devised in part as a *roman à clef*.[20] In the Rapper's introduction to mesmerism through magnetic exhibitions given in Boston in 1837 by "Doctor P———," Brownson recalled the lectures of Dr. Poyen, the French-man who had popularized the pseudoscience in New England.[21] Pris-cilla, the Rapper's feminist co-conspirator, was modeled after Fanny Wright, who for a time had been Brownson's own partner in reform.[22] And among the various seers and prophets were "Edgerton," a Yankee sage who advised men to plant themselves on their "imperishable in-stincts," and "the American Orpheus,"[23] who urged them to live as children.

---

[18] Brownson, *The Spirit-Rapper*, pp. 92, 140, 141.

[19] Ibid., p. 234.

[20] Arthur M. Schlesinger, Jr., *Orestes A. Brownson: A Pilgrim's Progress* (Boston, 1939), p. 225; Maynard, p. 224.

[21] Brownson, *The Spirit-Rapper*, pp. 4–7; Schlesinger, pp. 172–73.

[22] Maynard, p. 224. Perhaps Brownson cast a wider net with Priscilla than has been realized. The immediate cause of Priscilla's turn to women's rights—a London Anti-Slavery Congress's refusal to seat her as a delegate because of her sex—was evidently based on an incident which had helped make feminists of Elizabeth Cady Stanton and Lucretia Mott in 1840 (Brownson, *The Spirit-Rapper*, p. 44).

[23] Ibid., pp. 56–58.

That Brownson felt that less respect was due the spiritualists than these older friends and enemies is shown by his incorporation into the narrative, under their own names, of the Fox sisters and Andrew Jackson Davis as demonically inspired dupes. (The narrator also claimed to have known Joseph Smith in his youth and regarded the Book of Mormon as another piece of literary demonism.)[24] Nor was Brownson very accurate in his treatment of the Foxes. The Rapper claimed that he had given the magnetized flowers to the sisters, then fifteen and twelve years old, in 1843, whereupon he had gone off to Europe to foment the political troubles which climaxed in the revolution of 1848 (for which he took full credit). But the Hydesville disturbances, of course, had not taken place until 1848, at which time Margaret and Kate Fox were probably no more than thirteen and twelve.[25] Perhaps Brownson was suggesting that the Fox sisters were not so girlish as their publicists made them out to be.

More respectable figures in the movement were at least given the courtesy of transparent disguises. Increase Mather Cotton, a Presbyterian divine of august lineage, was subjected to poltergeist visitations like those inflicted on Eliakim Phelps of Stratford (and on J. V. Huntington's Doctor Cone). Cotton's was the only voice besides Merton's raised against the narrator's schemes, but even his old-fashioned Calvinism, though better by far than liberal Protestantism, was not strong enough to prevent the spirits from erecting a tableau of stuffed mannequins in which the central demonic figure was a preacher of Geneva, nor from causing Cotton's own Bible to knock him down during an attempted exorcism.[26]

One of the disputants in the debates about spiritualism toward the end of the book was "Minister Dodson," whose argument that séance phenomena were best explained by the science of "phreno-mesmerism,

24 Ibid., pp. 98–100.

25 Ibid., p. 81. The ages of Margaret and Kate at the time of the Hydesville disturbances have been variously given as fifteen and twelve, thirteen and twelve, twelve and nine, and by Margaret herself as eight and six. [Horace Greeley,] "Modern 'Spiritualism,'" *Putnam's* I (January 1853), 61; Robert Dale Owen, *Footfalls on the Boundary of Another World* (Philadelphia, 1860), p. 285; Podmore, I, 179; Reuben Briggs Davenport, *The Death-Blow to Spiritualism, Being the True Story of the Fox Sisters as Revealed by Authority of Margaret Fox Kane and Catherine Fox Jencken* (New York, 1897), p. 83.

26 Brownson, *The Spirit-Rapper*, pp. 84–87.

or electro-biology,"[27] was identical with the thesis advanced by John Bovee Dods in *Spirit Manifestations Examined and Explained: Judge Edmonds Refuted* (1854).[28] And Judge Edmonds himself, whose public career as a radical New York Democrat and later as a prominent Barn-Burner Brownson must have remembered from his own days in politics,[29] had the distinction of being doubly satirized. He was first referred to by name as a leading spiritualistic prophet of the "good time a-coming."[30] Later he was disguised as "Judge Preston," known to the Rapper as a former politician and legislator and now a jurist of high standing. With two others, an eminent physician and a former U.S. Senator named "Von Schaick," Preston had published a large, well-written account of spiritual manifestations. The occult physician of exaggerated reputation was George Dexter, of course, and "Von Schaick" was Brownson's mask for Nathaniel Tallmadge, the former governor of Wisconsin, whose spirited defense of the Judge had been printed as an appendix to the first volume of Edmonds and Dexter's *Spiritualism* (1853).[31] Sent by the ghost of Benjamin Franklin to visit the dying Rapper, Preston advanced the classical case for spiritualism against Merton with no more success than the latter's other opponents. Indeed, Merton found support for his own position in Preston's admission that "bad angels" as well as "good angels"[32] were sometimes heard rapping the séance table.

Merton's theory, and the episodes from earlier demonological history with which he supported it, were taken by Brownson from Jules Eudes de Mirville's *Pneumatologie: Des Esprits et de leure manifestations fluidiques* (1853),[33] a work which Robert Dale Owen was later to feel compelled to refute as the most effective expression of the Cath-

---

[27] Ibid., p. 162.

[28] John Bovee Dods, *Spirit Manifestations Examined and Explained: Judge Edmonds Refuted* (New York, 1854). To the great delight of the believers, Dods later became a spiritualist (Emma Hardinge Britten, *Modern American Spiritualism: A Twenty Years' Record of the Communion between Earth and the World of Spirits* [New York, 1870], p. 275).

[29] For Edmonds's political career, see Arthur M. Schlesinger, Jr., *The Age of Jackson* (Boston, 1946), pp. 179, 197, 341, 412, 438, 483.

[30] Brownson, *The Spirit-Rapper*, p. 140.

[31] Ibid., pp. 170–71; J. W. Edmonds and G. T. Dexter, *Spiritualism*, I (New York, 1853), 443–51.

[32] Brownson, *The Spirit-Rapper*, p. 176.

[33] J. E. de Mirville, *Pneumatologie* (Paris, 1853).

olic position on the subject.[34] Brownson admitted in his "Preface" that he had simply transferred the substance of de Mirville's work to his own. Thus de Mirville was probably the source of the Rapper's means of enslaving the Fox sisters, for according to Merton the famous nuns of Loudon had been bewitched in 1683 when the evil priest Urban Grandier had tossed a magnetized bouquet over the nunnery wall.[35] "Merton," of course, was a play on "Mirville."

Brownson's advocacy of the theory of demonic inspiration at the same time he was making humorous if sometimes heavy-handed sport of spiritualists and reformers gave *The Spirit-Rapper* a jarring tone of jocosity and seriousness which has puzzled its commentators. Both Schlesinger and Maynard have reacted much in the manner of the reviewer who found the poltergeists in *Alban* unfunny and undignified, Maynard stating that "we are never quite persuaded that Brownson is perfectly serious," and Schlesinger that "the humor was inappropriate if the reader was to presume that Brownson really believed his theory of diabolism."[36] Yet Brownson referred elsewhere to the work, without apparent irony, as the best statement of his opinions on the subject.[37] And as Schlesinger has noted, he later advanced the demonic theory in a thoroughly serious analysis of the planchette fad of 1869.[38] The truth is that few writers were able to treat spiritualism without some degree of humor; moreover, although Maynard may be right in saying that today's reader is unlikely to accept a demonic explanation of spiritual manifestations,[39] Brownson wrote at a time when that explanation was constantly before the public. Perhaps his attitude is best judged by his own prefatory remark that the work, "though affecting some degree of levity, is serious in its aims, and truthful in its statements. There is no fiction in it save its machinery." The weakness of *The Spirit-Rapper* as fiction resulted not from any insincerity on its author's part, but from the failure of his "machinery" to integrate the elements belonging to the novel, the romance, biography, the essay, the "dissertation," and the "regular treatise," all of which he admitted

[34] Owen, *Footfalls*, pp. 39–41.
[35] Brownson, *The Spirit-Rapper*, pp. 2, 158–61.
[36] Maynard, p. 224; Schlesinger, *Brownson*, p. 226.
[37] *Brownson's Quarterly Review*, 5th ser., I (April 1860), 265.
[38] Schlesinger, *Brownson*, p. 226; Brownson, *Works*, IX, 332–51.
[39] Maynard, p. 224.

to having "thrown together" in order to present his case against spiritualism.[40]

Approaching the book in the context of Brownson's entire career, Schlesinger and Maynard have dismissed it as a literary curiosity of little value.[41] But quite aside from its often amusing satiric edge, *The Spirit-Rapper* is a notable example of anti-spiritualistic and anti-reform satire. It was the first "novel" entirely devoted to spiritualism. Indebted to Huntington's *Alban*, it was the fullest fictive exposition of the demonic theory which Herman Melville was to laugh at in "The Apple-Tree Table." And its concatenation of spiritualism and reform made it the first in a series of satires which was to reach a high point three decades later. The Devil was to vanish from the scene during that period, but mediums and feminists were to persist in unholy alliance, most notably in *The Bostonians* of Henry James.

II | After *The Spirit-Rapper* the most immediate and explicit fictional partnership between spirits and reformers was the pseudonymous Fred Folio's *Lucy Boston; or, Women's Rights and Spiritualism, Illustrating the Follies and Delusions of the Nineteenth Century*.[42] Obviously indebted to Brownson, this satiric fantasy concerned a conspiracy of female spirits to extend the rule of women to earth through spiritualism—the Fox sisters having been controlled for this purpose. Lucy Boston, the beautiful, mannishly clad heroine elected state governor on a spiritualistic and women's-rights platform, was a caricature of feminist Lucy Stone, who wore bloomers and whose recent wedding, conducted by Thomas Wentworth Higginson, had omitted the vow of obedience and had included a formal "protest" against the legal subordination of woman and her property in the institution of marriage.[43]

The spiritualists were treated even more recklessly by Folio than they had been by Brownson. In a comic battle for control of the movement, a leading clairvoyant named Fungelhead (Andrew Jackson Davis) was deposed by the sensitive nose of J. Socrates Nozzleman, a

[40] Brownson, *The Spirit-Rapper*, p. 1.
[41] Schlesinger, *Brownson*, p. 225; Maynard, p. 226.
[42] See note 1.
[43] Anna Mary Wells, *Dear Preceptor: The Life and Times of Thomas Wentworth Higginson* (Boston, 1963), pp. 82, 92.

"smelling medium" whose medical practice depended on olfactory communication with the spirits. Nozzleman (Dr. Dexter) also shared authorship of a famous series of letters about spiritualism with Judge Addlehead (Judge Edmonds). At about the time that Lucy Boston's coalition of feminists, free-lovers, and mediums proved unable to govern and Lucy herself resigned her office in order to marry, Nozzleman was arrested for swindling and murdering his patients; the power of both spiritualism and women's rights was broken.[44] Despite the farcical nature of his satire, Folio insisted in prefatory remarks that both movements were fanatical humbugs, and the narrative demonstrated that free love was the inevitable result of their making common cause.[45] The feminist banner, moreover, carried the cipher "Th-Ede-vilto-Pa-y,"[46] and the book's illustration playfully linked both enthusiasms with demonic inspiration.

The Devil was given his due again in Timothy Shay Arthur's *Angel and the Demon: A Tale of Modern Spiritualism* (1858).[47] In condemning the movement as immoral and "demoniac," its mediums as "in mysterious league with evil spirits,"[48] this potboiler offered several varieties of mediumship. The unsuccessful effort of the snake-eyed English governess, Mrs. Jeckyl, to develop her impressible little charge, Madeline, as a "child medium," revived Hawthorne's evil magnetist and trance maiden in a contemporary spiritualistic context. Madeline was to be a "speaking" medium who would, in trance, give voice to spirit-dictated messages without the clumsy mediation of rapping or writing. Speaking mediums ("trance-lecturers") had become prominent in the movement as rappers fell into disfavor after the mid-1850's. Already the anonymous author of *Zillah, the Child Medium: A Tale of Spiritualism* (1857)[49] had described an insane medium's irreverent, futile attempt to restore life to the dead body of a similarly gifted girl.

Both Zillah and Madeline probably reflected the reputation of

---

44 Folio, *Lucy Boston*, pp. 198–210, 244–53, 288–94, 335–48, 373–89.
45 Ibid., p. vii.
46 Ibid., p. 228.
47 T. S. Arthur, *The Angel and the Demon: A Tale of Modern Spiritualism* (Philadelphia, 1858).
48 Ibid., p. 125.
49 *Zillah, the Child Medium* (New York, 1857).

Mrs. Cora L. V. Hatch, who delivered trance lectures to large crowds in Boston and New York during 1857 and 1858,[50] impressing if not convincing Cornelius Felton of Harvard, Henry Wadsworth Longfellow, and N. P. Willis.[51] Although by the end of 1858 Mrs. Hatch was in the process of obtaining a well-publicized divorce from her husband and magnetizer, a mesmeric physician named Benjamin Hatch, she had begun her career on "the spiritual rostrum" at the age of twelve, and under Hatch's astute management her eloquence and profuse curls had already made her, except for the Fox girls, the best-known "child medium" of the decade. (Her literary destiny was to be fulfilled in Henry James's *Bostonians*.)

Orestes Brownson and Fred Folio had dramatized the familiar charge that spiritualism fostered free love and sexual immorality. Such accusations were based on the tendency of spirits to confirm the doctrines of marital reformers and on the presence of spiritualists in free-love communities, and they made a general rule of scandals involving mediums.[52] The last half of 1858 saw a good many newspaper stories about such scandals, and about the Hatch case in particular. And that Arthur had Cora Hatch's situation in mind, or that he was prescient in his manipulation of polemical stereotypes, is apparent from the similarity of his case against spiritualism to that presented early in the following year by Cora's ex-husband, Benjamin Hatch, in a sensational pamphlet entitled *Spiritualists' Iniquities Unmasked, and the Hatch Divorce Case* (1859).[53] On the advice of Judge John Edmonds and other influential believers, Cora had left Hatch in August, 1858, alleging sexual abuse and misappropriation of her substantial earnings. Saying that Edmonds had maliciously intrigued against him,

---

[50] Harrison D. Barrett, *Life Work of Mrs. Cora L. V. Richmond* (Chicago, 1895), pp. 144–73; Earl Wesley Fornell, *The Unhappy Medium: Spiritualism and the Life of Margaret Fox* (Austin, Tex., 1964), pp. 80–83.

[51] Barrett, pp. 169–70; Samuel Longfellow, *Life of Henry Wadsworth Longfellow* (Boston, 1891), II, 347; N. P. Willis, *The Convalescent* (New York, 1859), pp. 303–6.

[52] E. W. Capron, *Modern Spiritualism: Its Facts and Fanaticisms, Its Consistencies and Contradictions* (Boston, 1855), pp. 380–81; Asa Mahan, *Modern Mysteries Explained and Exposed* (Boston, 1855), pp. 282–90; John B. Ellis, *Free Love and Its Votaries; or, American Socialism Unmasked* (New York, 1870), p. 411; Podmore, I, 292–93; Fornell, pp. 33–37.

[53] Benjamin Hatch, *Spiritualists' Iniquities Unmasked* (New York, 1859).

Hatch denied these accusations. He also claimed that mediums were possessed by demonic spirits intent on destroying society by inducing their victims to indulge in adultery, "promiscuous concubinage,"[54] and sexual immoralities of all sorts. Trance mediums, he alleged, were especially susceptible to such influences.

To document his case Hatch described such behavior on the part of over a dozen mediums, all of whom he named.[55] A once-upright clergyman, he said, had become a spiritualist editor and lecturer, had abandoned his sick wife in a "water cure . . . and started out on a lecturing tour with a Miss ———," and had written his wife "that he had found his true 'spiritual affinity,' and that she must cease to longer look upon him as her husband."[56] Hatch also charged an unnamed medium with engaging "in the sacrilegious mission of breaking up families and thereby ruining young wives."[57] As for Cora, she was the essence of pure womanhood—when not entranced by demons and surrounded by spiritualists. But now, he feared, she was in great danger, "sensitive to the last degree, and floating among most lecherous people."[58] For himself he hoped only that his pamphlet would save others from such bitter experiences.

These arguments apparently had not impressed the divorce court. But for the author of *The Angel and the Demon* and *Ten Nights in a Bar Room* (1854), as for the popular religious press whose audience he shared,[59] such alleged propensities constituted the spiritualists' gravest offense. And either he was acquainted with the Hatch scandal, or life imitated popular fiction. Cora's defenders and Hatch (the latter somewhat grudgingly) emphasized her youth, innocence, and value to the spiritualist movement. Like Cora, little Madeline was susceptible to magnetic control. She was the "most remarkable child-medium" ever seen by Mrs. Jeckyl, who predicted that the spirit messages received through Madeline would be of revolutionary importance for

---

[54] Hatch, *Spiritualists' Iniquities*, p. 15.
[55] Ibid., pp. 13–15.
[56] Ibid., p. 13.
[57] Ibid., p. 19.
[58] Ibid., p. 41.
[59] See, for instance, the Reverend William H. Ferris's condemnation of spiritualism for free-love immorality in "Review of Modern Spiritualism," *Ladies Repository* XVI (January-June 1856), 46–52, 88–92, 139–44, 229–33, 297–304, 364–70.

the world. And in the figure of Mrs. Jeckyl's accomplice, Dyer, a "getter-up of circles" and a sponger off foolish women, Arthur portrayed the medium as free-loving libertine, incoherent in his radical prophecies but dangerous in his magnetic ability to control and corrupt:

> Mr. Dyer sought influence over others—females particularly—by means of modern witchcraft, going from house to house 'and leading silly women captive,' and, by his devilish arts, withering or destroying the budding germs of rational freedom in little children, whenever they chanced to come within the sphere of his blasting influence. . . . It was a day of evil triumph with him when he discovered that he was a 'powerful medium,' and could subdue by means of his stronger will the consciousness of sickly, nervous women, and so control the wonderful organism of their spirits as to make them speak and act like mere automatons.[60]

A married man, Dyer had destroyed four other marriages with his influence before leaving his own wife because he felt a spiritual affinity for a prettier woman, thus committing "one of the most grievous sins in the crowded calendar of human wrongs." Fortunately, however, the "Angel" of the novel, a governess of devout purity, was able to frustrate Mrs. Jeckyl and Dyer in their attempt to enslave Madeline as a "neophyte priestess" in the "spiritual temple."[61]

The narrator of Bayard Taylor's "Confessions of a Medium" (1860)[62] was the victim of magnetic machinations instigated by a false spiritualistic prophet cast in the mold of Hatch's clergyman and Arthur's Dyer. Taylor's narrator had been easily mesmerized in his boyhood, and had impressed the Fox sisters in their early days with his power to attract spirits. (Like Linley, the narrator of Fitz-James O'Brien's "Diamond Lens," he had noted the matter-of-fact attitude taken by the sisters toward their mysteries; unlike Linley, he had realized that the spirits could answer his questions only when he was thinking of the answer himself.) Later, as a young man, he delivered

---

[60] Arthur, *The Angel and the Demon*, pp. 211, 193–94.
[61] Ibid., pp. 194–98.
[62] Taylor, "Confessions," pp. 699–715.

vocal spirit-messages to a circle of believers formed by a radical spiritualistic editor named Stilton. Once the circle had accepted Stilton's doctrine that spiritual affinity between man and woman transcends the institution of marriage, the spirits began to speak of one affinity between the narrator and Stilton's dull wife, and of another between Stilton and a young female medium whose spirits demanded grog. Finally the narrator realized that instead of being celestial in origin, these utterances were dictated to his passive trance-consciousness by the powerful mesmeric will of the editor, behind which sometimes lurked the darker presence of Satan—"that power . . . which had tempted me."[63] In a climactic séance the narrator wrestled with the Devil's will and unmasked Stilton's mesmeric deceit, but could not prevent the editor from eloping with his spiritual mate, leaving behind, as had Hatch's clergyman and Arthur's Dyer, a broken-hearted wife. And just as Hatch had been disturbed by the realization that spiritualism had "made victims of tens of thousands of its votaries,"[64] so the medium now wrote his "Confessions" to warn the "thousands and tens of thousands . . . still subject to the same delusion"[65] against further exposure to evil.

Although Taylor paid more attention to the mesmeric mechanics of trance, his analysis of spiritualism was not substantially different from that of Hatch or Arthur. He framed the character of Stilton, the editor, along the same lines of demonism and free love that the others had followed with their magnetic villains, imagined or supposedly real; the medium himself was a male counterpart to Cora Hatch and Madeline; and certainly the story as a whole was as melodramatic in outline as *The Angel and the Demon.*

But Taylor was a better writer than Arthur and knew more about his subject. Indeed, there was a vein of autobiography in the story. Like the medium, Taylor had more than once proved susceptible to mesmerization in his boyhood, before the advent of spiritualism.[66] Later, as Horace Greeley's assistant on the *Tribune,* he had observed

[63] Ibid., p. 708.
[64] Hatch, *Spiritualists' Iniquities,* p. 5.
[65] Taylor, "Confessions," p. 711.
[66] Marie Hansen-Taylor and Horace E. Scudder, eds., *Life and Letters of Bayard Taylor* (Boston, 1884), I, 19.

the editor's patronage of the Fox sisters and, again like his narrator, had attended some of their early séances. Either the spirits or the girls themselves had been impressed by Taylor, for he had written his dying first wife in December, 1850, that the ghost of Greeley's son, who wrote commendable poetry, had twice asked to communicate with him.[67] It is likely, therefore, that the narrator's memory of the Fox sisters, including Leah's remark that the spirits liked him because he seemed "to be nearer to them than most people,"[68] was drawn from Taylor's own experience. Perhaps also autobiographical was the narrator's interpretation of the sisters' talent as limited to reading the minds of their sitters. At the time, however, Taylor had only mentioned to his wife his inability to "believe that intelligent souls pass their future lives in such trifling occupations."[69]

Into the pattern of his narrator's confession Taylor wove not only his own and Benjamin Hatch's experiences, but also the career of Thomas Lake Harris, the Universalist minister turned spiritualist poet, preacher, editor, and community-founder. Harris had been one of the editors of an early spiritualistic journal, *Disclosures from the Interior and Superior Care for Mortals*, which had printed poems transmitted through him by the spirits of Coleridge, Southey, and Shelley. (Evil as Shelley was, a critic had said, he "ranked among the foremost of . . . the Satanic school of poets, and never wrote such trash as is here fathered upon him.")[70] The prophecies of Taylor's narrator were published by Stilton, the spiritualistic editor, in a magazine called *Revelations from the Interior*. And the narrator explicitly compared his own effusive trance-poetry to the verse found in *An Epic of the Starry Heaven* (1854),[71] one of Harris's several spirit-dictated volumes. Moreover, Harris, who was later to found his own communal societies on a basis of sexual mysticism, had already preached a high-minded version of Stilton's doctrine of spiritual affinity: according to

---

[67] Ibid., p. 194.
[68] Taylor, "Confessions," p. 702.
[69] Hansen-Taylor and Scudder, I, 194.
[70] "Literature and Logic of 'The Interior,' " *National Magazine* I (October 1852), 356; Podmore, I, 295.
[71] Taylor, "Confessions," pp. 705, 713. Harris's trance-poetry included *An Epic of the Starry Heaven* (New York, 1854), *A Lyric of the Morning Land* (New York, 1856), and *A Lyric of the Golden Age* (New York, 1856).

Harris each person, whatever his temporal situation, would be united in heaven with his true "counterpart."[72]

In addition, the confessional nature of the story and the narrator's thralldom to the Devil laid Harris as well as Benjamin Hatch under obligation. Harris's inability to share power amicably with others and his recurrent claims to a monopoly on divine inspiration had made him from the beginning a figure of controversy in the spiritualistic movement. In *The Wisdom of Angels* (1857)[73] he had recorded a clairvoyant journey during which he had seen the Harmonial Pantheists of Andrew Jackson Davis confined to hell and had received angelic sanction for his own "New Church." According to the spiritualist historian Emma Hardinge Britten, after failing in the winter of 1858–59 to take control of the movement in New York City, he had withdrawn from its "infidelic" body to form his own congregation of Christian Spiritualists. Moreover, in a new poem, *The Song of Satan* (1860), he supposedly confessed that infernal influences had controlled him during his mediumistic trances.[74] Both Harris and Hatch's recantations were the products of power struggles within the New York City movement and a widespread public revulsion against spiritualism in general. The defections of both men were particularly embarrassing because of the nature of their charges and their prominence within the movement.[75] To imitate just such "confessions," then, Taylor blended his own knowledge of mesmeric trance and the Fox sisters, Hatch's revelations of spiritualist "Iniquities," and Harris's career as medium, poet, and preacher of the doctrine of "spiritual counterparts."

Taylor was at pains to make his readers accept the narrative as the authentic autobiography of a genuine medium. The story was accepted for publication in the December, 1860, issue of the *Atlantic Monthly* by James Russell Lowell, who characteristically ignored its demonic implications in congratulating Taylor for having separated

---

[72] Podmore, I, 294. For Harris's more significant career as the mystical prophet of his own cults, see Herbert W. Schneider and George Lawton, *A Prophet and a Pilgrim* (New York, 1942).

[73] T. L. Harris, *The Wisdom of Angels* (New York, 1857), pp. 178–97.

[74] Britten, *Modern American Spiritualism*, pp. 213–14. Harris expressed the same views again in *Modern Spiritualism and the Power and the Glory of the Church of Christ* (London, 1860). For a description of Harris's *The Song of Satan* (New York, 1860), see Schneider and Lawton, pp. 22–24.

[75] Britten, pp. 213–14; Hatch, pp. 31–35, 39–40.

"self-deception from humbug—*me*-cheating from *thee*-cheating."[76] (In a different way than O'Brien's "The Diamond Lens," Taylor's story confirmed the verdict of the Harvard professors who had served on the *Boston Courier's* test committee.) Immediately Taylor wrote James T. Fields, the magazine's publisher, to request the unusual favor of "payment for turning state's evidence before said evidence is published." And although everything in the *Atlantic* appeared anonymously, he asked Fields not even to mention his identity: "I want it to be thought a *bona fide* confession, and was careful to give it that character. I think it will attract attention."[77]

He was repaid for his care in the following year when Thackeray told him in London that he had been "completely taken in by . . . 'Confessions.' "[78] Although Thackeray had witnessed the dancing table of Daniel Dunglas Home as George Bancroft's guest in New York,[79] it is unlikely that he knew very much about American spiritualism. But the skill with which Taylor shaped topical and autobiographical materials into a confession given psychological interest by its narrator's careful study of his own trance states made for a plausible representation of the same attitudes handled fantastically by Orestes Brownson, melodramatically by T. S. Arthur, and autobiographically by Benjamin Hatch and T. L. Harris—that spiritualism was radical, immoral, and ultimately from the Devil.

III | In Lowell, Taylor had an editor sympathetic to both serious supernatural fiction and attacks, humorous or otherwise, on spiritualism. In two other *Atlantic* stories Taylor dealt with material related to that of his "Confessions." The supernatural interest reflected by the menacing presence of Satan in that story expressed itself more fully in "The Haunted Shanty" (1861),[80] which told about an odd case of rural witchcraft. And the satiric attitude toward bizarre

---

[76] James Russell Lowell, *New Letters of James Russell Lowell*, ed. M. A. DeWolfe Howe (New York, 1932), p. 100.
[77] Hansen-Taylor and Scudder, I, 372.
[78] Ibid., p. 378.
[79] Katherine H. Porter, *Through a Glass Darkly: Spiritualism in the Browning Circle* (Lawrence, Kans., 1958), pp. 113–14.
[80] [Bayard Taylor,] "The Haunted Shanty," *Atlantic Monthly* VIII (July 1861), 57–72.

social experiment in the earlier story became lighthearted in "The Experiences of the A. C." (1862),[81] a good-natured fictional reminiscence about an attempt at communal living in the 1840's, the sponsors of which (a wealthy married couple) had since begun to "cultivate Mediums."[82]

This last story and "Confessions of a Medium" were preparations for Taylor's first novel, *Hannah Thurston: A Story of American Life* (1863), a satiric treatment of the previous decade's reform impulses set in the upstate New York town of "Ptolemy" (presumably Skaneateles).[83] Taylor exaggerated somewhat when he claimed in his "Preface" to treat native American materials which had "escaped the notice of novelists."[84] For in *Hannah Thurston* the spiritualistic and free-love movements which he had already attacked in "Confessions of a Medium" were again linked with women's rights and other reforms, as they had been by Orestes Brownson and Fred Folio. Taylor's thin plot was a love story: the rescue of Hannah Thurston, a sincere if parochial Quaker feminist, from a career of misguided reform oratory by Max Woodbury, a much-traveled and wealthy young man who was repelled by the two most popular enthusiasms of the day, "Spiritualism and Women's Rights."[85] The latter movement drew most of Taylor's serious attention. But uncritical belief in man-made millennia was most strongly dramatized in the person of the foolish Mrs. Merryfield, who depended on a fraudulent medium for communication with her dead son, himself a martyr to the water cure. And Hannah's eyes were opened to the possibility that her feminist cause could be perverted when Mrs. Merryfield, under the influence of the medium's attack on the enslavement of women in the marriage relation, attempted to run away from her husband in order to join the Aqueanda Community of Perfectionists.

Missing from this familiar synthesis of reform and spiritualism was the Devil. It would appear, in fact, that the satanic presence in "Confessions of a Medium" derived primarily from the recantations of

[81] [Bayard Taylor,] "The Experiences of the A.C.," *Atlantic Monthly* IX (February 1862), 170–88.
[82] Ibid., p. 188.
[83] Brownson, *Works*, XIX, 505.
[84] Taylor, *Hannah Thurston*, I, vi.
[85] Ibid., p. 111.

Benjamin Hatch and Thomas Lake Harris, with perhaps a contributory wish on Taylor's part to exploit the supernatural potential of his material. For in *Hannah Thurston* the spirits were contemptuously dismissed as owing to clairvoyance and deceit; indeed, a minister's attack on them as demonic was mentioned with amusement.[86] Dyce, the novel's sinister medium, was credited with a "powerful, uncanny magnetic force"[87] which perhaps allowed him to read his sitters' minds. But the most dramatic of the spiritual manifestations he elicited at the séance table were obviously fraudulent.

Taylor's description of Dyce's séance,[88] the longest such account in the serious fiction of the time, was a retrospective catalogue of manifestations common in the 1850's, here attributed to a single medium. Dyce asked each of his sitters to think of the spirit with whom he wished to communicate. First, like the spirit of Mrs. Horace Greeley's son, Absalom Merryfield pleased his mother by rapping out a greeting. Hannah Thurston was addressed directly through the throat of Dyce by a "faint, feminine voice" (probably belonging to the spirit of Margaret Fuller, one of Hannah's heroines). Woodbury, however, played a trick familiar to experienced mediums by failing to mention that the person whose "spirit" he sought was still alive, until after Dyce had claimed to see the spirit's apparition. Dyce met the challenge by insisting that either Woodbury's friend had died unknown to him or another spirit had been "unconsciously present" in Woodbury's mind; and he supported the latter supposition by displaying this second spirit's initials written in red on his own arm, which he had been holding under the table. Woodbury's observation that he had never heard of the second spirit caused an awkward moment, but could not shake the faith of the believers. (Taylor apparently did not feel it necessary to explain that such "blood-writing" could be produced by inscribing letters on the skin with a sharp point, then rubbing briskly.) The first part of the séance came to an end with spirit-writing through the medium's hand, including a message written by the ghost of Benjamin Lundy, the abolitionist, to his old friend Mr.

[86] Ibid., p. 213.
[87] Ibid., p. 217.
[88] Taylor, "Spiritual and Other Knockings," *Hannah Thurston*, I, 211–40.

Merryfield, about "light from the spirit world" and "the perfect day of Liberty" to come.[89]

With the exception of the patently fradulent blood-writing, Dyce's ability to supply the spirits desired by his sitters was explicable in terms of either clairvoyance or knowledge of his sitters' backgrounds. But Taylor left no room for doubt in describing the physical manifestations which next ensued.[90] In complete darkness rustling sounds and sharps raps were heard, the table was jolted up and down, and the sitters were touched "at random by invisible hands."[91] Finally the dismal melody of "Days of Absence" was picked out on the keys of an untuned piano at the side of the room, ostensibly by the spirit of Mrs. Merryfield's daughter, Angelina, who had just learned to play the song when she died.

Taylor followed a standard pattern in ordering his dark séance with table-tipping, invisible touch, and spirit music, each of them more tangible as evidence of mysterious agency than communications emanating from the medium's throat or pencil. Such physical phenomena had attracted notice in widely published accounts of séances involving the Fox sisters and members of Judge Edmonds's New York Circle.[92] In 1857 Thomas Wentworth Higginson had sworn to the authenticity, if not the spiritual origin, of a lifted table, the electric

[89] Ibid., pp. 219, 223, 226.
[90] Ibid., pp. 229–31.
[91] Ibid., p. 229.
[92] Judge Edmonds had sponsored a séance involving several mediums including the Fox sisters, in which roughly the same phenomena had been elicited. A skeptic present had described it as "a perfect pandemonium of noises, bangs on the table as loud as could be made by hand or foot, loud slaps, bells ringing loudly, the table creaking, flapping its leaves, and turning quite upside down. . . . Judge Edmonds continually exclaiming 'I'm touched—now I am tapped on the shoulder—now they are at my feet, now my head. . . .' After all the mediums and sitters had been forced by the spirits into a closet, those still outside had heard a chorus of Auld Lang Syne, sung by all the *closetees,* accompanied by raps on the door, and scrapings on an old violon-cello, which was in the closet. . ." (Charles Wyllys Elliott, *Mysteries; or, Glimpses of the Supernatural* [New York, 1852], pp. 167–68). As Greeley's assistant on the *Tribune,* Taylor was inevitably familiar with such goings-on during the early 1850's. Perhaps this was especially true after April, 1851, when Oliver Johnson (the "O. J." of Lowell's letter to Edward Davis about the Foxes), to replace whom Greeley had given Taylor his first job in 1848, returned to the newspaper's staff (Hansen-Taylor and Scudder, I, 115, 208; Podmore, I, 233).

touch of a hand on his foot under the table, and perfect accompaniment played on a guitar held by Higginson himself while he sang a Portuguese song probably unknown, he said, to more than a dozen other Americans, during two dark séances conducted by a Harvard divinity student who had been suspended for his mediumistic activities.[93]

Although these manifestations were more dramatic than rappings or spirit-writing, if they were fraudulent they required mediums to run great risks of being seized or suddenly illuminated as they moved about the table or manipulated extension rods bearing artificial hands made of guttapercha. At one of the séances of the Davenport brothers a sitter had seized a "spirit musician" in the dark, and had suffered in return a blow on the head from a tambourine; later he had suddenly turned up a lantern, revealing the Davenports playing a variety of instruments at once.[94] And P. T. Barnum was to write in *The Humbugs of the World* (1866)[95] that such exposures had forced the Davenports to devise the "spirit cabinet," in the privacy of which they could slip out of the ropes which held them in their chairs, play their instruments and throw objects out of the cabinet, and then tie themselves up again before inviting inspection from the sitters. Taylor was obviously acquainted with such tales about exposures of mediumistic fraud. For in *Hannah Thurston* when light returned to the séance and Dyce raised his face from his hands, he had a black eye. Although Dyce blamed the mishap on "unfriendly spirits,"[96] it was later learned that a skeptic, anticipating that under cover of darkness the medium would leave the table to play the piano, had rubbed chimney soot on the black keys.

[93] Higginson's account, dated April 15, 1857, was reprinted from the *Worcester Spy* by Emma Hardinge Britten, *Modern American Spiritualism*, pp. 183–85. The young medium, Frederick L. H. Willis, was a close friend of the Alcott family, and his posthumous memoirs, omitting any mention of his mediumistic activities, were to claim that he had served as the model for Laurie in *Little Women*. Taking up medicine while remaining a spiritualist, he was evidently to treat Robert Dale Owen during the latter's final years (Edith Willis Lynn and Henry Bazin, eds., *Alcott Memoirs, Posthumously Compiled from Papers, Journals, and Memoranda of the Late Dr. Frederick L. H. Willis* [Boston, 1915], pp. 24, 40; Richard W. Leopold, *Robert Dale Owen: A Biography* [Cambridge, Mass., 1940], p. 407).
[94] Ferris, "Review of Modern Spiritualism," 142–43.
[95] P. T. Barnum, *The Humbugs of the World* (London, 1866), pp. 49–55.
[96] Taylor, *Hannah Thurston*, I, 230–31, 238–39.

Taylor thus trivialized the powers of the medium by discarding demonic inspiration and minimizing clairvoyance in favor of gross fraud evident to all but deluded believers such as Mrs. Merryfield. He retained, however, the conception of the spiritualist as sinister radical evident in his own and T. S. Arthur's earlier treatments of the subject. Stilton, the spiritualistic editor of "Confessions of a Medium," had mesmerically victimized the story's narrator in order to justify his own libertinism. T. S. Arthur's Dyer had gone from home to home, "leading silly women captive" with his magnetic arts and breaking up marriages with his doctrines. Taylor traced Dyce from the same pattern, as shown by Mr. Merryfield's thoughts upon realizing that the medium had induced his wife to run away:

> The evil influence of Dyce, strengthened by his assumed power, as a medium, of bringing her children near to her; the magnetic strength, morbid though it was, of the man's words and presence; the daily opportunities of establishing some intangible authority over the wife . . . until she became, finally, the ignorant slave of his will—all this, or the possibility of it, presented itself to Merryfield's mind. . . .[97]

But Taylor attempted to fill out the villainous stereotype with topically realistic strokes. Thus the detailed account of the séance. Thus, too, the satirical but recognizable history of Dyce as an itinerant medium:

> He led a desultory life, here and there, through New York and the New England States, presiding at spiritual sessions in the houses of the believers, among whom he had acquired a certain amount of reputation as a medium. Sometimes his performances were held in public (admittance ten cents), in the smaller towns, and he earned enough in this way to pay his necessary expenses. When he discovered a believing family, in good circumstances, especially where the table was well supplied, he would pitch his tent, for days or weeks, as the circumstances favoured. Such an oasis in the desert of existence he had found at Mr. Merryfield's. . . .[98]

[97] Ibid., II, 108.
[98] Ibid., p. 55.

Thus Dyce was to some extent a compound of both the sensational villain of T. S. Arthur (and Benjamin Hatch) and the inane parasite attacked by Artemus Ward for "destroyin the piece of mind of evry famerlee he enters. . . . a cuss to society & a pirit on honest peple's corn beef barrils."[99]

Dyce's ideas were as topically conceived as his manifestations. In his parasitic wanderings he preached the doctrines of the Perfectionists at Aqueanda, a utopian community where "those selfish institutions, marriage and the right of property," had been replaced by free love and communal labor. ("Good God! Is this true?" was Max Woodbury's reaction.) Aqueanda was also a haven for spiritualists, and Dyce's most compelling argument in persuading Mrs. Merryfield to assert her "rights" by going there was the possibility that in "the pure and harmonious life of the Community, she might perhaps attain to the conditions of a medium, and be always surrounded by angelic company."[100] Artemus Ward had noted a similar convergence of interests in the free-love society at Berlin Heights, Ohio, whose members, he said, "believed in affinertys and sich, goin back on their domestic ties without no hesitation whatsomever. They was likewise spirit rappers and high-presher reformers on gineral principles."[101] Probably both Ward and Taylor had read in Greeley's *Tribune* about Kiantone, the Harmonial utopia directed by John Murray Spear, who under the direction of spirits had been advocating ever more radical reforms of various sorts since the early 1850's. Marriage and property were unknown in the short-lived settlement at Kiantone, where the colonists lived in pentagonal houses and drank water drawn from springs certified as magical by the spirits. As the *Tribune* noted, however, the spirit child born to Spear's female associate, who had left her husband to become the prophet's scribe, behaved like an ordinary baby and, said some, looked like Spear.[102]

---

[99] Charles Farrar Browne, *The Complete Works of Artemus Ward* (London, 1884), p. 50.
[100] Taylor, *Hannah Thurston*, II, 52, 129.
[101] Browne, *The Complete Works of Artemus Ward*, p. 159.
[102] *New York Weekly Tribune*, July 3, 1858, pp. 2–3; October 2, 1858, p. 7; *New York Tribune*, January 5, 1859, p. 3. First known as a prison-reformer, Spear was among those whom Bronson Alcott proposed inviting to form the group which eventually became the Town and Country Club. Others on Alcott's list included

But by naming a free-love, communistic society "Aqueanda," placing it near "Ptolemy," and calling its members "Perfectionists," Taylor must have suggested to many of his readers the Oneida Community of Perfectionists, which John Humphreys Noyes had founded near Skaneateles in 1848 on a basis of communal enterprise and "complex marriage" derived from his own interpretation of primitive Christianity. It would appear, however, that Taylor erred in implying that Oneida was a center of mediumistic activity. For spiritualism was not to be important in the Community until toward the end of Noyes's reign, perhaps in the late 1870's; and it was to be criticized as nothing but "Swedenborgianism Americanized" in Noyes's own *History of American Socialisms* (1870).[103] Whatever the allusive significance of their name and location, then, the Aqueanda Perfectionists were nothing more than a composite of critical stereotypes of free-loving, spiritualistic, and communistic societies.

Perhaps recognizing the literary lineage from which *Hannah Thurston* had sprung—a lineage probably more analogical than genetic—Orestes Brownson, who thought the book's love story silly, praised that part of it which criticized women's rights and demonstrated "the vain pretensions and immoral tendencies of Mesmerism, spiritism, and free-lovism. . . ."[104] Perhaps, too, the absence of any mention of demonism in Brownson's review was a silent recognition of the modulation effected by Taylor in this kind of anti-reform satire. Writing during the Civil War, when the energy of the spiritualists was temporarily in abeyance, and when it perhaps seemed no longer topically relevant to warn the "thousands and tens of thousands" of satanically deluded believers at whom his earlier medium's "Confessions" had (rhetorically, at least) been directed, Taylor approached the relationship of spiritualism to reform from a social rather than religious point

---

Emerson, Thoreau, Lowell, Garrison, Oliver Johnson (Lowell's "O. J."), and Adin Ballou of the Hopedale Community. Alcott was on good terms with a number of spiritualists, especially Andrew Jackson Davis, whose efforts he described as paralleling his own. See *The Letters of A. Bronson Alcott*, ed. Richard L. Herrnstadt (Ames, Iowa, 1969), pp. 147–48, 150, 164, 202–7, 210, 219.

[103] John Humphrey Noyes, *History of American Socialisms* (Philadelphia, 1870), p. 540. A chapter on "The Spiritualistic Communities," pp. 564–76, surveyed communal attempts to combine spiritualism and socialism.

[104] Brownson, *Works*, XIX, 506.

of view. This relationship had appeared as demonic or supernatural conspiracy in the treatments of T. S. Arthur, Fred Folio, and Brownson, and the alliance of mesmerism and social millenarianism had aroused a morbid shudder in Nathaniel Hawthorne. In *Hannah Thurston*, however, Taylor regarded this bundle of "-isms" as original and occasionally grotesque "peculiarities of development in American life," more particularly of life in the rural towns of the North and West. Attributing the prevalence of feminists and spiritualists in Ptolemy to the narrowness of provincial culture, where intellect was marked "by activity rather than development,"[105] he presented the Merryfields as products of that culture easily attracted to faddistic enthusiasms, of which spiritualism was only one of the more grotesque.

Similarly, Taylor naturalized the persistent figure of the magnetic and prophetic villain, who can be traced back through his more demonic appearances as editor in Taylor's own "Confessions of a Medium," as free-loving medium in Arthur's *Angel and the Demon*, and as archrevolutionist in Brownson's *Spirit-Rapper*, to Hawthorne's Westervelt, who has been described by Harry Levin as "the diabolical mesmerist of *The Blithedale Romance*."[106] In Taylor's hands the medium became a recognizable figure, clearly if satirically placed in society. Still a caricature, he represented the qualities of both the melodramatic and humorous stereotypes, dangerous with his magnetic ability to corrupt the deluded, but also resembling, with his trivial and fraudulent manifestations, the inane rappers ridiculed by Q. K. Philander Doesticks and Artemus Ward. He had lost his Gothic aura. And it only remained for Henry James, in *The Bostonians*, to delineate him as an authentic social type in the person of Selah Tarrant, once a medium and participant in the "Cayuga" experiment, and presently a mesmeric healer and promoter of his daughter's career as a feminist trance-lecturer.

It would appear, then, that just as the humorous sketch of the séance had run its course by the end of the Civil War, so had the satirical and melodramatic treatment of spiritualism as demonically inspired. Taylor's handling of medium and believers in *Hannah Thurston* incorporated some of the comic and polemic attitudes of his predecessors. But

---

[105] Taylor, *Hannah Thurston*, I, vi, 192.
[106] Harry Levin, *The Power of Blackness* (New York, 1958), p. 13.

his exorcism (by omission) of the Devil, and his study of the movement as just one of several enthusiasms characteristic of a particular culture at a particular time, furnish evidence that it was becoming possible for the writer of fiction to examine spiritualism in a relatively objective manner. Two decades later, after the rise and fall of a new wave of spiritualistic excitement in the 1870's, this opportunity would be realized by William Dean Howells and Henry James, writers who were growing up during the reign of the Fox sisters, in *The Undiscovered Country* (1880) and *The Bostonians* (1886).

V: "PHENOMENAL PROOF
OF A LIFE TO COME" [1]

American Spiritualism from 1860 to 1900

I | By the end of the 1850's the spiritualistic epidemic had
noticeably subsided. The Fox sisters had retired from public
mediumship; spiritual manifestations had lost their novelty; the
public had become apathetic and skeptical. And although some mediums later claimed to have played important roles in the Union
victory, the movement continued at low ebb throughout the Civil
War. Postwar efforts to revive hopes of achieving social millennium
under spirit direction collapsed when Victoria Woodhull, after cap-
turing the presidency of the American Association of Spiritualists in
1871, alienated many believers with her strident feminism, her defense
of free love, and her involvement in the Beecher-Tilton scandal.

During these same postwar years, however, there was a resurgence
of popular interest in the consolatory and religious promise of spiritualism. The death of half a million people in the war had stimulated
a widespread search for consolation among their survivors. One manifestation of this impulse was the vogue of such works as *The Gates
Ajar* (1869),[2] whose heroine, mourning the death of her brother in the
war, was able, by thinking and talking about heaven, to assure herself

[1] Robert Dale Owen, "Lecture," *Religio-Philosophical Journal* XVI (July 11,
1874), 5.
[2] Elizabeth Stuart Phelps, *The Gates Ajar* (Boston, 1869).

of its existence and of his happy life there. *The Gates Ajar* differed from spiritualistic visions of the hereafter only in its admitted fiction and its more conventional piety. (Although Elizabeth Stuart Phelps wrote the novel at Andover Seminary, where her father was professor of sacred rhetoric and homiletics, she had already written a short story sympathetically based on the experiences of her grandfather, Eliakim Phelps, during the Stratford rappings of 1850.)[3] And in any event the war had magnified the wish (basic to spiritualism) to know that loved ones had ascended to immortality. For some of the war-bereaved it was doubtless but another step to attempt to communicate with the dead.

War or no war, the religious crisis to which spiritualism was in part a response had intensified. Since the time that Judge Edmonds had advocated spiritualism as a defense against skepticism, confidence in traditional answers to the question of immortality had further eroded under the impact of higher criticism and science. And three years before John Fiske attempted the reconciliation of Christianity and Darwinism in his *Outlines of Cosmic Philosophy* (1874),[4] Robert Dale Owen, himself once a free-thinker, suggested in *The Debatable Land between This World and the Next* (1871)[5] that spiritualism could mediate between faith and science by providing empirically verifiable evidence of immortality. Later, in the *Atlantic Monthly* of December, 1874,[6] Owen explained his acceptance of the Biblical account of the risen Christ on the ground that during the previous summer he himself had "seen and touched and conversed with a materialized spirit. . . ."[7]

During the same years the public's imagination was caught by a new repertoire of mediumistic manifestations. A popular fad of 1868 was a predecessor of the ouija board called planchette, a small hand-rest fitted with wheels and a pencil so as to produce spirit-writing under the touch of a magnetic hand. Requiring no professional medium for

---

[3] Elizabeth Stuart Phelps, "The Day of My Death," *Men, Women, and Ghosts* (Boston, 1869), pp. 113–60.
[4] John Fiske, *Outlines of Cosmic Philosophy* (Boston, 1874).
[5] Robert Dale Owen, *The Debatable Land between This World and the Next* (Philadelphia, 1871).
[6] Robert Dale Owen, "Some Results from My Spiritual Studies. A Chapter of Autobiography," *Atlantic Monthly* XXXIV (December 1874), 719–31.
[7] Ibid., p. 722.

its operation, this device was particularly attractive to some of the feminine writers involved in the postwar search for psychical consolation. Harriet Beecher Stowe interested herself in planchette;[8] Elizabeth Stuart Phelps wrote an article about it;[9] and Kate Field published her experiences as a medium for automatic writing in *Planchette's Diary* (1868).[10] Meanwhile, "spirit photographers" took pictures showing the bereaved watched over by glowing but indistinct loved ones. J. V. Mansfield, the "spirit postmaster," mailed to his clients messages which he had transcribed from their dead relatives. And in dark séances "trumpet mediums," tied to their chairs, elicited the voices of spirits from metal speaking-trumpets which floated over the heads of the living.[11]

Skeptics attributed planchette-writing to involuntary motion on the part of the amateur mediums holding the device. And they explained the rest of these manifestations as fraudulent. In order to identify the spirits with whom his customers sought to communicate, Mansfield evidently employed various methods to read their letters of inquiry without appearing to have tampered with the envelopes, which he then returned apparently unopened, along with the requisite spirit-messages. Trumpet mediums were allegedly able to slip in and out of the knots which held them in their chairs.[12] But despite such charges, Mansfield's operation as a mail-order medium, begun in the late 1850's, was still flourishing when Mark Twain attacked him as "Man-

[8] Mrs. Stowe planned to write an article on planchette in the winter of 1868, according to a passage from Kate Field's diary printed in Lillian Whiting, *Kate Field: A Record* (Boston, 1899), p. 197. Eventually Mrs. Stowe did tell of her experiences with planchette in her brother Charles Beecher's *Spiritual Manifestations* (Boston, 1879), pp. 25–36.

[9] Elizabeth Stuart Phelps, "Planchette," *Watchman and Reflector* XXXIX (September 3, 1868), 5.

[10] Kate Field, *Planchette's Diary* (New York, 1868).

[11] Frank Podmore, *Modern Spiritualism: A History and a Criticism* (London, 1902), II, 117–25; Emma Hardinge Britten, *Modern American Spiritualism: A Twenty Years' Record of the Communion between Earth and the World of Spirits* (New York, 1870), pp. 185–94; Britten, *Nineteenth Century Miracles; or, Spirits and Their Work in Every Country of the Earth* (New York, 1884), pp. 551–52.

[12] P. T. Barnum, *The Humbugs of the World* (London, 1866), pp. 49–55, 59–60; [Horace Howard Furness,] *Preliminary Report of the Commission Appointed by the University of Pennsylvania to Investigate Modern Spiritualism in Accordance with the Request of the Late Henry Seybert* (Philadlphia, 1887), pp. 128–47.

chester" in *Life on the Mississippi* (1883).[13] And Lafcadio Hearn, who as a Cincinnati reporter unmasked several fraudulent mediums and wrote a definitive analysis of the methods of spirit photographers,[14] was nonetheless baffled in 1874 by a trumpet medium who elicited a message from his dead father for which Hearn could suggest no mundane origin. (Eighteen years later the same medium so impressed Hamlin Garland that he went on to assign her talents to the heroine of his first psychical romance, *The Tyranny of the Dark*.)[15]

But the most dramatic of all manifestations—and the basis of Robert Dale Owen's strongest claims for spiritualism—was the "materialization" of spirits in the flesh. In the early 1860's Owen had seen Kate Fox elicit the first silent "full form" materialization. Meanwhile the Davenport brothers, needing protection from aggressive skeptics, had devised the "spirit cabinet," a roofless closet within which, tied to their chairs, they could induce the spirits to play musical instruments and to show spectral faces at small apertures. The advantages of the spirit cabinet led to its widespread adoption in the late 1860's. And sometime in 1871 spirits in white robes began to issue forth from cabinets to talk with and embrace their mediums' clients.[16]

When reports of this development reached England, British mediums immediately began to evoke similar manifestations. The best-known of these English spirits—indeed, the most famous single spirit

[13] Samuel Clemens, *Life on the Mississippi* (Boston, 1883), pp. 481–85.
[14] [Lafcadio Hearn,] "Spirit Photography," *Cincinnati Commercial*, November 14, 1875, pp. 1, 3.
[15] In addition to the mysterious intonations of Hearn's dead father, the voices of "Maudie" (an affectionate child) and "Mitchel" (an articulate, deep-voiced male) were elicited by "Mrs. Smith," a young Cincinnati medium, in a séance reported by Hearn in "Among the Spirits," *Cincinnati Enquirer*, January 25, 1874, p. 8. Garland was to write at length of his 1892 encounter in California with a medium from Ohio named "Mrs. Smiley," and of her séances visited by "Maudie" and "Mitchell" [*sic*], in *Forty Years of Psychic Research* (New York, 1936), pp. 32–107. Garland was so impressed by these sessions that he took the medium back to Boston for further study by the American Psychical Society. A decade later spirits and sitters almost duplicating those of "Mrs. Smiley" attended the trumpet-speaking séances conducted by the heroine of Garland's first occult novel, *The Tyranny of the Dark* (London, 1905), pp. 201–12, 283–306. And in 1908 he presented "Mrs. Smiley" herself, along with her familiars "Maudie" and "Mitchel," in a composite fictional account of his psychical experiences, *The Shadow World* (New York, 1908), pp. 50–70.
[16] Podmore, II, 95–96; Barnum, pp. 49–55.

of the century—was "Katie King," who was originally the familiar of a pretty young London medium named Florence Cook. Paid a retainer by a wealthy believer, Miss Cook held invitational rather than public séances, and at first there was little to distinguish her performances from those of other materializing mediums. But during the first half of 1874 William Crookes, a rising young physicist later to be knighted for his contributions to science, asserted publicly that he had seen both Katie and Florence in the cabinet at the same time and had photographed Katie, thus proving beyond all doubt her spiritual identity.[17] Such testimony from a reputable young Fellow of the Royal Society seemed to the spiritualists to vindicate their strongest claims (it is cited to the present day).[18] A few years ago, however, in *The Spiritualists: The Story of Florence Cook and William Crookes* (1962),[19] Trevor H. Hall argued very persuasively that Florence Cook, about to lose her substantial subsidy because of suspicion of fraud, somehow compromised Crookes, thus forcing him to bear public witness for her. In any event, Katie bade her friend Florrie a tearful farewell in May, 1874, never to appear for her again.

But the earthly ministry of Katie King was not yet complete. For almost immediately she reappeared in Philadelphia. There, during the next six months, she brought to American spiritualists in general, and to Robert Dale Owen in particular, one of their greatest triumphs and, ultimately, one of their greatest humiliations.

II | At the age of seventy-three Robert Dale Owen could look back on a richly diversified career. The son of Robert Owen, the English reformer, he had come to America as a young man in 1825 to assist in the founding of his father's socialist community at New Harmony, Indiana. Between 1829 and 1831 he had edited free-thought and labor newspapers in New York City, numbering among his associates Fanny Wright and, briefly, Orestes Brownson. Back home again in Indiana, he had turned from radical to more conventional Democratic politics, serving as a representative to both state and na-

---

[17] Podmore, II, 97–99, 152–66.

[18] See, for instance, Norman Blunsdon, *A Popular Dictionary of Spiritualism* (New York, 1962), p. 114.

[19] Trevor H. Hall, *The Spiritualists: The Story of Florence Cook and William Crookes* (London, 1962).

tional legislatures, in which latter capacity he had helped establish the Smithsonian Institute in 1846. Still later he had been the American minister to the Court of Naples from 1854 to 1858. His political career had closed with important service as a leading War Democrat on Stanton's Ordnance and American Freedmen's Inquiry Commissions.[20]

Since 1856, however, his chief interest had been the study and promulgation of spiritualism. Easily the best-known American yet to declare his unequivocal belief, Owen had established his authority as a leading spokesman for the movement with *Footfalls on the Boundary of Another World* (1860),[21] a collection of carefully documented accounts of spontaneous rather than mediumistic spiritual phenomena, together with a temperate argument for the "spiritual hypothesis." Shunning public séances and professional mediums, he had gained a reputation for careful investigation and cautious conclusions, and he had warned against Victoria Woodhull's attempt to mingle spirits and reform.[22] His goal, in fact, was to establish spiritualism as an intellectually and socially respectable adjunct of Protestant Christianity.

Owen's most successful effort in this direction had been *The Debatable Land between This World and the Next* (1871). This second work had advised the Protestant clergy that spiritualism could halt both secularism and Catholicism, and it had dealt with mediumistic phenomena, including Kate Fox's silent materializations of the previous decade. At a time of increasing spiritual excitement the book had elicited interested and polite, if usually skeptical, notice. Mrs. Stowe had seen it as the spiritual equivalent of Darwin's *Voyage of the Beagle*, and Alfred Russel Wallace, a recent convert to the spiritual hypothesis, had praised its scientific approach.[23] *The Debatable Land* was for the 1870's what Judge Edmonds's *Spiritualism* had been

---

[20] The preceding account of Owen's career and the following narrative of his involvement in the Katie King affair are based in large part on Richard W. Leopold's excellent study, *Robert Dale Owen: A Biography* (Cambridge, Mass., 1940). Despite its necessarily narrow focus, Leopold's discussion of Owen as a spiritualist constitutes the best (and almost the only) scholarly treatment of the post-Civil War fortunes of the movement (ibid., pp. 321–39, 379–416).

[21] Robert Dale Owen, *Footfalls on the Boundary of Another World* (Philadelphia, 1860).

[22] Leopold, p. 382.

[23] Ibid., pp. 391–93.

for the 1850's, with the important difference that Owen's reputation, scientism, and prudence had so far spared him ridicule and invective. Moreover, he had demonstrated that he was not a one-idea crank by writing *Beyond the Breakers* (1870),[24] a novel of Indiana life, and *Threading My Way: Twenty-seven Years of Autobiography* (1874),[25] a collection of reminiscences originally undertaken for the *Atlantic Monthly* at the suggestion of William Dean Howells.[26]

Nourished by the onset of cabinet materializations and by *The Debatable Land*, public interest in spiritualism steadily mounted in the early 1870's. Once again the press was paying close attention. Hardly realizing that theosophy would come out of his encounter there with Helena Blavatsky, the *New York Daily Graphic* dispatched Colonel Henry Olcott to Chittenden, Vermont, where the Eddy brothers were materializing whole groups of spirits in their farmhouse.[27] Grand claims as to the prevalence of believers were once more abroad. The *Chicago Daily Times* named monarchs, clergymen, and writers as spiritualists, including Victor Emmanuel, Henry Ward Beecher, Thomas Carlyle, Josh Billings, Mark Twain, Herman Melville, and Edna Dean Proctor.[28]

But the most significant news was that of William Crookes's endorsement of Katie King in England. For here was the scientific proof of spirit survival demanded by Owen in *The Debatable Land*.[29] Hence Katie's reappearance in Philadelphia soon after her London farewell was an occasion for celebration. And the most notable celebrant, having come to Philadelphia upon learning that Katie had asked for him, was Robert Dale Owen.

According to his own account Owen witnessed, in June and July, 1874, forty séances during which Katie King talked to him and other invited guests, called him "Father Owen" and kissed him, gave him a

[24] Robert Dale Owen, *Beyond the Breakers: A Story of the Present Day* (Philadelphia, 1870).

[25] Robert Dale Owen, *Threading My Way: Twenty-seven Years of Autobiography* (New York, 1874).

[26] Ibid., p. iii.

[27] Arthur Conan Doyle, *The History of Spiritualism* (New York, 1926), I, 254, 260–61.

[28] Article dated June 11, 1874, reprinted from the *Chicago Daily Times* as "Spiritualism in New York," *Religio-Philosophical Journal* XVI (July 11, 1874), 4–5.

[29] Owen, *The Debatable Land*, p. 280.

lock of her hair, and accepted gifts from the living. Unlike Florence Cook, Mr. and Mrs. Nelson Holmes, a pair of professional mediums who had just returned from England, remained outside their cabinet and in full view of their audience during Katie's appearances, thus rendering apparently irrelevant the usual suspicion that medium and spirit were identical. Sometimes a "luminous" hand and arm appeared to assist Katie. And once she "levitated"—rose into the air in a manner recalling to Owen "some of the old paintings of the Transfiguration." When in July Katie said goodbye until autumn, the sitters wept.[30]

Abandoning his usual caution, Owen announced to a group of spiritualists midway through this course of séances that he planned to describe the wonders he had seen in a work to be entitled "Phenomenal Proof of a Life to Come": "If we can trust to what we see, to what we hear under the very strictest of test conditions, then we have the phenomenal proof of a life to come."[31] This lecture and a letter from Owen to the spiritualist press were happily received by the believers.[32] The man who had always avoided professional mediums and early disclosures of the results of his investigations was now finding with the Holmeses the proofs he had sought for eighteen years.

As Katie's séances resumed in the fall of 1874, Owen was readying his record of "phenomenal proof" for the *Atlantic Monthly*. A November article described his initial European investigations.[33] In December he briefly compared the Philadelphia materializations to the Resurrection.[34] Meanwhile he rode over all doubts, publicly staking his reputation "as a dispassionate observer, on the genuine character of the phenomena."[35] Finally, in January, 1875, alongside poems by Longfellow and Aldrich, essays by Oliver Wendell Holmes and Bayard Taylor, and the first installments of "Roderick Hudson" and "Old Times on the Mississippi," appeared "Touching Spiritual Visitants from a Higher Life," Owen's story of his summer with Katie

[30] Robert Dale Owen, "Touching Spiritual Visitants from a Higher Life. A Chapter of Autobiography," *Atlantic Monthly* XXXV (January 1875), 57–69.
[31] Owen, "Lecture," p. 5.
[32] "Materializations in Philadelphia," *Religio-Philosophical Journal* XVI (July 25, 1874), 5; Leopold, p. 401.
[33] Robert Dale Owen, "How I Came to Study Spiritual Phenomena. A Chapter of Autobiography," *Atlantic Monthly* XXXIV (November 1874), 578–90.
[34] "Some Results from My Spiritual Studies," p. 722.
[35] Leopold, p. 402.

King. His logic was irrefutable: either Katie was a supernatural being or she was a flesh-and-blood fraud; and because human beings could not have passed through walls and partitions into an empty cabinet which Owen himself had repeatedly examined, she was necessarily a spirit.[36]

But Owen's triumph had turned to acute embarrassment by the time his article reached the public. For early in December he had learned that Katie was in reality a confederate of the mediums and that she entered their spirit cabinet in the dark from behind a secret panel in the wall of the séance room. Owen had promptly announced the withdrawal of his endorsement and had later explained the situation in a letter to the *New York Tribune*. But the truth had come too late for Howells to withdraw "Touching Spiritual Visitants" from the *Atlantic*; there had only been time for the insertion of an editorial disclaimer of responsibility. Owen's retraction had thus preceded the appearance of his evidence for "the phenomenal proof of a life to come." And his reputation as an effective spokesman for spiritualism had been forever destroyed.[37]

Owen's confinement for temporary insanity during the following summer and his death in 1877 were both connected in the public mind with a supposed loss of faith in spiritualism resulting from the Philadelphia episode. But as his biographer, Richard W. Leopold, has clearly shown, Owen himself never wavered in his belief; he attended séances until the end, and of his earthly accomplishments his gravestone referred only to his books on spiritualism. Even spiritualists agreed, however, that great harm had been done to their movement. For the wave of public interest which had reached a crest in the excitement over Katie subsided sharply after her exposure as a fraud and her most prominent defender's humiliation. Never again was the nineteenth-century movement to regain that interest.[38]

III | The Katie King fiasco was the most serious of a number of scandals which plagued spiritualism on both sides of the Atlantic after the successes of the early 1870's. Mediums began to

---

[36] Owen, "Touching Spiritual Visitants," p. 66.
[37] Leopold, pp. 402–6.
[38] Ibid., pp. 406–7, 412.

find themselves the frequent targets of newspaper exposés and legal harassment. Conjurors exhibited the techniques of fraudulent manifestations. And the open-minded interest which a few serious journals had taken in Katie gave way to hostility and inattention. The net result of this pattern of events was both to confirm the movement's status as a minor quasi-religious cult promising individual consolation rather than social millennium, and to stimulate the formation of Societies for Psychical Research in which the growing scientific interest in the possibility of spirit survival, and the workings of the medium's mind, could presumably be pursued with less risk of fraud. Indeed, during the last two decades of the century the spiritualistic medium played a significant role in the field of psychology by providing such pioneer investigators as Pierre Janet, Theodore Flournoy, William James, and F. W. H. Myers with data for their theories of multiple personality, hysteria, and the unconscious.[39]

Many believers satisfied themselves that the Philadelphia exposure had itself been concocted by the press, and that Owen had acted in foolish haste.[40] Materialization continued, therefore, to play a regular part in the séance. In 1892 an anonymous medium's *Revelations* explained the techniques with which "hundreds of 'materializing mediums' doing business in this country" were building "a good-sized bank account."[41] And a "Blue Book" supposedly circulated among mediums with information about convinced believers and their favorite spirits.

That there was either supernatural or human communication is suggested by Florence Marryat's account of her American spiritual experiences in *There Is No Death* (1891).[42] The daughter of the English novelist and herself an actress and writer, Miss Marryat had become a spiritualist upon seeing her dead daughter materialized at London séances conducted by Mrs. Nelson Holmes and Florence Cook. Coming to America for a dramatic tour in 1884, she visited a New York me-

[39] Henri F. Ellenberger, *The Discovery of the Unconscious: The History and Evolution of Dynamic Psychiatry* (New York, 1970), pp. 83–85, 120–21, 138, 173–74, 313–18, 338, 358–60, 755–56, 780.
[40] Leopold, p. 406.
[41] Harry Price and Eric J. Dingwall, eds., *Revelations of a Spirit Medium*, Facsimile ed. (London, 1922), p. 246.
[42] Florence Marryat, *There Is No Death* (New York, 1891), pp. 207–65.

dium anonymously and encountered the spirit of her daughter. At three séances in Boston she recognized first her daughter and brother-in-law, then the spirit of a British officer she had known years before in India, and finally the officer's mother. And when she returned to New York, the officer stepped forth from a medium's cabinet dressed in the uniform of the Twelfth Madras Native Infantry. Miss Marryat concluded that "the dry atmosphere of the United States is far more favorable to the process of materialization."[43] But few people paid attention to such claims any longer. The *Nation*, which a decade earlier had welcomed Owen's *Debatable Land* as a serious contribution to a field of investigation neglected by science,[44] now described a Boston séance of the sort attended by Miss Marryat as an imposture in which spirits and seekers cooperated in a display of familiar affection.[45]

Other forms of mediumship also retained their hold on believers. One of the longest-lived was the inspirational trance-lecture, in which the medium, under spirit direction, spoke on subjects chosen by her audience. Indeed, in long-range terms one of the most successful American mediums of the century was Mrs. Cora L. V. Hatch (later Mrs. Tappan and Mrs. Richmond), the blond "child medium" of the 1850's. Although her first husband had charged after their divorce that she was the victim of demonically inspired free-lovers,[46] the medium herself continued in demand as a pietistic trance-speaker, uttering in girlish tones the thoughts of spirits on everything from "The Romish Church" to Darwinism and "the social evil." These utterances, of course, were beyond the reach of simple tests for fraud, and even skeptics thought her gift remarkable, whatever its nature. Untouched by changes in séance fashion, Mrs. Hatch delivered thousands of such lectures and was still at work in 1895 as pastor of a spiritualist congregation in Chicago.[47]

More illustrative of the movement's decline were the misfortunes of Margaret and Kate Fox, with whom it had all started at Hydesville in

[43] Ibid., p. 213.
[44] "The Debatable Land," *Nation* XV (October 24, 1872), 269–70.
[45] "Among the Materializers," *Nation* XXXVIII (January 3, 1884), 9–10.
[46] Benjamin Hatch, *Spiritualists' Iniquities Unmasked, and the Hatch Divorce Case* (New York, 1859), pp. 24–43.
[47] Harrison D. Barrett, *Life Work of Mrs. Cora L. V. Richmond* (Chicago, 1895), pp. 177, 434, and passim; Podmore, II, 134–39.

1848. Unable to gain recognition from his family (and the world) as Elisha Kent Kane's widow, "Margaret Fox Kane" had become a Catholic in 1858, professing a deep aversion to spiritualism. But sometime after the Civil War she returned to the séance table in order to earn a living. Kate later did the same thing after her own husband died. Both sisters were habitually intemperate. And they blamed their troubles on their older sister Leah, the first promoter of spiritualism, who as the wife of a wealthy banker and a private medium for respectable friends increasingly found her sisters an embarrassment. Finally in 1888 Margaret told the New York press that the Hydesville disturbances had been nothing but childish efforts to tease their superstitious mother, and that the Rochester rappings and all that had followed had been the product of Leah's realization that in the toe joints of Margaret and Kate lay publicity and profit. Later Margaret claimed that these revelations had subjected her to persecution at the hands of Leah and such believers as John L. O'Sullivan (once Hawthorne and Brownson's friend as editor of the *Democratic Review*). Nonetheless, on October 21, 1888, before a packed house at the Academy of Music, she delivered what the press erroneously called the "death blow" to spiritualism by eliciting distinct rappings from her stockinged feet. Her authorized version of all these matters was then published by Reuben Briggs Davenport as *The Death-Blow to Spiritualism, Being the True Story of the Fox Sisters* (1888).[48] Margaret attempted to capitalize on this publicity with a series of exhibitions of her skeletal gift. But these appearances proved uninteresting to the public. And before long, claiming that she had recanted under newspaper and financial pressure, she became a medium again, eking out a wretched existence until 1893, when she followed Leah and Kate to the grave.[49]

The entire episode, however, was anticlimactic, a tabloid sensation merely confirming the public skepticism already in force since the too-materialistic materializations of Katie King. Generally speaking, the movement was to continue in relative obscurity, without a great deal

[48] Reuben Briggs Davenport, *The Death-Blow to Spiritualism, Being the True Story of the Fox Sisters as Revealed by Authority of Margaret Fox Kane and Catherine Fox Jencken* (New York, 1897), pp. 30–103, 234–36. As an outgrowth of a newspaper crusade against spiritualism, this account must be taken with a grain of salt. [49] Earl Wesley Fornell, *The Unhappy Medium: Spiritualism and the Life of Margaret Fox* (Austin, Tex., 1964), pp. 174–75.

of popular appeal, until given a new impetus by the deaths of American and British soldiers in World War I. And even then it would attract neither the vigorous public support nor the serious discussions of its religious urgency that it had received during the 1850's and 1870's.

But just as under the aegis of the Fox sisters the spirits had manifested themselves in the literature of the 1850's, so youthful memories of early spiritualism and its literary effects combined with observations of the movement's second rise and fall after the Civil War to influence some of the writings of the three major novelists of the postwar generation—William Dean Howells, Mark Twain, and Henry James.

VI: "NO TRAVELER RETURNS"[1]

William Dean Howells and *The Undiscovered Country*

I | The first phase of the spiritualistic movement left deep impressions in the youthful minds of William Dean Howells, Mark Twain, and Henry James. Each was also familiar with some of the early literary responses to spiritualism or mesmerism. Howells and Twain, moreover, witnessed certain episodes of postwar spiritualism from close vantage-points. And all three, whether for topical or highly personal reasons, turned this experience to literary use. First Twain imitated the humorous journalists of the 1850's in reporting postwar séances in San Francisco. Then James drew on his reading of Hawthorne for "Professor Fargo" (1874).[2] Both men continued to utilize earlier spiritual manifestations and literary models during the 1880's— Twain in *Life on the Mississippi* (1883)[3] and evidently in *Adventures of Huckleberry Finn* (1885),[4] James in *The Bostonians* (1886).[5] But by this time Howells, turning to his own personal and literary expe-

---

[1] William Dean Howells, *The Undiscovered Country* (Boston, 1880), p. 373, where the lines from *Hamlet* from which Howells took his title were given in full: "The undiscover'd country from whose bourn/No traveler returns. . . ."
[2] Henry James, "Professor Fargo," *Galaxy* XVIII (August 1874), 233–53.
[3] Samuel Clemens, *Life on the Mississippi* (Boston, 1883).
[4] Samuel Clemens, *Adventures of Huckleberry Finn* (New York, 1885).
[5] Henry James, *The Bostonians* (London, 1886).

riences, had already written the first sustainedly serious novel about American spiritualism, *The Undiscovered Country* (1880).

No writer of note had yet been willing to treat the spiritualistic attempt to establish an empirical basis for religious belief with anything but laughter or satiric contempt. Howells's attitude toward the movement was more complex, however, than that of either his predecessors or, at this point of their careers, Twain and James. Like earlier writers he criticized spiritualism as misguided in its aims, morbid in its human effects, and trivial in its results. But his experiences as editor of the *Atlantic Monthly* during the Katie King episode of 1874–75 had given him a compassionate understanding of the leading prophet of spiritualism, Robert Dale Owen, and of the issues Owen had raised. Serving as the catalyst in the creation of *The Undiscovered Country*, these experiences led Howells not only to criticize the spiritualistic movement, but also to depict it as a poignant if grotesque response to personal bereavement and to the religious crisis of the agnostic 1870's.

These attitudes took shape in *The Undiscovered Country* in three interrelated actions: the unsuccessful search for tangible evidence of immortality undertaken by Dr. Boynton, a sincere but deluded spiritualist whose beautiful daughter Egeria was his spellbound medium; the development of sympathetic if still critical understanding of Boynton's goal and character on the part of Ford, a skeptical young journalist and amateur scientist whose first intention was to expose Boynton as a charlatan; and the liberation of Egeria from mediumistic servitude through the powers of nature and Ford's love. Unfolded against the seedy backdrop of Boston spiritualism and the pastoral setting of a celibate Shaker commune, these actions touched on a variety of Howellsian themes in ways that made the novel a rehearsal for its better-known successors. But the chief concern of *The Undiscovered Country*, from its title to its parting injunction that for news of immortality "we must all wait,"[6] was the problem of spiritualism. Howells later said so himself.[7]

Boynton and his quest therefore dominated the novel. As a young man he had rebelled against a Calvinistic upbringing by turning to

[6] Howells, *The Undiscovered Country*, p. 419.
[7] Howells to J. G. Holland, February 18, 1881, in William M. Gibson's "Introduction" to William Dean Howells, *A Modern Instance* (Boston, 1957), p. vii.

materialistic atheism. At his wife's death, however, he had sensed an "incorporeal presence,"[8] and had become an ardent spiritualist, dedicating his mesmerically sensitive daughter to the search for physical proof of immortality. The absurdity of Boynton's obsession was emphasized by humorous touches. When he saw a diver working in the Charles River, for instance, he seriously considered the possibility of isolating a medium from hostile influence by submerging her for an underwater séance.

But Boynton was more than a crank deluded by personal grief. His aim was to resolve the conflict between religious faith and scientific agnosticism by providing an experimentally verifiable alternative to doubt. To Ford, the skeptical journalist and scientist, he defined this conflict in terms of the contradictory answers given by spiritualism and evolution to the questions of man's origin and destiny—"whether we came from the Clam or the Ancient of Days, whether we shall live forever, or rot forever. . . ."[9] And he warned an audience of Shakers that the loss of faith which he saw spreading through "the whole Christian world" could have catastrophic moral consequences:

> Priests in the pulpit and before the altar proclaim a creed which they hope it will be good for their hearers to believe, and the people envy the faith that can so confidently preach that creed; but neither priests nor people believe. As yet, this devastating doubt has not made itself felt in morals; for those who doubt were bred in the morality of those who believed. But how shall it be with the new generation, with the children of those who feel that it may be better to eat, drink, and make merry, for to-morrow they die forever? Will they be restrained by the morality which, ceasing to be a guest of the mind in us, remains master of the nerves? Will they not eat, drink, and make merry at their pleasure, set free as they are, or outlawed as they are, by the spirit of inquiry, by the spirit of science, which has beaten down the defenses and razed the citadel of the old faith? . . . In view of this calamitous future, I, as a spiritualist, cannot refrain from *doing*. . . .[10]

[8] Howells, *The Undiscovered Country*, p. 179.
[9] Ibid., p. 288.
[10] Ibid., pp. 235–36.

While Boynton's mode of "doing" may have been eccentric, his concern was certainly not unusual. Indeed, the extent to which it was also the concern of the novelist himself was shortly to be demonstrated in *A Modern Instance* (1882).

Set in Boston, the first of the three sections into which *The Undiscovered Country* can be divided established the pattern of Boynton's failure.[11] Having proclaimed that a glowing blue hand, presumably elicited by Egeria during a dark séance, had provided "the key to the mystery"[12] of immortality, he then discovered that it had been a chemical trick on the part of Ford, who had come to the séance with his dilettantish friend Phillips in hopes of detecting an imposture. Later Mrs. Le Roy, the professional medium in whose studio the séance was held, admitted to Boynton that she had assisted the innocent Egeria by counterfeiting the voices and touches of invisible spirits. Thus defeated by both skepticism and spiritualistic chicanery, Boynton took the advice of Hatch, a friendly half-believer for whom séances were merely social occasions, that he and his daughter flee the city. Ford and Phillips were left to wonder whether "the Pythoness and her papa"[13] were conscious or unconscious frauds.

In the second section of the novel the same pattern repeated itself more emphatically.[14] Boynton's optimism was revived at a country inn by what he reported as rapping noises, a lifted tabletop, a picture swinging on the wall, a brush flung across a room by an unknown force, and a single discharge of ground lightning—all of which he happily attributed to Egeria's occult powers. Egeria, however, lay in troubled sleep during the alleged occurrences, and the landlord of the inn later denied Boynton's story. In response to the pastoral environment of the Shaker village of Vardley, to which the pair wandered from the inn, Egeria threw off her father's supposedly mesmeric influence. And when a demonstration of her mediumship was attempted in order to persuade the Shakers to join Boynton in his spiritualistic crusade to save Christianity from cankering doubt, she was unable even to go into

[11] Ibid., Chs. 1–7.
[12] Ibid., p. 33.
[13] Ibid., p. 108.
[14] Ibid., Chs. 8–17.

simple magnetic trance. Boynton was again humiliated, but before he could flee a second time he discovered that Ford had arrived in Vardley. Blaming Egeria's failure on his enemy's presence, he harmlessly assaulted him, suffering a stroke himself from which he was never to recover.

The last part of the novel brought relative spiritual wisdom not only to the dying Boynton, but also to Ford, who stayed on in Vardley out of a sense of responsibility for the other's plight.[15] Boynton came to realize that he had "played the vampire"[16] with his daughter. He was disillusioned by a magazine article about a girl so "surcharged with electricity"[17] that (until her bedposts were insulated) she caused manifestations much like Egeria's. In Boston, Ford had used scientific knowledge to mislead Boynton with his chemically glowing hand, and in return Boynton had attacked him as a sacriligious evolutionist.[18] But now in Vardley, when science (the "electric girl" theory) caused Boynton to despair at the thought of dying without faith, it was Ford who sympathetically reminded him that he still had recourse to "the hope that the world has had for eighteen hundred years."[19] Characteristically constructing an optimistic new theory on the basis of Ford's remark, Boynton found in the Bible a promise of immortality befitting man's good or evil motives on earth. Convinced at last that spiritualism was a materialistic attempt to demonstrate the undemonstrable, he faced death eager for its certain knowledge.

Unable to share this passion for final certainty, Ford turned instead to the possibilities of married life with Egeria "in the full sunshine of our common day."[20] But in giving spiritual comfort to the dying prophet he had, in effect, renounced the skeptical hostility which in Boston had led him to treat the faith of the spiritualists as a fraudulent joke. Instrumental in this change of attitude was the admiration which he had come to feel for Boynton's character and altruism: "I liked him. It isn't a logical position; he never squared with my ideas; but I know

[15] Ibid., Chs. 18–25.
[16] Ibid., p. 319.
[17] Ibid., p. 360.
[18] Ibid., p. 57.
[19] Ibid., p. 364.
[20] Ibid., p. 419.

now that he was a singularly upright and truthful man. . . . I want to say that when I interfered with him there in Boston he had a noble motive, and I had an ignoble one."[21] Perhaps Ford had also learned that science was best applied to mundane improvement, for he went on to make his fortune with a chemical compound "known to all housekeepers."[22] And although he and Egeria cherished her father's memory, they did so without impatience: "If Boynton has found the undiscovered country, he has sent no message back to them, and they do not question his silence."[23] This policy found approval in Howells's last words as narrator: "They wait, and we must all wait."[24]

In *The Undiscovered Country*, then, Howells criticized as morbid and irrelevant the spiritualistic demand for physical proof of immortality. But at the same time he vindicated the motives and character of a single quixotic spiritualist through the changing attitude of an unbeliever whose skepticism was humanized in the process. The novel was not without its faults of disproportion and improbability, and the nature of Egeria's trances was never made clear. But by developing the full implications of spiritualism as a response to personal grief and general religious crisis, and especially by creating in Boynton a spiritualist whose human complexity transcended the usual satiric or comic stereotypes, Howells gave a new literary depth to the subject.

From the time his novel began to appear in the *Atlantic* until after its publication in book form, Howells's serious handling of his materials and his delineation of Boynton found favor, first with friends and then with reviewers. Mark Twain professed to have been moved by the story of "that old man,"[25] and he congratulated Howells for his mastery of spiritualistic jargon. Thomas Gold Appleton, Longfellow's brother-in-law and long a Brahmin spiritualist himself, told the novelist that his realistic method was superior to Zola's.[26] Charles Eliot

21 Ibid., p. 394.
22 Ibid., p. 416.
23 Ibid., p. 419.
24 Ibid.
25 Clemens and Howells, *Mark Twain-Howells Letters: The Correspondence of Samuel L. Clemens and William Dean Howells, 1872–1910*, ed. Henry Nash Smith and William M. Gibson (Cambridge, Mass., 1960), I, 288.
26 Appleton to Howells, February 23, 1880. MS at Houghton Library.

Norton wrote Howells that the work had deep autobiographical significance and pronounced Boynton his best character to date.[27] Even Henry James, who was rather unenthusiastic about the novel (but whose *Bostonians* was perhaps to show how closely he had read it), saw that it was his friend's most serious work and granted that Boynton was excellent in conception.[28]

Similar praise came in reviews by Brooks Adams and Thomas Wentworth Higginson. Adams found Boynton to be a long-overdue demonstration that Howells was capable of vigorous masculine portraiture—something Adams thought still lacking in Ford.[29] Although Higginson felt that the work was rather anachronistic (perhaps because over twenty years had passed since his own efforts in behalf of F. L. Willis, the divinity-school medium),[30] he knowledgeably commended the fidelity with which the spiritualists were drawn, and he, too, singled out as Howells's finest characterization the "pitiable and heroic"[31] figure of Boynton.

In spite of this favorable reception, the novel soon languished in the shadow of the greater works which followed from Howells's pen during the 1880's; for years it attracted only occasional attention as a minor occult romance or topical satire.[32] Within the past fifteen years, however, *The Undiscovered Country* has been rediscovered as an important early stopping-place on Howells's road to realism, and as a significant religious and psychological novel in its own right.[33] The

27 Norton to Howells, June 24, 1880. MS at Houghton Library. Norton also praised the book to James Russell Lowell (Charles E. Norton, *Letters of Charles Eliot Norton*, ed. Sarah Norton and M. A. DeWolfe Howe [Boston, 1913], II, 110).

28 James to Howells, July 2, 1880. MS at Houghton Library.

29 Brooks Adams, "The Undiscovered Country," *International Review* IX (August 1880), 151.

30 T. W. Higginson, "Howells' 'Undiscovered Country,'" *Scribner's* XX (September 1880), 793.

31 Ibid., p. 794.

32 Delmar Gross Cooke, *William Dean Howells: A Critical Study* (New York, 1922), pp. 183–85; Everett Carter, *Howells and the Age of Realism* (Philadelphia, 1954), p. 106.

33 Edwin H. Cady, *The Road to Realism: The Early Years, 1837–1885, of William Dean Howells* (Syracuse, 1956), pp. 197–98; Olov W. Fryckstedt, *In Quest of America: A Study of Howells' Early Development as a Novelist* (Cambridge, Mass., 1958), pp. 183–91; George N. Bennett, *William Dean Howells: The Development*

influences of Turgenev and Hawthorne have been traced in it, along with similarities to Henry James's "Professor Fargo" (1874).[34] The net effect of these efforts has been to rescue the novel from critical oblivion.

Yet neither the literary nor the autobiographical matrices of Howells's treatment of spiritualism have received much attention. Parallels with specific works of Hawthorne and James have generally been viewed in isolation, without reference to the "tradition" of topical romance and satire which was available for Howells to use and to modify. Analysis of Howells's own knowledge of spiritualism has confined itself to his genial remarks about the movement's impact on the Western Reserve in his youth and about discussions of the subject which he had listened to in Cambridge.[35] No doubt these experiences formed part of the spiritualistic background of the novel. But Howells wrote of them without implying any sense of personal involvement and without shedding much light on his characterization of Boynton.[36] As a result, Boynton's own spiritualism has been treated merely as a convenient topical reflector for deeper religious and psychological themes.[37]

---

of a Novelist (Norman, Okla., 1959), pp. 96–105; Van Wyck Brooks, *Howells: His Life and World* (New York, 1959), pp. 119–22; Kermit Vanderbilt, "The Undiscovered Country: Howells' Version of American Pastoral," *The Achievement of William Dean Howells: A Reinterpretation* (Princeton, 1968), pp. 11–48.

[34] Fryckstedt, pp. 183–91; Bennett, pp. 99, 104–5; Smith and Gibson, eds., *Twain-Howells Letters*, I, 289; Martha Banta, "'The Two Worlds of Henry James: A Study in the Fiction of the Supernatural'" (Ph.D. diss.: Indiana University, 1964), pp. 158–60; Vanderbilt, p. 46.

[35] Carter, p. 106; Bennett, pp. 98–99; Smith and Gibson, eds., *Twain-Howells Letters*, II, 288–89. It has been suggested that Howells and James may have drawn the father-daughter relationships of *The Undiscovered Country* and *The Bostonians* from a story they could have heard from the Holmes family about a farcical séance staged by a father and daughter in Boston in 1866 (Eleanor M. Tilton and Thomas Franklyn Currier, eds., A *Bibliography of Oliver Wendell Holmes* [New York, 1953], p. 488). In view of both authors' knowledge of spiritualism, their probable awareness of each others' writings on the subject, and their reading of Hawthorne, this possibility does not seem very important.

[36] William Dean Howells, *Impressions and Experiences* (New York, 1896), pp. 20–21; William Dean Howells, *Years of My Youth* (New York, 1916), p. 106; William Dean Howells, *Life in Letters of William Dean Howells*, ed. Mildred Howells (New York, 1928), I, 110, 166.

[37] Bennett, pp. 98–100; Vanderbilt, pp. 13–14.

The truth is, however, that *The Undiscovered Country* originated in Howells's painful experiences as Robert Dale Owen's editor and friend during the Katie King controversy of 1874–75. In his letter to Howells praising the portrayal of Boynton, Charles Eliot Norton said that his calling the novel an autobiography would be justly resented were he a reviewer rather than a friend, and he tactfully refrained from specifying what he had in mind.[38] But Norton's old friend Tom Appleton, who would have known, was more direct. "I do not like to ask questions," he wrote, "nor is it fit;—but if your old man isn't *Owen*, I mean the living, not the dead one, it might be."[39] (Appleton must have been trying to distinguish Robert Dale Owen, dead only three years, from his better-known father Robert Owen, the English socialist, who had died in 1858; when Appleton and Howells had been acquainted with the younger Owen in Boston, the latter had been "the living" and his father "the dead one.")[40] There is no record of Howells's reply, if any. But Appleton's guess was correct. For it is quite clear that in his portrait of Boynton, the novelist was criticizing the quest and vindicating the character of Robert Dale Owen.

II | It is not surprising that Tom Appleton should have recognized Boynton as Owen. Appleton had long been a knowledgeable spiritualist, and he had been present at the first meeting between Howells and Owen early in 1872. One of the more convivial members of the Dante and Saturday Clubs, he was also known as an art collector, having donated over six thousand engravings of Italian paintings to the Boston Public Library.[41] At his death in 1884 Oliver Wendell Holmes was to pay tribute to him as both a connoisseur and "the favorite guest of every banquet."[42] Appleton's spiritualism had

---

38 Norton to Howells, June 24, 1880.
39 Appleton to Howells, February 23, 1880; quoted by permission of Harvard College Library.
40 It is unlikely that Appleton was acquainted with Robert Dale Owen's son Ernest, who lived in Indiana.
41 Boston Public Library, *The Tosti Engravings: The Gift of Mr. Thomas G. Appleton, Esq.* (Boston, 1873). Cf. Susan Hale, ed., *The Life and Letters of Thomas Gold Appleton* (New York, 1885), pp. 319–20.
42 Oliver Wendell Holmes, "Thomas Gold Appleton," *Atlantic Monthly* LIII (June 1884), 850.

always reflected his gregarious nature. In the early 1850's he had helped introduce table-tipping to Paris as a fashionable social diversion.[43] And Longfellow once said that his brother-in-law was so well-liked by Boston's mediums that one of them, asked by the poet to identify the author of a medieval spiritual treatise and given the clue "T-h-o-m-a-s A-," had immediately volunteered "Tom Appleton!"[44]

Howells knew Appleton as both Brahmin *bon vivant* and spiritualist. He remarked in a letter to his father after his first meeting with Owen that Appleton "has never done anything but eat good dinners and say witty things."[45] Years later, in *Literary Friends and Acquaintance* (1901), he was to write of the vigor with which the spiritualist, ready to enjoy "a joke at the expense of his doctrine,"[46] had argued his cause against the skeptical Holmes and Agassiz. Howells also may have read "At the Medium's" (1873),[47] an urbane dialogue in which Appleton had not only displayed his sense of humor in describing a séance, but also hoped quite seriously that spiritualism would reconcile faith and science, pointing to Alfred Russel Wallace's endorsement of "Mr. Owen's fascinating book."[48]

Edwin H. Cady has suggested that Appleton "must surely have served as one of the models for Bromfield Corey"[49] in *The Rise of Silas Lapham* (1885). And probably Appleton, who had once resided in Phillips Place in Cambridge,[50] could have recognized himself in *The Undiscovered Country*, divided into connoisseur and spiritualist as the minor characters Phillips and Hatch. Phillips was a patrician bachelor and diner-out who was also an appreciative patron of the arts. When Boynton identified the rapping spirit of "Giorgione" as that of "a Viennese painter,"[51] Phillips was quick to correct him. Ford himself linked Phillips to Hatch, the breezy spiritualist, by identifying the lat-

[43] Hale, ed., *Life and Letters of Thomas Gold Appleton*, pp. 281, 284–85.
[44] E. S. Nadal, *A Virginian Village and Other Papers* (New York, 1917), p. 164.
[45] Howells, *Life in Letters of William Dean Howells*, I, 166.
[46] William Dean Howells, *Literary Friends and Acquaintance* (New York, 1901), pp. 152–53, 186.
[47] *Old and New* VIII (September 1873), 309–14; reprinted in Thomas Gold Appleton, *A Sheaf of Papers* (Boston, 1875), pp. 289–301.
[48] Ibid., p. 298.
[49] Cady, *The Road to Realism*, p. 198.
[50] Hale, ed., *Life and Letters of Thomas Gold Appleton*, p. 288.
[51] Howells, *The Undiscovered Country*, p. 9.

ter as "a brother *dilettante*" who dabbled in "ghosts" rather than "bricabrac" and "Bonifazios."[52] There was a sharp edge to the characterization of the effete Phillips, who with his malicious friend Mrs. Perham represented polite Boston society in the novel. Perhaps Appleton detected this, for in his letter of praise he told Howells that "our unconscious bad manners serves [*sic*] you well."[53] Hatch, on the other hand, was presented as a friend who remained loyal to Boynton even after commonsensically rejecting spiritualism. Appleton, too, had turned away from spiritualism by the time he wrote to praise Howells's novel.[54] In any event, Appleton's cultivation of the séance interested the novelist not nearly so much as did the attempt of their mutual acquaintance, Robert Dale Owen, to establish physical proof of immortality.

The editorial relationship of Howells and Owen had begun well.[55] After their first meeting in Appleton's presence, Howells wrote his father that the occult conversation of the two spiritualists had seemed trivial. Yet he thought Owen personally "charming," and noted a "real light of peace . . . in his face."[56] As an editor, moreover, he recognized the journalistic potential of Owen's diverse experiences and encouraged him to reminisce about his early years in eleven articles carried by the *Atlantic Monthly* in 1873 and later collected by Owen in *Threading My Way* (1874).[57] In the foreword to his book Owen thanked his "good friend" Howells for having "incited" him to the task.[58] Howells's proprietary *Atlantic* review was a tribute to Owen's character:

[52] Ibid., p. 86.
[53] Appleton to Howells, February 23, 1880; quoted by permission of Harvard College Library.
[54] Hale, ed., *Life and Letters of Thomas Gold Appleton*, p. 322.
[55] None of Howells's biographers mention this episode of his *Atlantic* career. It has been treated as part of Owen's last years in Richard W. Leopold's excellent *Robert Dale Owen: A Biography* (Cambridge, Mass., 1940), pp. 398, 403, 408, 413. Using Leopold's calendar of events and his analysis of Owen's behavior, I have attempted to define Howells's role in the Katie King affair by reexamining the relevant data cited by Leopold, especially the letters of Owen to Howells, and by supplementing it with evidence gathered from my own research.
[56] Howells, *Life in Letters of William Dean Howells*, I, 166.
[57] Robert Dale Owen, *Threading My Way: Twenty-seven Years of Autobiography* (New York, 1874). The eleven articles appeared in the *Atlantic Monthly* XXXI (January–June 1873) and XXXII (July–November 1873).
[58] Owen, *Threading My Way*, p. iii.

"Through all runs the sweetest and gentlest spirit; a lenient judgment, a generous sympathy, a high morality, a shrewd and humorous self-perception. It is as Christian a book as ever was written, and is to be praised as much for its blameless conscience, as for its blameless manner."[59] The review noted with anticipation that Owen promised another volume telling how he had become "part of our political, social, and religious history."[60] Meanwhile, three more autobiographical pieces had appeared in the *Atlantic* by midsummer, 1874.

Owen, forced to live by his pen in his old age, had thus proved to be a productive contributor.[61] But he was also the leading spokesman for spiritualism at a time of rising public interest in the subject. And although Howells had never displayed any editorial sympathy for the movement—he had given *The Debatable Land* to the elder Henry James for an astringent review[62]—and although one of his publishers apparently was averse to the magazine's taking any interest in spirits,[63] he now accepted Owen's offer of a series of reminiscences about his career as an occult investigator.[64]

What followed was one of Howells's greatest editorial ordeals. For by the time Owen began to write these pieces he had fallen under the spell of the beautiful Katie King, with the consequence that in the December, 1874, and January, 1875, issues of the *Atlantic* he cited her materializations as the proof of immortality capable of halting the religious and moral decline of the nineteenth century.[65] But only ten days after informing Howells that the December essay was attracting friendly notice, Owen attempted, too late, to withdraw the January

[59] [William Dean Howells,] "Recent Literature," *Atlantic Monthly* XXXIII (February 1874), 232.

[60] Ibid.

[61] Leopold, p. 396.

[62] Henry James, Sr., "Spiritualism New and Old," *Atlantic Monthly* XXIX (March 1872), 358–62.

[63] Howells to Francis Jackson Garrison, May 21, 1874. MS at Princeton University Library.

[64] Owen to Howells, September 14 and September 18, 1873. MSS of all letters from Owen to Howells cited here are at the Houghton Library.

[65] Robert Dale Owen, "Some Results from My Spiritual Studies. A Chapter of Autobiography," *Atlantic Monthly* XXXIV (December 1874), 719–31; also "Touching Spiritual Visitants from a Higher Life. A Chapter of Autobiography," *Atlantic Monthly* XXXV (January 1875), 57–69.

article because of his discovery that Katie was a flesh-and-blood fraud.[66] Howells had time only to insert an interleaved disclaimer which probably did nothing but call further attention to the fiasco: "The Editors and Publishers of The Atlantic desire to advertise their friends of the Press and Public that with Mr. Robert Dale Owen rests all responsibility for the statements of his articles on spiritual phenomena."[67]

As if the situation were not bad enough, Owen's "blameless conscience," which Howells had so admired, proceeded to make matters worse. In advance of the January *Atlantic's* appearance, Owen felt it his duty to make public his withdrawal of support from Katie and her mediums.[68] Then, despite Howells's request for a period of silence,[69] he went on to explain as much as he knew of the deception in a letter to the *New York Tribune*.[70] The result of this mistimed forthrightness was that the press took great delight in comparing his claims in the *Atlantic* with his simultaneous disclosures of fraud. In its extended coverage of the incident, the *Springfield Union* referred several times to Owen's "laughable yet pathetic plight"[71] in this vein: "But poor Mr. Owen! One is really sorry for the old gentleman. If it wasn't for that article in the Atlantic it wouldn't be so bad, but as it is a man could not occupy a more preposterous position before the public than does this venerable witness for Spiritualism."[72] Although it praised Owen's candor, the *Union* attacked his "extraordinary powers of credulity"[73] and accurately predicted that his testimony for spiritualism would henceforth be without value.[74]

Not all of the criticism was directed at Owen, however. Some of it was reserved for the *Atlantic*. The *Springfield Union* (whose young assistant editor, Edward Bellamy, had discounted Katie months before

[66] Owen to Howells, November 24, December 4, and December 7, 1874.
[67] Leopold, p. 403.
[68] Owen to Howells, December 7 and December 12, 1874.
[69] Memorandum by Howells on Owen's letter of December 7, 1874; Owen to Howells, December 12, 1874.
[70] Leopold, p. 403.
[71] *Springfield Union*, December 22, 1874, p. 4.
[72] Ibid., December 18, 1874, p. 2.
[73] Ibid., December 16, 1874, p. 4.
[74] Ibid., December 15, 1874, p. 4.

her exposure) said that the magazine had left "poor Owen in the lurch,"[75] and it warned against similar blunders in the future:

> It is all very well for the editor and publishers of The Atlantic Monthly to advertise that they are not responsible for the religious views of Robert Dale Owen, but they must and will be held responsible for giving up their magazine (supposed to be devoted to what is best in literature), to the most ridiculous twaddle, if they print any more articles from Mr. Owen, or anybody else, of the character of his paper in the January number. . . .[76]

Howells himself, in returning a collection of journalistic comments sent to him by Francis Jackson Garrison, agreed with the opinion of a Rochester newspaper that the *Atlantic*'s disclaimer had been unwise.[77] At the time the affair must have promised as much embarrassment for the magazine as Mrs. Stowe's defense of Lady Byron had caused a few years before.

Howells was probably relieved when Owen apologized for his inability to attend the annual dinner for *Atlantic* contributors in mid-December.[78] Yet the editor's letter to Garrison showed that even at the height of the controversy his respect for Owen's character remained high. Indeed, the other's plight seems to have troubled him as much as his own did:

> The general vulgar clamor against us in the press for publishing a matter which but for the unlucky denouement would be regarded as of very singular interest, and the coarse jeers at Owen, are enough to make a spiritualist of a man out of hand. If I *were* a spiritualist, the . . . fraud would not shake my faith in the principle that the dead can communicate with the living, in the least. As it is, I'm sorry from the bottom of my heart, for Mr. Owen, whose high character and courage merit the respect of every one.[79]

[75] Ibid., December 22, 1874, p. 4.
[76] Ibid., December 16, 1874, p. 4.
[77] Howells to Garrison, December 28, 1874. MS at Princeton University Library.
[78] Owen to Howells, December 12, 1874.
[79] Howells to Garrison, December 28, 1874; quoted by permission of Professor William White Howells. Permission to quote this passage in full or in part must be requested from Professor Howells.

Perhaps this sympathy lay behind the appearance of a political reminiscence by Owen in the June, 1875, *Atlantic.*[80] But his plans for further articles were either ignored or rejected.[81] Finally, late in 1876, he inquired whether the magazine was forever closed to him because of his religious notions.[82] Evidently it was.

Yet if Owen's plight received no public sympathy from his editor, it took deep root in the imagination of the novelist. As usual, Howells's personal experience did not immediately bear fruit; perhaps it could not while Owen still lived. But the spiritualist's death in June, 1877—an event recalling his name to national attention in editorial tributes to his political rather than occult achievements[83]—may well have suggested to Howells the possibility of using Owen's search for proof of immortality, with its dramatic pathos and its wide-ranging implications of spiritual and social malaise, as the vehicle of his first comprehensive novel of American life. For it was during the following winter that Howells asked Thomas Sergeant Perry to read *The Undiscovered Country* in manuscript.[84]

Howells did not, of course, write a novel "about" Owen. Born in Scotland, educated in Europe, and well-known in America, Owen had been a figure of cosmopolitan experiences, diverse interests, and urbane temperament. Needing both to conceal the source of his painfully bought inspiration and to create a native heterodox prophet representative of spiritual crisis in New England, Howells drew Boynton as a Yankee villager, narrow in education, cut off from Puritan tradition and helplessly adrift in the city (the same Boston so resistant to the provincials of other Howells novels in the 1880's), single-minded yet subject to mercurial changes in mood. Boynton's character, moreover, and his relationships with his daughter and Ford owed something to

[80] Robert Dale Owen, "Political Results from the Varioloid," *Atlantic Monthly* XXXV (June 1875), 660–70.

[81] Owen to Howells, December 29, 1874, and November 4, 1876. In the first of these letters Owen offered to write an article either about his marriage, as had previously been planned, or about the susceptibility of benevolence to imposture, and he wondered whether delay of payment for the January article was inadvertent or intentional.

[82] Ibid.

[83] Leopold, p. 415.

[84] Perry to Howells, February 6, 1878. MS at the Houghton Library.

treatments of similar types by Hawthorne and perhaps Henry James. And the morbidity of such relationships, seen here as part of the spiritualistic milieu, was something to which Howells would often return as a psychological novelist.

Boynton was more, then, than the sum of Howells's memories of Owen. Yet it is a relatively simple matter, keeping in mind Howells's involvement with Owen, to trace parallels in backgrounds, religious ideas, occult adventures, and ultimate failures which indicate the great extent to which Howells modeled his fictional spiritualist on the real one he had known.

Both men came from backgrounds of strict piety. Owen had written in *Threading My Way* of his youthful renunciation of the Calvinism in which he had been raised;[85] and a controversial phase of his early career in America had been devoted to the cause of free thought.[86] Similarly, Boynton told the Shakers of his own rejection of Calvinism in his youth, and of his adoption for many years thereafter of an aggressively materialistic point-of-view.[87] Both thanked spiritualism for rescuing them from atheism. During his Indiana years, moreover, Owen had published an account of Joseph Rodes Buchanan's experiments with medical mesmerism;[88] Boynton was a mesmeric physician.

More fundamental was the similarity of their spiritualistic goals. Each assumed a prophetic role in seeking an answer to the question of immortality. For Owen the solution to this problem had seemed of "inestimable importance to mankind,"[89] while Boynton felt that his researches were "profoundly interesting to the race."[90] In both cases this sense of urgency stemmed from the fear that apathy, doubt, and scientific materialism threatened to bring on moral chaos by eroding the ethical sanctions of organized religion. Just as this fear had been a

[85] Owen, *Threading My Way*, pp. 52–65. Howells, of course, had published the articles which made up the book he favorably reviewed.
[86] Robert Dale Owen, "An Earnest Sowing of Wild Oats," *Atlantic Monthly* XXXIV (July 1874), 67–78.
[87] Howells, *The Undiscovered Country*, p. 178.
[88] Robert Dale Owen, *Neurology: An Account of Some Experiments in Cerebral Physiology, by Dr. Buchanan* (London, 1842). Joseph Rodes Buchanan, the medical mesmerist, had long since become a spiritualist.
[89] Owen, "Touching Spiritual Visitants from a Higher Life," p. 57.
[90] Howells, *The Undiscovered Country*, p. 165.

major concern of Owen's "Address to the Protestant Clergy" in *The Debatable Land* (1871),[91] and of his *Atlantic* article, "Some Results from My Spiritual Studies" (1874),[92] so it was the theme of Boynton's speech to the Vardley Shakers.[93] Neither prophet wanted a return to Calvinism. Rather, they preached a nonsectarian, spiritualistic doctrine of love, progress, and immortality for all.

As spiritual researchers, moreover, both characterized themselves as scientists. In the *Atlantic* Owen had contrasted the superstitious first century's requirement of an awesome miracle with the scientific nineteenth century's need for "the facts"[94] of immortality. Boynton, who asserted the need for a "spiritistic science,"[95] took a similar historical view: "Shall one revelation suffice for all time? . . . Are we less worthy of communion with supernal essences than those semi-barbarous Jews? . . . How shall hope and faith be rekindled?"[96] Like Owen, Boynton both berated contemporary scientists for ridiculing spiritualism and praised the courage of William Crookes, the English physicist who had dared endorse the London Katie King.[97] There seems little doubt, in short, that Boynton's philanthropic message was firmly grounded in Owen's.

Even the séance phenomena which misled Boynton may have been suggested by Owen's experiences. Howells could not have called up another Katie King, of course, without laying bare his source. Yet as the Boston séance began, Boynton looked forward to visible spirits in the near future, and Mrs. Le Roy, the professional medium who assisted Egeria at that séance, elicited materialized hands from a small box in the center of her table. Even Boynton realized that these were probably only stuffed gloves.[98] But the appearance of a glowing hand at the end of the dark séance led him to proclaim that the "key to the

91 Robert Dale Owen, *The Debatable Land between This World and the Next* (Philadelphia, 1871), pp. 109–32.
92 Owen, "Some Results from My Spiritual Studies," pp. 720–21, 724–26.
93 Howells, *The Undiscovered Country*, pp. 235–37.
94 Owen, "Some Results from My Spiritual Studies," p. 725.
95 Howells, *The Undiscovered Country*, p. 237.
96 Ibid., p. 218.
97 Owen, "Some Results from My Spiritual Studies," p. 722; Howells, *The Undiscovered Country*, p. 57.
98 Howells, *The Undiscovered Country*, pp. 10, 23–28, 52–53.

mystery"[99] had been found. Owen had reported a few such manifestations in *The Debatable Land*.[100] More pertinently, he had been led to utter similar claims in the *Atlantic* by the appearances of Katie King, who on two occasions had been assisted by a "luminous"[101] hand. Just as Katie and presumably her helping hand had proved fraudulent, so the hand which Boynton witnessed turned out to have been Ford's, chemically treated. Ford did not explain what made his fingers give off blue light, but P. T. Barnum's *Humbugs of the World* (1866) specified a dash of phosphorous and carbon bisulphide.[102]

For both men, at any rate, the immediate causes of failure were the same. Until venturing into spiritualistic society in Boston, Boynton had displayed throughout his occult researches the same distrust of professional mediums and group séances that had characterized Owen's cautious investigations before his meetings with Katie in Philadelphia.[103] And just as Owen had been abused not only by mediumistic fraud but also by what Howells had termed "the coarse jeers"[104] of the press, so Boynton was driven from Boston by Mrs. Le Roy's deceit and by Ford's hostility and misleading trick. Consistent with the resentment which Howells had displayed in remarking that newspaper attacks on Owen and the *Atlantic* were "enough to make a spiritualist of a man out of hand,"[105] he was much harsher in his treatment of the journalist's fraud than he was with Mrs. Le Roy's. The professional medium, in fact, came off as a kindly sort of charlatan. But Boynton attacked Ford for the sacrilege of his interference with the reverent aspirations of the believers, and Ford himself finally admitted that the spiritualist's motive had been "noble," his own "ignoble."[106] It would appear, then, that if Howells dramatized Owen's plight in the figure of Boynton, he almost wishfully drew in Ford a representative of hostile

[99] Ibid., p. 33.
[100] Owen, *The Debatable Land*, pp. 270, 272–74.
[101] Owen, "Touching Spiritual Visitants from a Higher Life," pp. 58–59.
[102] P. T. Barnum, *The Humbugs of the World* (London, 1866), pp. 95–96.
[103] Howells, *The Undiscovered Country*, pp. 95–96; Leopold, p. 381.
[104] Howells to Garrison, December 28, 1874; quoted by permission of Professor William White Howells. Permission to quote this passage must be requested from Professor Howells.
[105] Ibid.; quoted by permission of Professor William White Howells. Permission to quote this passage must be requested from Professor Howells.
[106] Howells, *The Undiscovered Country*, p. 394.

press and skeptical science who by the story's end had been converted to the novelist's own attitude of criticism for the cause and respect for the man.

Late in December, 1874, Owen had written Howells that his chief regret in the Philadelphia affair was for having exposed the *Atlantic* to criticism.[107] Professing a mistaken confidence that his own reputation could not be damaged by a single innocent blunder, he had defended himself by placing greater value on his reverent and benevolent aspiration, despite its susceptibility to abuse by imperfect men in an imperfect world, than on the kind of suspicious temperament which might have avoided embarrassment. In the hope that it might indirectly place the affair in perspective, he had offered to write an essay for Howells, based not on the immediate event but on his experiences of a lifetime, dealing with the subject of "Righteous Sentiment in presence of Worthless Object."[108] But he had understood that under the circumstances Howells might not wish to print such an article.

Owen had never been able to vindicate himself in the pages of the *Atlantic*. Nor had he ever given up his belief in spiritualism. It had remained for Howells to do both for him, in a novel about a prophet who finally realized that his righteous sentiment had been misdirected not toward a single fraudulent spirit, but toward the worthless object of spiritualism itself. Nowhere in the novel, it must be emphasized, did the search for physical evidence of immortality elicit anything but criticism from Howells. In *The Debatable Land* Owen had called for proof "that intercourse from beyond the bourn is not forbidden to man."[109] At the end of his life a now-wiser Boynton quoted Hamlet in full: "The undiscovered country, from whose bourn no traveler returns."[110] Perhaps in his Shakespearean title lay Howells's final answer to the spiritualist whose gravestone bore the equally geographical titles of the works by which he wished to be remembered: *Footfalls on the Boundary of Another World* and *The Debatable Land between This World and the Next*.[111]

---

[107] Owen to Howells, December 29, 1874.
[108] Ibid. Quoted by permission of Harvard College Library.
[109] Owen, *The Debatable Land*, p. 280.
[110] Howells, *The Undiscovered Country*, p. 373.
[111] Leopold, p. 414.

III | In giving form to these "autobiographical" materials in *The Undiscovered Country*, Howells had two sorts of literary prec- edent as far as spiritualism was concerned. For one thing, his novel was the latest in the series of anti-spiritualistic fictions initiated by Lowell with "The Unhappy Lot of Mr. Knott" (1851), and its opening scene resembled the satiric séances of an earlier generation of writers. More fundamental was his obvious reliance, recently noted by several schol- ars, on patterns of occult romance taken from Hawthorne. Henry James had already blended similar occult and satiric elements in "Pro- fessor Fargo" (1874). But Howells departed significantly from the conventions of both anti-spiritualistic satire and Hawthornesque ro- mance, for those conventions were incapable of shaping his reflections on the plight of Robert Dale Owen.

Howells's account of Egeria and Mrs. Le Roy's séance in his long opening chapter gave promise of beginning a typical satire in the style of the spiritualistic episode of Bayard Taylor's *Hannah Thurston*.[112] There was the shabby professional medium. There was the familiar sequence of phenomena which began with rappings and included the voices, touches, and embraces of spirits in the dark, along with a music box which played as it presumably floated in the air. There was the skeptical hero regarding the proceedings with disgust; in *Hannah Thurston* the hero's servant had coated the keys of the piano in ad- vance with soot which came off on the fraudulent medium's hand, and in *The Undiscovered Country* Ford himself attempted to catch Mrs. Le Roy out of her chair in the dark, grasping instead the innocent Egeria and revealing the glowing hand which he, too, had prepared beforehand. Finally, there was the flock of silly believers who joyously received saccharine messages from the spirits, just as Taylor's Mr. and Mrs. Merryfield and their friends had done.

That a couple named "Merrifield"[113] attended Mrs. Le Roy's séance may not have been entirely coincidental, for Howells, who recognized Taylor as an early voice of realism in American fiction, had read *Han-*

---

[112] Howells, *The Undiscovered Country*, pp. 1–34; Bayard Taylor, *Hannah Thurs- ton: A Story of American Life* (London, 1863), I, 211–40.
[113] Howells, *The Undiscovered Country*, p. 16.

nah Thurston.[114] For that matter, though, Tom Appleton had humorously sketched a séance given by a lady medium and characterized by sentimental believers and communications in "At the Medium's" (1873).[115] Rather than suggesting specific genetic relationships, these similarities underscore the persistence of the séance pattern in literary and journalistic satire, some of which Howells inevitably knew.

There was an important difference, however, in Howells's handling of this material. Bayard Taylor had characterized Dyce, his medium, as a home-wrecking libertine who attempted to lure Mrs. Merryfield away to a free-love commune, but there had been no trace of carnality in Dyce's séance itself. What Howells brought anew to such scenes, in the sobbing and giggling excitement with which his Mrs. Merrifield and the other ladies responded to the invisible but material kisses and embraces of masculine spirits counterfeited in the dark by Mrs. Le Roy, was a dramatic rather than editorial demonstration of repressed sexuality emerging as spiritual longing.[116] In fact, if the séance provided some believers with a social means of releasing sexual feelings, it perhaps also gave the realistic novelist a satiric setting in which he could treat such matters without offending an audience long accustomed to denunciations of spiritualistic immorality.

But Howells told Charles Dudley Warner that he was fortunately not required by his story to explain the trick by which Mrs. Le Roy was able to materialize groping hands in a box in the middle of her table:[117] clearly his major intention was not to ridicule or "expose" spiritualism. And the satiric séance, while adequate for that purpose, did not lend itself to the serious exploration of Boynton's situation. Indeed, as Boynton's only venture into the studio of the professional medium, Mrs. Le Roy's séance placed him in a false light very much like that in which, after years of cautious private investigation, Robert Dale Owen had found himself as a result of the Katie King fiasco.

114 [William Dean Howells,] *"The Story of Kennett,* by Bayard Taylor," *Atlantic Monthly* XVII (June 1866), 775, 777.
115 Appleton, *A Sheaf of Papers,* pp. 289–93.
116 Howells, *The Undiscovered Country,* pp. 21–31. For an excellent discussion of this aspect of Howells's novel, see Vanderbilt, pp. 24–26.
117 Howells to Warner, December 27, 1879 (MS at the Watkinson Library); Howells, *The Undiscovered Country,* pp. 52–53.

Against such a background Ford, whose initial judgments were those of a skeptical satirist, could only think Boynton a charlatan or a fool. For the spiritualist's ideas to be seen in proper perspective and for his personal honor to be redeemed in Ford's eyes, it was necessary that he be taken out of the sentimental, fraudulent milieu of Boston spiritualism, and that the attitudes of the satiric literary séance be abandoned. (Ford's subsequent visit to a spiritualistic meeting at Walden Pond emphasized the contrast between Boynton's poignant sincerity and the tired inspiration of professional trance-speakers.)[118]

Clearly a more basic literary influence on *The Undiscovered Country* than that of anti-spiritualistic satire was Hawthorne's, which manifested itself in the magnetic relationship of father and daughter, in the romance of skeptic and trance maiden, and in the obsessive nature of the spiritualist's quest. In the opening section of the novel these themes were developed in counterpoint to the satiric matter of the séance. But when Boynton and Egeria fled Boston to wander the countryside, when Ford began to have second thoughts about their presumed deception, and when his friend Phillips judged "worthy of Hawthorne"[119] his own conjecture that Egeria might be innocent amid fraud, the note of "Rappaccini's Daughter" and *The Blithedale Romance* became insistent.

The occult psychological themes, the love story, and the pastoral structure of *The Undiscovered Country* resembled in outline those of *The Blithedale Romance*.[120] Both works began in the city with a specious demonstration of occult powers; both then shifted to a pastoral communist utopia where a social or religious reformer hoped to bring his ideas to fruition; both involved the vampiristic domination of an innocent trance-maiden by a prophetic magnetist; in both that dominance failed while on public exhibition in a village hall; and in both the trance maiden was ultimately liberated by the power of love. Similarly, the romantic conflict caused by the intrusion of Ford into the twilight world of the trance maiden and her father was reminiscent of the situation of the medical student who had wandered into the gar-

[118] Ibid., pp. 254–56.

[119] Ibid., p. 110.

[120] The pastoral structure of Howells's novel has been thoroughly discussed, and its similarity to that of *The Blithedale Romance* touched upon, by Vanderbilt, pp. 41–48.

den of the poison maiden and her father in "Rappaccini's Daughter." And Dr. Boynton's desire for forbidden knowledge was something like the scientific passion of Dr. Rappaccini.[121]

It is possible, then, that Howells found Hawthorne's studies of single-minded, deluded prophecy compatible with his wish to create a character based on Robert Dale Owen. Certainly he looked to the pattern of Hawthorne's occult love-stories as something which could lend romantic interest to the struggle between spiritualist and skeptic. At the same time, he seems also to have seen in the sinister bond between Hawthorne's mesmerists and trance maidens a morbid relationship which could illustrate the emotional perils of mediumship even in the service of high motives.

In Howells's hands, however, the mechanism of Egeria's subjection to her father became less magnetic and more psychological. Hawthorne had accepted the reality of mesmeric clairvoyance and had analyzed the mediumship of Ada Shepard, his children's governess, as a waking dream controlled by her sitter's mind.[122] Similarly, Boynton's control over Egeria was taken to be mesmeric by both father and daughter, Egeria approximating Hawthorne's diagnosis by suggesting that she was perhaps "not a medium, but only a dreamer"[123] whose dreams were dictated by her father. Evidently Howells agreed that Boynton's power was mesmeric—at least in the early stages of composition. For after reading the novel in manuscript, Thomas Sergeant Perry argued that its only flaw was the uncertain nature of this relationship, and he urged that it be removed from the realm of mesmerism and placed on the more definite ground of filial obedience.[124] Whatever his revisions, at no point did Howells categorically define Boynton's influence over Egeria as either magnetic or paternal charisma; but he did show that the result of that influence was nervous disorder in the girl. And he may have been following Perry's advice in the latter part of the story, where mesmerism was forgotten as Egeria threw off the spell amidst the burgeoning spring of the Shaker village.

---

[121] The resemblance of Boynton to Rappaccini has been pointed out by George Bennett, pp. 100, 104–5.
[122] Nathaniel Hawthorne, *Passages from the French and Italian Note-Books* (Boston, 1893), p. 395.
[123] Howells, *The Undiscovered Country*, p. 68.
[124] Perry to Howells, February 6, 1878.

In demonstrating that Howells saw spiritualism as a reflection of psychological as well as religious malaise, Kermit Vanderbilt has persuasively argued that the novelist developed the father-daughter relationship as an unconsciously incestuous one in which Boynton treated Egeria as a surrogate for his dead wife, reunion with whom had originally motivated his quest.[125] The degree to which Howells used Boynton to dramatize Robert Dale Owen's prophetic career may weaken the force of Vanderbilt's contention that spiritualism served Boynton as a "censor" which gave him "a respectable excuse for controlling Egeria and rebuffing Ford, all in the name of spiritual progress for the race."[126] Yet curious if not incestuous psychological undercurrents had figured in the occultism not only of Owen himself, but also of his daughter Rosamond. In fact, memories of Owen and his daughter may have suggested the neurotic ambience of Howells's opening chapters, in which the nobly intentioned Boynton devoted the sickly Egeria to the quest for truth amidst the necromantic surroundings of Mrs. Le Roy's establishment. Sometime before Owen's humiliation, Rosamond Dale Owen had visited him in his Boston boardinghouse. Long afflicted with neurasthenic illnesses to the point of semi-invalidism, she had been so incapacitated during her visit that her father had carried her up and down stairs despite his age. But as she later remembered in *My Perilous Life in Palestine* (1928),[127] she had accompanied him to one or two gatherings of his new literary acquaintances from Boston and Cambridge, of whom Longfellow had impressed her most favorably; perhaps she had also met her father's fellow spiritualist Tom Appleton (Longfellow's brother-in-law), and Howells, her father's editorial benefactor. Not a séance medium herself, she was nevertheless a spiritualist who occasionally lectured on her otherworldly experiences, and while in Boston she had consulted a professional medium about a romantic problem. Surely Howells could never have imagined for Egeria Boynton anything so melodramatic as Rosamond Dale Owen's later marriage to the dying Laurence Oliphant (the British diplomat, novelist, and apostate from Thomas Lake Har-

---

[125] Vanderbilt, pp. 24–40.
[126] Ibid., p. 30.
[127] Rosamond Dale Owen, *My Perilous Life in Palestine* (London, 1928), pp. 126–27, 134–37.

ris's communal mysticism), or her turbulent life in Palestine after Oliphant's death. But Rosamond's neurasthenia and the spiritualism she shared with her father could have suggested something of the emotional strain of the occult life which repeatedly prostrated Howells's heroine (at one point forcing Ford to carry her up to her room) until she recovered in the pastoral environment of the Shaker village.

As for Owen himself, he had written in the November, 1874, *Atlantic* of having been encouraged in his early investigations by a message from the spirit of "Violet," a girl whose death had caused him grief as a young man.[128] In his January, 1875, article he had said that shortly before his invitation to meet Katie King in Philadelphia, Violet had predicted through a Boston medium (obviously a collaborator in the Philadelphia conspiracy) that he would soon see and talk with visible spirits, including Violet herself.[129] (In the wake of the Katie King scandal, Violet's Boston medium had been exposed by a skeptic who by putting coloring material on his hand had proved that the ghostly fingers which touched his own in a dark séance belonged to the medium;[130] such, of course, were the spiritual caresses counterfeited by Howells's Mrs. Le Roy, and such was the trick by which Ford hoped to expose the spiritualists.) In pursuance of Violet, Owen had later given a long-treasured lock of her hair to Katie, but that beautiful spirit, who had embraced him and called him "Father Owen," had returned the keepsake with the message that Violet wished him to wait until called to join her in the next world.[131]

The Undiscovered Country, of course, was an early indication of Howells's keen interest in morbid familial and sexual relationships, especially as effects of religious and social change—an interest shown again most immediately with Squire Gaylord, his daughter Marcia, and her husband Bartley Hubbard in *A Modern Instance* (1882), and

[128] Robert Dale Owen, "How I Came to Study Spiritual Phenomena. A Chapter of Autobiography," *Atlantic Monthly* XXXIV (November 1874), 584.
[129] Owen, "Touching Spiritual Visitants from a Higher Life," pp. 57–58. In a chapter devoted to Violet in his second book on spiritualism, Owen had noted that after first mentioning her in the earlier *Footfalls* (1860) he had been notified by many American mediums that Violet was communicating with them (*The Debatable Land*, pp. 345–58). Violet has been identified by Leopold (p. 165) as Fanny Wright's sister Camilla.
[130] *Springfield Union*, December 24, 1874, p. 4.
[131] Owen, "Touching Spiritual Visitants from a Higher Life," pp. 57–58.

later in such occult and psychological fiction as *The Shadow of a Dream* (1890), *Questionable Shapes* (1902), *The Son of Royal Langbrith* (1904), and *Between the Dark and the Daylight: Romances* (1907). Here at the outset of the realistic 1880's, with Boynton and Egeria as with the Boston séance, Howells was using the patterns of occult romance and anti-spiritualistic satire to explore on a subtler, more clinical level the sinister sexual implications which Hawthorne had feared in mesmerism, and which Orestes Brownson and Bayard Taylor, among others, had melodramatically denounced in spiritualism.

More recently than these other writers, in fact, Henry James had dramatized some of the same implications in "Professor Fargo" (1874). James had united elements of anti-spiritualistic satire with the mesmeric melodrama of *The Blithedale Romance*. While ridiculing the paltry mediumistic performance of Professor Fargo, James's ironic narrator watched him gain control over the beautiful deaf-mute daughter of Colonel Gifford, an idealistic mathematical wizard who shared the platform with Fargo in New England village halls. Fargo was quite clearly cut from the pattern of Hawthorne's Westervelt, and the sexual nature of his conquest of Miss Gifford was made obvious. Colonel Gifford, on the other hand, was a quixotic crank who preached world reform through a new method of arithmetical calculation; it was his denial of Fargo's claim to "spiritual magnetism"[132] which led to his daughter's mesmeric ravishment. Howells would never have found in James's tale a serious treatment of the religious significance of spiritualism. But he could have remembered, perhaps unwittingly at first, a struggle for possession of a passive young woman between her father, who was both a deluded idealist and a scoffing critic of spiritualism, and a fraudulent medium who was also a genuine magnetist. Significantly, although *The Undiscovered Country*'s conflict between skeptic and spiritualist could have been an independent recombination of elements already taken from Hawthorne by James, Howells's manuscript revisions included the shortening of his skeptical reporter's name from "Gifford" to "Ford."[133]

[132] Ibid., p. 247.
[133] Vanderbilt, p. 47. Martha Banta has pointed out similarities among *The*

But anything which Howells may have derived by osmosis or design from Hawthorne or James underwent marked change. As we have seen, magnetism became more a psychological than a mesmeric influence, though not completely so. Modeled on Owen, moreover, the magnetic prophet lost his explicitly villainous status, in this respect resembling Westervelt or Fargo less than he did the characters based on Seymour Kirkup, the Florentine necromancer, in Hawthorne's last romances. And the pastoral experience itself, which had debilitated or at best disappointed the reformers of *The Blithedale Romance*, now became, in the sojourn of Boynton, Egeria, and Ford among the Shakers, a means of attaining spiritual wisdom and human love. (Howells had first vacationed among the Shakers during the summer following his and Owen's embarrassment.) [134] Even the deluded prophet, finally judged innocent by Ford because his motives were noble, [135] realized his error before dying. In short, the happy ending of Howells's agnostic novel allowed for the forgiveness and correction of error.

Howells's refusal "to make a Hawthornesque tragedy out of *The Undiscovered Country*" has been ascribed by George Bennett to the novelist's "temperamental optimism" and to an ethic which rejected the concept of unpardonable sin. [136] In a general sense Bennett's explanation is sound. Surely, though, the Howellsian ethic was elicited in this work by the task of indirectly vindicating the "blameless conscience" of Robert Dale Owen. And just as Owen and the problem he represented could not have been altogether dealt with in the context of the anti-spiritualistic satire of Bayard Taylor, neither could they have been handled adequately in terms of the villainous magnetists and Faustian scientists of Hawthorne. In the final analysis, Howells's

---

Blithedale Romance, "Professor Fargo," *The Undiscovered Country*, and *The Bostonians*, without explicitly suggesting any genetic relationship among the latter three (Banta, "The Two Worlds of Henry James," pp. 158–72).

[134] Howells, *Life in Letters of William Dean Howells*, I, 209–10. Vanderbilt's suggestion that the inspiration for the novel came from Howells's summer among the Shakers is valid insofar as the Vardley setting is concerned. But the novelist's treatment of the sect's celibate and communal life was subsidiary to his overabiding concern with Boynton's spiritualism (Vanderbilt, pp. 12–13).

[135] Howells, *The Undiscovered Country*, pp. 319, 362.

[136] Bennett, pp. 104–5.

powerful study of Boynton and the spiritual crisis of the 1870's owed less to the writer's literary models or ethical views than it did to his emotional commitment to Owen's memory.

IV | Writing *The Undiscovered Country* may have freed Howells from that commitment, for late in 1883 he and Mark Twain used spirit materialization for comic effect in their stage farce, "Colonel Sellers as a Scientist" (1883).[137] That Howells was amused by the ludicrous extremes to which the pursuit of immortality could lead had been revealed by Boynton's thought of submerging a medium clad in a diving suit for an underwater séance. But Colonel Sellers's absurd attempt to raise ghosts by means of electric batteries rather than the devices of the spiritualists ("those crazy, rapping, table-tipping, planchette, music in the air . . . frauds") bore the stamp of Twain's inspiration; so did the situation which resulted when a young man was mistaken for a materialized spirit by the Colonel, who was aghast at the sight of his daughter embracing the "materializee" (surely Twain's term).[138] And it was Twain who would return to Sellers's occult technology for thematic as well as slapstick purposes in *The American Claimant* (1892),[139] the novel which eventually grew out of the play.

But the literary legacy of Katie King had not exhausted itself with *The Undiscovered Country*. Through that novel, in fact, it extended to Edward Bellamy's *Miss Ludington's Sister: A Romance of Immortality* (1884),[140] in a way that places in new perspective the initial stage of the well-known "mutual indebtedness"[141] of Bellamy and Howells. For to trace this line of descent is to discover that Bellamy composed his curious tale of spiritualism expressly for Howells, its first reader and reviewer.

In a letter of August, 1881, praising Bellamy's *Dr. Heidenhoff's Process* (1880), Howells offered to read and perhaps recommend to

---

[137] William Dean Howells, "Colonel Sellers as a Scientist," *The Complete Plays of W. D. Howells*, ed. Walter J. Meserve (New York, 1960), pp. 205–41.

[138] Ibid., pp. 215, 238.

[139] Samuel Clemens, *The American Claimant* (New York, 1892).

[140] Edward Bellamy, *Miss Ludington's Sister* (Boston, 1884).

[141] Joseph Schiffman, "Mutual Indebtedness: Unpublished Letters of Edward Bellamy to William Dean Howells," *Harvard Library Bulletin* XII (Autumn 1958), 363–74.

his own publisher, Osgood, any new romance Bellamy might have on hand. Bellamy replied deferentially that he would take advantage of the opportunity when he had the time. Two and a half years later, in March, 1884, Howells received the manuscript of *Miss Ludington's Sister*, along with a reminder of his earlier kindness.[142]

In that manuscript Howells read the strange story of young Paul De Riemer's love affair first with the "spirit" of the girlhood portrait of his elderly aunt, Miss Ida Ludington; then with the fleshly embodiment of the young Ida as materialized in séances conducted by Mrs. Legrand, a New York medium; and finally with the quite mortal Ida who confessed to playing the spirit's part in a scheme designed by her parents and Mrs. Legrand, her aunt, to defraud Paul and Miss Ludington. Always the speculative romancer, Bellamy interwove with this spiritualistic intrigue the hypothesis that personal identity is actually a succession of separate selves, each with its own afterlife and each innocent of the sins of the others.[143] Thus Paul could argue that the spirit of his aunt's youth still lived; thus the spiritualists could take advantage of him by falsely verifying his theory; and thus, abandoning the occult foolishness of his theory in favor of its moral truth, Paul could forgive the spiritualists and marry Ida on the ground that her previous self, now departed, had been the agent of fraud.

True to his word, Howells brought *Miss Ludington's Sister* to Osgood's attention.[144] Not stopping there, in a *Century* review he hailed the story as an important "realistic" romance by the only American of the day worth comparing with Hawthorne. Without giving the mystery away, he described the situation of the beautiful spirit called back to earth as breathtakingly suspenseful. And he claimed that Bellamy had "taken some of the crudest and most sordid traits of our life, and . . . produced from them an effect of the most delicate and airy romance."[145]

[142] Bellamy to Howells, August 21, 1881; March 18, 1884; March 22, 1884; MSS at Houghton Library. What Howells wrote to Bellamy must be inferred from Bellamy's letters.

[143] Bellamy, *Miss Ludington's Sister*, pp. 182, 26–29.

[144] Bellamy to Howells, April 10, 1884; MS at Houghton Library.

[145] William Dean Howells, "Two Notable Novels," *Century* XXVIII (August 1884), 632–34. The other work under review was Ed Howe's *Story of a Country Town* (Boston, 1884).

From first to last, of course, Howells liked most of Bellamy's books, and in this instance he was promoting one which he had solicited for Osgood. In his campaign for native realism, moreover, he was pleased that even a romancer could deal with "democratic levels" of American experience without obeisance to British reviewers' notions of social and literary propriety. Nonetheless, Howells's admiration for Bellamy's thinly textured and hardly "realistic" fable has seemed inexplicably extravagant; Joseph Schiffman, in chronicling the "mutual indebtedness" of the two men, could attribute such enthusiasm only to Howells's general interest "in the question of immortality."[146] The likelihood is, however, that very specific personal considerations motivated Howells's excessive praise. The only "crude and sordid" reality of American life visible in *Miss Ludington's Sister* was one quite familiar to him as a result of the Katie King episode—fraudulent spiritualism. And although he did not say so in his review, he must have realized that Bellamy had pondered both Katie's case and the reviewer's own *Undiscovered Country*.

Bellamy was well acquainted with the story of Katie King. As assistant editor of the *Springfield Union*, he had presciently dismissed her as humbug—"the leading miracle of the season"—at the height of her popularity in the summer of 1874;[147] a few months later his newspaper had devoted a good deal of space to the scandal which broke when Robert Dale Owen exposed her deception.[148] As for the literary possibilities of such events, in the summer of 1875 Bellamy had reviewed Florence Marryat's English thriller *Open! Sesame!* (1875)[149] in terms prophetic of *Miss Ludington's Sister*: "The hero is a victim of Spiritualistic delusions, his weakness being taken advantage of for selfish ends, by a set of designing persons, from whose devices he is

[146] Schiffman, p. 367.

[147] [Edward Bellamy,] "Recent Miracles," *Springfield Union*, August 11, 1874, p. 4. Bellamy has been identified as the author of this article by Sylvia E. Bowman in *The Year 2000: A Critical Biography of Edward Bellamy* (New York, 1958), p. 61.

[148] "The End of a Notable Humbug," *Springfield Union*, December 18, 1874, p. 2; "Last Phases of the Philadelphia Sensation," *Springfield Union*, December 22, 1874, p. 4; and untitled stories and editorials, December 15, 1874, p. 4; December 16, 1874, p. 4; December 17, 1874, p. 4. Bellamy could have had a hand in these stories, although they were not mentioned by Professor Bowman.

[149] Florence Marryat, *Open! Sesame!* (London, 1875).

rescued and the materialization sham exposed by his devoted wife."[150] Ironically, Bellamy had ignored the presence of genuine spirits in the story, doubtless unaware that Captain Marryat's daughter would never renounce the English Katie King she had often admired in person, or that she had been satisfied with the London séances of the very mediums under whose auspices Katie had crossed the Atlantic to appear for Robert Dale Owen; nor could he have foreseen that shortly after the publication of *Miss Ludington's Sister*, Miss Marryat's dead daughter would be materializing for her at séances in New York and Boston.[151] But that Bellamy could adapt Miss Marryat's aristocratic melodrama to the American scene had been prefigured by his observation as a reviewer that *Open! Sesame!* dealt with "a 'materialization' fraud of the Katie King order."[152]

In his own romance Bellamy stayed close to the pattern of the American Katie's séances as described in the *Springfield Union*. The *Union* had reported that the pretty young woman who impersonated Katie entered her medium's spirit cabinet (which Robert Dale Owen made a point of examining before each performance) from a secret recess in the wall of the darkened séance room; then, with the lights turned up, she emerged from the cabinet to dazzle her admirers.[153] Bellamy merely shifted the point of surreptitious entry to a concealed trapdoor in the roof of Mrs. Legrand's cabinet, through which the beautiful Ida, clad like Katie in white raiment which revealed her well-modeled shoulders, descended from the room above.[154] In a reportorial sense, at least, Bellamy's account of Mrs. Legrand's materializations of Ida—the most vivid episode of his story and the one specifically mentioned in Howells's review—was quite "realistic."

Against this background the reasons for Howells's enthusiastic response to *Miss Ludington's Sister* begin to emerge. Having been em-

---

[150] [Edward Bellamy,] "Literary Notices," *Springfield Union*, August 21, 1875, p. 6. Sylvia E. Bowman identified this review as Bellamy's and pointed to its importance in *The Year 2000*, p. 61.

[151] Florence Marryat, *There Is No Death* (New York, 1891), pp. 17–22, 83–96, 139–46, 207–65.

[152] [Bellamy,] "Literary Notices."

[153] "The End of a Notable Humbug," p. 2.

[154] Bellamy, *Miss Ludington's Sister*, pp. 79–89, 113–20.

barrassed by publishing Robert Dale Owen's rhapsodic article about Katie King in the *Atlantic Monthly* at the very moment that newspapers like the *Springfield Union* were describing her fraud and attacking the *Atlantic*, Howells cannot have avoided recognizing Bellamy's artful modification of Katie's séances in those conducted by Mrs. Legrand. Quite by accident, moreover, Howells may have been in a receptive frame of mind for a story of love between mortal and false spirit, for only a few months had passed since he and Mark Twain had made farcical capital of Colonel Sellers's horror at seeing his daughter infatuated with a "materializee"; both in a letter to Twain about their play and in his review of Bellamy's romance, Howells spoke of the climactic "*eclaircissement*" of the ghost's identity.[155]

It was no accident, however, that Bellamy sent the author of *The Undiscovered Country* a manuscript bearing such clear traces of Katie. Bellamy may have directed neither the *Springfield Union's* coverage of Katie's downfall, nor its attack on "the editor and publishers of The Atlantic Monthly" for foisting Owen's "twaddle" on their readers and then "leaving poor Owen in the lurch" by denying responsibility for his claims.[156] But as the newspaper's assistant editor and the author of an earlier denunciation of Katie, Bellamy was inevitably aware of Howells's involvement in Owen's fiasco. True, a decade separated Katie King and the completion of *Miss Ludington's Sister*. But *The Undiscovered Country* appeared only a year before Howells offered to read Bellamy's manuscript. Did Bellamy (like Charles Eliot Norton and Tom Appleton) perceive that Howells had transformed his memory of the sorry episode into the compassionate examination of Dr. Boynton's spiritualistic quest? That might explain the absence of harshness in Bellamy's treatment of his own hero's occult obsession and Mrs. Legrand's fakery, especially as contrasted with his earlier contempt for Katie's entourage. His tale did resemble Howells's novel—itself a "realistic" canvas stretched on a frame of Hawthornesque romance—in tracing a shift from delusive preoccupation with the hereafter to a healthy reliance on the qualities of earthly love and forgiveness which liberated the heroines of both works from

155 Clemens and Howells, *Mark Twain-Howells Letters*, I, 453; Howells, "Two Notable Novels," p. 633.
156 *Springfield Union*, December 16, 1874, p. 4.

morbid servitude in familial séances. And surely Howells would have noticed vestiges of his own easygoing fraud, Mrs. Le Roy, in Bellamy's benevolent charlatan, Mrs. Legrand.

In short, it is hard not to conclude that Howells's offer of assistance in 1881 prompted Bellamy to illustrate his fancy of multiple identity with a tale of spiritualism which would appeal to his benefactor by sympathetically reflecting both the Katie King affair and its assimilation in *The Undiscovered Country*. And in the *Century* review which praised Bellamy for treating "our reality" with "boldness," and for extracting a "delicate and airy" effect from "some of the crudest and most sordid traits of our life," we can read Howells's pleasure that Bellamy had profited by the example of *The Undiscovered Country* in making artistic sense out of the spiritualistic scandal which so vividly figured in Howells's own vision of American "reality."

Howells himself continued to treat the subject of spiritualism from time to time. In *The Landlord at Lion's Head* (1897),[157] he used planchette writing both to lend an occult touch to the thematic riddle of Jeff Durgin's character—"the broken shaft"[158]—and to characterize the otherworldly interests of rural Yankees who were quite hardheaded in everyday matters. The planchette device itself, which curiously enough had been introduced in America by Robert Dale Owen, set the novel's opening scene at about the year 1870, but Yankee susceptibility to exotic religious impulse in the aftermath of Puritanism was something that Howells was at the same time and in much the same way remembering from his Western Reserve boyhood in *Impressions and Experiences* (1896).[159]

Still later, the interest attracted at the turn of the century by the investigations of occult and psychological phenomena conducted by the Society for Psychical Research manifested itself in the occult tales Howells collected in *Questionable Shapes* (1903)[160] and *Between the Dark and the Daylight: Romances* (1907).[161] Spiritualism was mentioned only once in these stories, and then as a vulgar contrast to what

157 William Dean Howells, *The Landlord at the Lion's Head* (New York, 1897).
158 Ibid., pp. 27, 69, 92–99, 192–94, 365, 387, 419, 444.
159 Howells, *Impressions and Experiences*, pp. 20–21.
160 William Dean Howells, *Questionable Shapes* (New York, 1903).
161 William Dean Howells, *Between the Dark and the Daylight: Romances* (New York, 1907).

Howells's characters thought was a genuinely supernatural occurrence.[162] Yet in some of the studies of love and marriage in *Questionable Shapes* he was still exploring problems of morbid psychology like those he had treated in the relationship between the spiritualistic Boynton and the mediumistic Egeria. Almost until the end of his life he now and then dealt sympathetically yet critically in his magazine columns with believers like Sir Oliver Lodge, a latter-day counterpart of Owen.[163] But Howells never again wrote about spiritualism with the power which his "autobiographical" point of view had conferred upon *The Undiscovered Country*.

[162] Howells, *Questionable Shapes*, p. 5.
[163] William Dean Howells, "Editor's Easy Chair," *Harper's* CIX (October 1904), 803–6; CXXV (November 1912), 958–61; CXXX (February 1915), 472–75; CXXXV (November 1917), 882–85; CXXXIX (August 1919), 445–48.

VII: "SPERITS COULDN'T A DONE BETTER" [1]

Mark Twain and Spiritualism

I | Mark Twain, like Howells, first became aware of the spiritu-
alistic movement during his youth. If he did not witness at
first hand the rapping séances which came to Hannibal sometime in
the 1850's, he must have heard of them. In 1853 he wrote his mother
from New York that "Rochester, famous on account of the 'Spirit
Rappings' was of course interesting."[2] Already, in the manner of the
humorous journalists he was studying in his brother's printshop, he
had borrowed two items about spirits and believers from the newspaper exchanges for his short-lived column in the *Hannibal Daily
Journal*.[3] It was only natural, therefore, that when the mature Twain
turned to spiritualistic materials, he handled them in terms of the
comic séances and rascally ghosts of the literary comedians with whom
he had served his apprenticeship. This he did whether reporting a wave
of spiritual excitement in San Francisco,[4] or castigating the medium
J .V. Mansfield in *Life on the Mississippi* (1883),[5] or making scampish

[1] Samuel Clemens, *Adventures of Huckleberry Finn* (New York, 1885), p. 351.
[2] Minnie M. Brashear, *Mark Twain, Son of Missouri* (Chapel Hill, N.C., 1934),
pp. 154, 142.
[3] Ibid., pp. 131, 133.
[4] Samuel Clemens, *The Washoe Giant in San Francisco*, ed. Franklin Walker (San
Francisco, 1938), pp. 119–37.
[5] Samuel Clemens, *Life on the Mississippi* (Boston, 1883).

| 155

poltergeists out of Tom Sawyer and Huck Finn in *Adventures of Huckleberry Finn* (1885). As late as 1898 he created a comic rapping séance in the unfinished Mysterious Stranger manuscript, "Schoolhouse Hill."[6]

Spiritualism first made popular headway in California when the "inspirational lecturer" Emma Hardinge (later Mrs. Britten) spent over a year there as missionary for the cause in 1863 and 1864. Public interest reached a high point a year later when Mrs. Ada Hoyt Foye, called by Emma Hardinge "the best test medium of the age,"[7] arrived in San Francisco. Mark Twain had missed Emma Hardinge's appearance on behalf of the Virginia City Sanitary Fund,[8] having left Nevada partly in consequence of his difficulties with the ladies of that organization. But when Ada Foye's weekly public séances created a journalistic sensation in San Francisco during the winter of 1865–66, Twain was on hand as the correspondent of the *Virginia City Territorial Enterprise*. And early in 1866 the *Golden Era* reprinted six *Enterprise* pieces in which he burlesqued a "true" ghost story, defended the spiritualists against charges of immorality and insanity, and told of his own experiences at three séances.[9]

Before attending a séance Twain took note of the spirits in "The Kearny Street Ghost Story"[10] by burlesquing a spiritualistic report about the ghostly persecution of servant girls in one local household. The alleged incidents provided him with the materials for a sketch resembling the previous decade's comic accounts of spiritual manifestations. There was nothing new about either frightened servants or spirits who flung furniture about the room. One poltergeist even supplied the conventional ghost-story device of leaving behind concrete verification of his earthly visit—in this case, nine bloody kittens deposited on a terrified servant's pillow. "What would you think of

[6] Samuel Clemens, *Mark Twain's Mysterious Stranger Manuscripts*, ed.William M. Gibson (Berkeley, 1969), pp. 175–220.

[7] Emma Hardinge Britten, *Autobiography*, ed. Margaret Wilkinson (Manchester, 1900), p. 253. For the rise of spiritualism in California, see Emma Hardinge Britten, *Modern American Spiritualism: A Twenty Years' Record of the Communion between Earth and the World of Spirits* (New York, 1870), pp. 439–58.

[8] Britten, *Autobiography*, p. 187.

[9] Clemens, *The Washoe Giant*, pp. 119–37.

[10] Ibid., pp. 120–21.

that?" asked the obviously skeptical Twain. "What would you think of a ghost that came to your bedside at dead of night and had kittens?"[11]

In reporting Ada Foye's weekly test séances, however, Twain displayed a surprisingly friendly interest as well as a sense of the ludicrous. For the title of his first report he or his editors altered Artemus Ward's "Among the Spirits"[12] to "Among the Spiritualists."[13] But whereas Ward had attacked professional mediums as an "ornery set of cusses,"[14] Twain treated Mrs. Foye with genial objectivity and described with only half-facetious puzzlement her spirit-rapping, spirit-writing, and "pellet reading." Fingering through a pile of folded slips of paper on which people in her audience had written the names of spirits with whom they wished to speak, the medium would be seized by a spirit to write its name backwards and upside-down; she would then pick up the paper pellets, one at a time, until three raps rang out; unfolding the pellet in her hand, she would reveal that it contained the very name which she had written at spirit direction. The seeker in the audience would then question the spirit, who would reply through raps or Mrs. Foye's pencil. In this way a dead gambler named "Gus Graham" amazed Twain by answering perfectly the questions put by another reporter as to the year (1854), cause (shooting), and place (Randolph County, Illinois) of his death.[15]

As a literary comedian himself, Twain burlesqued this exchange after reporting it. Asking for the spirit of "John Smith," he was answered by the rappings of a host of "Smiths" claiming to have perished in every possible place and of every known cause of death. All of them were unhappy in their infernal abode, which they called "the Smithsonian Institute." Twain finally discovered that "John Smith" had been talked to death by his wife. But in closing his account on a serious note, Twain made it clear that not even clairvoyance could

---

[11] Ibid., p. 121.

[12] Charles Farrar Browne, *The Complete Works of Artemus Ward* (London, 1884), pp. 48–51.

[13] Ivan Benson, *Mark Twain's Western Years* (Stanford, Calif., 1938), p. 71. The sketch was printed as "Among the Spirits" in Clemens, *The Washoe Giant*, pp. 122–24.

[14] Browne, *The Complete Works of Artemus Ward*, p. 51.

[15] Clemens, *The Washoe Giant*, pp. 122–23.

explain all of the correct answers given by "Gus Graham" and other spirits.[16]

He learned nothing more at Mrs. Foye's next séance, which he reported in "Mark Twain, Committee Man."[17] Having engineered his election to the committee which was to insure honesty in the proceedings, he could detect no trickery, and he testified that Mrs. Foye's inspired spirit-autographs were indeed identical to the names sent up from the audience. Once again he was at a loss to account for the power which supplied the spirits with correct answers to questions about their earthly existence. Whether that power was ghostly he expected never to know, nor could he believe in what he did not know. But he promised to continue investigating so long as he retained his sanity.

Twain insisted that this second account was completely factual, and instead of inventing humorous material he contented himself with jocose reportage, treating as an amusing debate a dispute between Mrs. Foye and an angry German who claimed (in thick dialect) that the man from whose spirit he had just received a message was still alive. Without apparent irony Twain recorded Mrs. Foye's indignant reply that the deceitful unbeliever had been answered by an equally deceitful spirit, and that she would halt the séance were her religion to be further insulted. In this same account, however, Twain did interject his own ironic responses to a description of the hereafter according to the spirit of another "Smith"—a Unitarian-Universalist clergyman. The spirit refused to evaluate his own behavior on earth ("the shrewd old waterproof nonentity!"), bragged of his swift ascent through the spheres since his death ("Go slow, old man, go slow—you have got all eternity before you"), and said that the spirits had no sense of temperature ("which militates somewhat against all my notions of orthodox damnation—fire and brimstone").[18] Spiritual progress through the spheres had long been a subject for humorous comment: Doesticks's uncle had praised the liquor served in the second sphere and had looked forward to apple dumplings in the

16 Ibid., p. 124.
17 Ibid., pp. 125–29.
18 Ibid., p. 128.

third.[19] Here a reporter as well as a funnyman, Twain merely poked commonsensical fun at the vagueness of the spirit's remarks. Not until he took a personal dislike to another medium, J. V. Mansfield, was he to wax vitriolic over such communications.

In thus making humorous capital of spiritualism with the methods of facetious reportage and burlesque already employed by the literary comedians, Twain was notably gentler than his predecessors. Doesticks and Ward had portrayed mediums as cheats, believers as fools, but Twain made sport only of the spirits. He showed no awareness of such skeptical explanations of mediumistic pellet-reading as that given two years earlier in San Francisco to Artemus Ward and his manager by a conjuror who used sleight-of-hand and mechanical contrivance to read the folded slips of paper and to produce rappings.[20] Indeed, Twain handled potentially scandalous material—the spirits' mistakes, their requests for further interviews with the living in the medium's private studio, the German's claim of fraud—without suggesting that he doubted Mrs. Foye's honesty.

It would appear that personal friendship and Twain's professional role as defender of the underdog had something to do with his friendliness to the spiritualists. Two of his colleagues, Charles Warren Stoddard and Prentice Mulford, were deeply interested in the movement. Stoddard, with whom Twain went to at least one séance, was later to imply that he had been the target of an attempted seduction by Laura Cuppy, an inspirational lecturer whose little group, the Friends of Progress, combined spiritualism with feminist and free-love exhortation.[21] Whether on personal or journalistic grounds, Twain did not like the *San Francisco Bulletin*'s charges that spiritualism was causing insanity and immorality among the Friends of Progress. In a sketch about "Spiritual Insanity,"[22] he facetiously applied the *Bul-*

[19] Mortimer Thomson, "An Evening with the Spiritualists," *Doesticks What He Says* (New York, 1855), pp. 253–61.

[20] Edward P. Hingston, *The Genial Showman, Being Reminiscences of the Life of Artemus Ward, and Pictures of a Showman's Career in the Western World* (New York, 1870), pp. 106–9.

[21] Franklin Walker, *San Francisco's Literary Frontier* (New York, 1939), pp. 201–6; Clemens, *The Washoe Giant*, pp. 119–20.

[22] Clemens, *The Washoe Giant*, pp. 129–31.

letin's diagnosis of spiritualistic delusion to the behavior of the San Francisco Board of Supervisors. And in "The New Wildcat Religion"[23] he explicitly chided the *Bulletin*, observing that in former years Methodist and Campbellite enthusiasms had sent people to the asylum without causing public indignation. With every evidence of seriousness he said that while he had no special love for "the wildcat," he could not think the *Bulletin*'s attacks fair in view of the many sensible and respectable believers with whom he was personally acquainted.

To this mild partisanship must be added the fact that Twain had evidently detected no mediumistic imposture himself. This was again true of his last recorded California séance, which he described in "More Spiritual Investigations."[24] He joined a medium, her husband, and two others at a table which tipped so as to cause a pointer to spell out messages on an alphabetical dial. Twain felt sure that the medium could not agitate the table on which her hands lightly rested, and he knew two of the sitters well enough to rule out fraud on their part. But while the spirit dial itself interested him, its ethereal manipulators were trivial and vague in their communications, with none of "Gus Graham's" perspicuity. Another "Smith," egged on by the medium, chaffed the reporter for his abuse of the Smith family. And although Twain promised in closing to ignore the *Bulletin*'s warnings, and to exchange pleasantries with the "Smiths" whenever possible on the ground that they were "better company than a good many live people,"[25] he was clearly losing his interest in spiritualism.

From the first that interest had probably been as much journalistic as personal, its benevolence partially determined by newspaper rivalries. Yet if Twain's efforts as an occult investigator had failed to reveal the nature of the power which twirled the dial, rapped intelligently, and controlled Mrs. Foye's pencil, his need for copy had provided a convenient opportunity for reworking some of the themes and devices of the literary comedians. By the time his last spiritualistic sketch appeared in the *Golden Era*, he had already sailed for the Sandwich Islands, his apprenticeship over.

23 Ibid., pp. 133–34.
24 Ibid., pp. 135–37.
25 Ibid., p. 137.

II | Mark Twain left San Francisco evidently still on good terms with spirits, mediums, and believers. Over the next decade and a half, however, his journalistic goodwill for "the wildcat" gave way to private contempt. Perhaps what he learned about mediumistic fraud cast new light on the séances he had so tolerantly reported in California. Certainly what he saw of spiritualistic belief at Nook Farm in Hartford annoyed him. But what finally provoked him to public wrath in *Life on the Mississippi* (1883) was the inept attempt of James Vincent Mansfield, the "spirit postmaster," to impersonate the spirit of Twain's brother Henry Clemens.

During the 1870's Twain probably came across skeptical explanations of some of the mediumistic phenomena which had compelled his respect in San Francisco. An admirer of P. T. Barnum, he may have read the showman's exposure of such mediums as Mansfield, the Fox sisters, and the Davenport brothers in *The Humbugs of the World* (1866).[26] Of particular interest to Twain would have been Barnum's disclosure of the way a young western medium manipulated a spirit dial with her feet while her arms rested casually on the table. As for Ada Foye's exhibitions, Barnum described a format almost identical to hers in explaining the sleight-of-hand involved in successful pellet-reading.[27] A Professor Baldwin staged the same feat in the "lectures" which he gave from St. Louis to Boston demonstrating how spiritual manifestations could be accomplished through conjuring and showmanship. Lafcadio Hearn jokingly hoped that Baldwin's show would prevent the spread of spiritual insanity,[28] and in 1877 Herman Melville's wife expressed interest in the professor's exposure of pellet reading in Boston.[29]

Twain need not have been aware of these specific revelations, of course. As early as 1869 he mentioned in the *Buffalo Express* an instrument-maker who constructed electrical rapping-devices for mediums. Another of his *Express* items was simply a variation of his

[26] P. T. Barnum, *The Humbugs of the World* (London, 1866).
[27] Ibid., pp. 71–75, 64–65.
[28] [Lafcadio Hearn,] "Artful Ambidexterity: The Mysterious Manifestations of Spiritualism Exposed," *Cincinnati Enquirer*, July 4, 1874, p. 8.
[29] Victor Paltsits, ed., *Family Correspondence of Herman Melville, 1830–1904, in the Gansevoort-Lansing Collection* (New York, 1929), p. 46.

earlier conversation with the "Smith" whose wife had talked him to death; this time Twain wrote that the departed husband of a Hartford woman had disappointed her at a séance by showing no wish to return to her—it was hot enough where he was.[30]

This joke might not have amused two well-known Hartford ladies whose neighbor Twain soon became at Nook Farm. Although Harriet Beecher Stowe's public remarks about spiritualism tended to be non-committal if friendly, she had been quietly interested in séance communication since her first son's death in 1857; her husband Calvin, of course, was subject to visions of persons living, dead, and imaginary throughout his life.[31] In 1868 Mrs. Stowe evidently went so far as to plan or prepare a magazine article about her conversations, through an amateur medium's planchette, with what purported to be the spirits of Charlotte Bronte and the Duchess of Sutherland.[32] Her account of these dialogues did not appear, however, until her brother Charles Beecher included it in his *Spiritual Manifestations* (1879),[33] and if she continued to dabble in the occult she did so privately. But her half-sister, Isabella Beecher Hooker, acquired a faith in mediums and spirits which at times proved troublesome to her family and her neighbors, Twain among them. He amused Mrs. Hooker by mistaking for a footman one of the mediums she had invited to an 1877 party.[34] Whether she was equally amused by his reference to a "Gammer Hooker"[35] possessed of devils, in a later discarded chapter of *The Prince and the Pauper* printed in a Hartford newspaper in 1880,[36] is not on record.

More vexsome to the Nook Farm community than Mrs. Hooker's

---

[30] Samuel Clemens, *The Forgotten Writings of Mark Twain*, ed. Henry Duskis (New York, 1963), pp. 129, 104.

[31] Harriet Beecher Stowe, "Spiritualism," *Christian Union*, n.s., II (September 3, 1870), 129–30; (September 10, 1870), 145–46; (September 24, 1870), 177–78; Forrest Wilson, *Crusader in Crinoline: The Life of Harriet Beecher Stowe* (Philadelphia, 1941), pp. 150, 166–71, 388, 436, 450–51, 463, 534, 562, 573–76, 598; Kenneth R. Andrews, *Nook Farm: Mark Twain's Hartford Circle* (Cambridge, Mass., 1950), pp. 62–65.

[32] Lilian Whiting, *Kate Field: A Record* (Boston, 1899), p. 197.

[33] Charles Beecher, *Spiritual Manifestations* (Boston, 1879), pp. 25–36. Mrs. Stowe's biographers do not seem to have noticed this report.

[34] Andrews, pp. 53–65.

[35] Ibid., p. 244.

[36] Ibid., pp. 243–46.

own occultism was her friendship during the early 1870's with the notorious feminist and spiritualist, Victoria Woodhull. In January, 1871, not long after launching her lively newspaper, *Woodhull and Claflin's Weekly,* the pretty Mrs. Woodhull stole the thunder of a suffragette convention in Washington by independently petitioning a congressional committee for the right to vote. Many established feminists considered her a lately arrived opportunist with questionable personal morals and dangerous ideas. But at first, devoting her newspaper to the cause and speaking on "the woman question" to packed houses, she carried the day. And when it was learned that she attributed her oratorical prowess to the spiritual guidance of Demosthenes, the American Association of Spiritualists invited her to its 1871 meeting and elected her president.[37]

As chairman of the 1870 suffragette convention, Isabella Beecher Hooker was immediately and permanently captivated by Victoria Woodhull's charm and eloquence.[38] Harriet Beecher Stowe, however, caricatured the new luminary as the wrong kind of feminist and spiritualist—"Audacia Dangereyes"—in *My Wife and I* (1871).[39] (*Woodhull and Claflin's Weekly* retaliated with a rambling serial entitled "My Friends and I.")[40] And when Mrs. Woodhull, stung by attacks on her advocacy of sexual freedom, made public the Beecher-Tilton scandal in the fall of 1872 by charging Henry Ward Beecher with practicing adultery in private while attacking free love from the pulpit, most of Beecher's family rallied to his defense. But Isabella Hooker, although she refrained from supporting Mrs. Woodhull's 1872 campaign for the White House on an equal rights platform combining women's rights with spiritualism, socialism, and free love, vocally endorsed the accusation against her brother, thus estranging herself from Mrs. Stowe.[41]

---

[37] Emanie Sachs, *The Terrible Siren: Victoria Woodhull* (New York, 1928), pp. 66–78, 121.
[38] Ibid., pp. 75–87; Andrews, pp. 36, 55.
[39] Harriet Beecher Stowe, *My Wife and I* (New York, 1871). That Audacia Dangereyes published a radical weekly like Mrs. Woodhull's was pointed out by Andrews, p. 264, n. 48.
[40] *Woodhull and Claflin's Weekly* III (July–November 1871).
[41] *Woodhull and Claflin's Weekly* VI (November 2, 1872), 8–13; Wilson, pp. 579–81; Andrews, pp. 33–41, 134–37; Sachs, pp. 168–77, 207, 217–18, 312–16.

Paying close and disgusted attention to the Beecher-Tilton scandal, Twain knew of Mrs. Woodhull's involvement in the affair, and he must have been aware of her leadership of organized spiritualism.[42] Indeed, she received vociferous support from the same Laura Cuppy who only a few years before had angered the *San Francisco Bulletin* by preaching spiritualism and passional freedom to the Friends of Progress.[43] As a western journalist Twain had genially protested against the *Bulletin*'s imputation of immorality and insanity to the spiritualists. But as a resident of Nook Farm, although he came to believe Henry Ward Beecher guilty as charged, he followed the example of Mrs. Stowe by refusing for a time to allow his wife to have anything to do with their other neighbor, Isabella Hooker.[44]

There is no record of any awareness on Twain's part of the embarrassment suffered by the spiritualists and by his friend Howells in the Katie King scandal. He probably knew of it, however. His first *Atlantic* contribution, "A True Story" (1874),[45] immediately adjoined Robert Dale Owen's first occult reminiscence;[46] and "Old Times on the Mississippi" (1875)[47] began two months later next to Owen's claims for Katie, responsibility for which the *Atlantic* denied with a special insert in the same issue.[48] At any rate, by 1880 Twain's former tolerance had soured to the point that he congratulated Howells for the mastery of "the nauseating professional slang of spiritism"[49] exhibited in *The Undiscovered Country*.

Perhaps most responsible for this caustic remark was Twain's own encounter with another professional spiritist. In *Mr. Clemens and*

---

[42] Justin Kaplan, *Mr. Clemens and Mark Twain: A Biography* (New York, 1966), pp. 157–58, 188–89; Andrews, pp. 134–37.

[43] Sachs, pp. 195, 207, 217–18.

[44] Andrews, pp. 39–40; Kaplan, pp. 157–58.

[45] Samuel Clemens, "A True Story," *Atlantic Monthly* XXXIV (November 1874), 591–94.

[46] Robert Dale Owen, "How I Came to Study Spiritual Phenomena. A Chapter of Autobiography," *Atlantic Monthly* XXXIV (November 1874), 578–90.

[47] Samuel Clemens, "Old Times on the Mississippi," *Atlantic Monthly* XXXV (January 1875), 69–73.

[48] Robert Dale Owen, "Touching Spiritual Visitants from a Higher Life. A Chapter of Autobiography," *Atlantic Monthly* XXXV (January 1875), 57–69.

[49] Clemens and Howells, *Mark Twain-Howells Letters: The Correspondence of Samuel L. Clemens and William Dean Howells, 1872–1910*, ed. Henry Nash Smith and William M. Gibson (Cambridge, Mass., 1960), I, 288.

Mark Twain: A Biography (1966), Justin Kaplan has concluded from an 1879 entry in Twain's notebook that the writer attempted to communicate with the spirit of his brother Henry Clemens through the mediumship of Mansfield.[50] Kaplan did not mention any literary consequence of this meeting. Yet although Twain disguised its personal nature, he recalled this very séance with evident anger in an anecdote about a fraudulent medium named Manchester in *Life on the Mississippi* (1883).[51]

There Twain told of learning in New Orleans in 1882 that an old river-pilot friend had become one of Manchester's gulls. For five dollars each, the pilot had received for over fifteen years weekly letters, via Manchester's inspired pen, from a dead relative in the spirit world. In a suppressed manuscript passage first printed by Willis Wager in 1944,[52] Twain recalled his own meeting with the medium: "I called on him once, ten years ago, with a couple of friends, to inquire after a distant relative, killed in a cyclone. I asked the questions, and my late relative wrote down the replies by the hand of the medium—I mean the medium *said* it was my relative. The conversation went something like this. . . ."[53] The questions and answers of seeker and spirit followed in the form of a dramatic dialogue.

Before publishing the book, however, Twain revised and expanded this introduction so as to indulge in invective against Manchester, to exaggerate the cause of his "distant relative's" death in tall-tale fashion, and (most pertinently) to pass himself off as merely an observer rather than the spirit's kin. The writer still claimed to have visited the medium with two friends ten years before. But now he said that one of his companions had tried to converse through spirit-writing with an uncle who had died after being blown three miles by a cyclone against a large tree which toppled in the process. Calling Manchester "the paltriest fraud alive," Twain proceeded to illustrate the medium's "sloppy twaddle"[54] by recapitulating his own questions and the inane answers of his relative in the guise of a dialogue between his friend

---

[50] Kaplan, p. 203; Kaplan, letter to the author, October 9, 1966.
[51] Clemens, *Life on the Mississippi*, pp. 481–85.
[52] Clemens, *Life on the Mississippi*, ed. Willis Wager (New York, 1944), pp. 416–17.
[53] Ibid., p. 416.
[54] Clemens, *Life on the Mississippi* (1883), p. 482.

and the friend's deceased uncle. The uncle described an afterlife of vapid conversation among the spirits. And although known while alive for his keen mind and perfect memory, as a ghost he was able to remember neither the date nor "the particularly violent and unusual"[55] circumstances of his cyclonic passing. The séance was a threadbare fraud.

It is plain that the medium whom Twain named as Mansfield in his notebook and then attacked as Manchester in *Life on the Mississippi* was James Vincent Mansfield, "the spirit postmaster." A participant in the Boston test séances of 1857 which had led Professors Peirce, Agassiz, and Horsford to condemn spiritualism as dangerous "to the truth of man and the purity of woman,"[56] Mansfield had welcomed Emma Hardinge to San Francisco in 1863 but evidently had returned to New York before Twain took an interest in Ada Foye's séances.[57] The mail-order scheme described in *Life on the Mississippi* was clearly Mansfield's. Twain wrote that Manchester's postage was "graduated by distance: from the local post-office in Paradise to New York, five dollars; from New York to St. Louis, three cents."[58] In 1872 Mansfield had advertised almost identical rates in Victoria Woodhull's newspaper: "Test Medium, answers sealed letters, at 361 Sixth Avenue, New York. Terms $5 and four three-cent stamps."[59] And in 1884 he was still passing along the messages he received "from the post-office of the soul across the silent sea, bounded by the coast lines of earth and the realms of immortality."[60]

Mansfield demonstrated his mediumistic power by returning, presumably unopened, his clients' "sealed" inquiries about dead loved ones, along with appropriate spirit-replies transcribed by his own pen. For customers like Twain's pilot, the medium continued to turn out spiritual effusions on a regularly scheduled basis. Before the Civil War

---

[55] Ibid., pp. 485, 482.
[56] "The Spiritualists Checkmated," *Harper's Weekly* I (July 11, 1857), 438; Britten, *Modern American Spiritualism*, pp. 185–94.
[57] Britten, *Modern American Spiritualism*, p. 456; Barnum, *Humbugs of the World*, p. 59.
[58] Clemens, *Life on the Mississippi* (1883), p. 481.
[59] *Woodhull and Claflin's Weekly* V (May 18, 1872), 13.
[60] Emma Hardinge Britten, *Nineteenth Century Miracles; or, Spirits and Their Work in Every Country of the Earth* (New York, 1884), p. 551.

Cornelius Felton of Harvard had accused him of opening the sealed letters, and P. T. Barnum had described several methods of doing so in *The Humbugs of the World* (1866), wryly noting that repeated exposure had not put this "humbug" out of business.[61] Indeed, not long after Twain attacked him in *Life on the Mississippi,* the medium's old friend Emma Hardinge Britten could testify to his continuing success: "Though the snows of many winters have bleached the once raven locks, the heart and hand of the good 'postmaster' are as devoted to the service of the angels, as in days of yore." Mansfield estimated, she said, that over a thirty-year period "he must have written over one hundred thousand answers to sealed letters at the direction of Spirits!"[62] No wonder, then, that Twain excoriated not only the medium, but also his foolish clients.

But what seems to have irritated Twain more than the pilot's gulling was the memory it recalled of his own visit to Mansfield. How well he remembered and how accurately he reported the occasion is open to question. His anecdote was consistent with Barnum's description of Mansfield's spirit-writing séances, even as to the test questions with which the medium had difficulty;[63] but the spirit replies recalled by Twain were far less imaginative than those which the Shakespearean scholar H. H. Furness was to receive (some in dialect) during his investigation of Mansfield in 1885 for the University of Pennsylvania's Seybert Commission on Spiritualism.[64] Comic touches throughout Twain's anecdote make it unlikely that he provided anything like an exact transcript of his encounter with the medium. Still, it is clear that the dialogue between Twain's unnamed friend and his friend's dead uncle (or, in the suppressed manuscript version, between Twain and his "distant relative") was actually a fictional account of Twain's own conversation with the spirit of Henry Clemens through Mansfield's mediumship. According to Justin Kaplan, Twain had jotted a brief reminder of that conversation in his 1879 notebook. Now he identified the medium with a pseudonym so flimsy as

61 Britten, *Modern American Spiritualism*, p. 252; Barnum, p. 60.
62 Britten, *Nineteenth Century Miracles*, pp. 551–52.
63 Barnum, pp. 60, 65–66.
64 [H. H. Furness,] *Preliminary Report of the Commission Appointed by the University of Pennsylvania to Investigate Modern Spiritualism in Accordance with the Request of the Late Henry Seybert* (Philadelphia, 1887), pp. 128–47.

to suggest that it was not for Mansfield's sake that the anecdote was revised for publication. Less obviously, he gave traces of Henry's identity to the dead uncle. In beginning the latter-day portion of *Life on the Mississippi*, Twain had quickly brought to an end the story of his antebellum life as a river pilot with a chapter called "A Catastrophe"[65] —an account of Henry's death as the result of a steamboat explosion. In remembering the séance he hyperbolically disguised that explosion as the uncle's "peculiarly violent and unusual" collision with a tree during a cyclone, and to his friend he delegated the question of whether the deceased had perished from natural causes or "a catastrophe." He exaggerated less in describing the uncle's memory as having been "absolutely defectless"[66] while he lived, for the studious Henry had possessed a reputation for total recall.[67]

Thus the real reason for Twain's indignation was probably his memory of the palpable imposture in which Mansfield had involved the spirit of the brother whose death had caused the humorist much grief and guilt. He had not wanted either his father or Henry to be misrepresented by sentimental gravestones when their remains were transferred to a new cemetery in 1876.[68] Particularly galling, then, must have been the inanities to which (if the séance was reported accurately) Henry had been reduced through the pencil of the spasmodically jerking Mansfield. As Twain reconstructed the occasion, his friend's uncle had told of an afterlife consisting only of conversation among the spirits about "how happy we are; and about friends left behind in the earth, and how to influence them for their good."[69] Eating, drinking, smoking, reading—all were unnecessary in the realm of virtuous souls.

When a clergyman's spirit in San Francisco had described a similar hereafter, Twain had attempted with good-natured irony to find out whether he was destined for the same place. Since that time, however, he had become impatient with such conceptions of immortality. For years he had been working intermittently on a manuscript—eventually

[65] Clemens, *Life on the Mississippi* (1883), pp. 236–45.
[66] Ibid., pp. 484, 485.
[67] Dixon Wecter, *Sam Clemens of Hannibal*, ed. Elizabeth Wecter (Boston, 1952), p. 130.
[68] Ibid., p. 119.
[69] Clemens, *Life on the Mississippi* (1883), p. 482.

published as *Extracts from Captain Stormfield's Visit to Heaven*
(1909)[70]—which was in part a burlesque of the sentimental version of
the afterlife he had noticed in Elizabeth Stuart Phelps's best-selling
The Gates Ajar (1869).[71] For his own brother to indicate through a
fraudulent medium that he was, as Twain put it, "content to spend
an eternity in frivolous employments"[72] might easily have provoked
the irascible writer to invective. In the manuscript version of the
séance, he remembered asking how long the spirit had been "a beati-
fied vegetable."[73] As he retold it in print, his friend had inquired
what he could do while still alive to make sure that he would avoid
such a heaven.

"Gus Graham" and some of the other spirits summoned by Ada
Foye in San Francisco had at least offered satisfactory proof of identity. But the spurious Henry had apparently lapsed into idiocy, for in
Twain's anecdote the ghostly uncle forgot even the date of his own
death and claimed (after much hesitation on the part of the medium's
pencil) to have died of natural causes. Upon receiving these responses
the nephew brought the séance to a close by sarcastically complaining
to the medium that his uncle had been permitted to take beyond the
grave not even a remnant of his powerful intellect and perfect memory. At this point Twain returned to the present to express further
anger at the medium's continued success at the expense of fools.

Twain's reconstruction of Mansfield's séance echoed the comic
séances of the literary comedians with such devices as the tall-tale
version of Henry's catastrophe, the casting into dramatic form of the
conversation between seeker and spirit, and the sarcasm of the seeker
mounting to a denunciation of the spirit's stupidity and the medium's
fraud. As for the fictional veil of the anecdote, a generation earlier
Charles Farrar Browne had attended at least one séance as a reporter
before sending Artemus Ward among the spirits to chat with his

---

[70] Samuel Clemens, *Extracts from Captain Stormfield's Visit to Heaven* (New
York, 1909).

[71] Elizabeth Stuart Phelps, *The Gates Ajar* (Boston, 1869). For Twain's reminiscence of burlesquing *The Gates Ajar*, see Samuel Clemens, *Mark Twain in Eruption*, ed. Bernard DeVoto (New York, 1940), pp. 246–47, and Samuel Clemens,
Report from Paradise, ed. Dixon Wecter (New York, 1952), p. xiii.

[72] Clemens, *Life on the Mississippi* (1883), p. 482.

[73] Clemens, *Life on the Mississippi*, ed. Willis Wager (1944), p. 416.

father; and Mortimer Thomson may have used his own experience as a basis for Q. K. Philander Doesticks's talk with *his* spurious uncle. By revising the episode so as to pose as an observer rather than a participant, Twain allowed his invective against Manchester to seem impersonally motivated, and perhaps thereby established the psychic distance from which he could make comically exaggerated satiric capital of an incident involving the death of his beloved Henry (that "distant relative") without risking public impropriety or private guilt.

Mansfield was just the sort of cheat already being or shortly to be delineated by Twain in the persons of the Duke and the Dauphin in *Adventures of Huckleberry Finn*. Although the novel was set too early in time for the two sharpers to lay claim to mediumship, some of their talents closely resembled Mansfield's. The Duke had been both mesmerist and phrenologist, and the Dauphin bragged of telling fortunes with the aid of an accomplice "to find out the facts"[74] about his customers ahead of time. Mansfield's methods of obtaining information about his correspondents and their dead relatives from "sealed letters" were similarly devious; on at least one occasion he was accused of furnishing a photographer with descriptions of the spirits their mutual customers sought to have photographed.[75]

Mansfield was not the only professional spiritualist Twain had met who fit the Dauphin's type. Walter Blair has suggested that the Dauphin's claim to experience in the "layin' on o' hands"[76] may have been a humorous allusion on Twain's part to J. R. Newton, the faith healer who had cured Olivia Clemens's adolescent neurasthenia.[77] Newton, who died in 1883, had once told Twain that his powers might be electrical in nature.[78] But whether or not he claimed spiritual inspiration when talking to Twain or dealing with Jervis Langdon, Newton was known to admiring believers and suspicious legal authorities alike as a spiritualistic physician. While in trance he had assured an audience of believers that through him Pythagoras, Socrates, and

[74] Clemens, *Huckleberry Finn*, p. 162.
[75] "Want of Confidence," *Religio-Philosophical Journal* XIII (October 5, 1872), 8.
[76] Clemens, *Huckleberry Finn*, p. 162.
[77] Walter Blair, *Mark Twain and Huck Finn* (Berkeley, 1960), pp. 21–22, 276; Samuel Clemens, *Mark Twain's Autobiography*, ed. Albert Bigelow Paine (New York, 1924), I, 104–5.
[78] Ibid.

Plato still walked the earth. His achievements, as well as those of Ada Foye and Mansfield, had been recorded in *Modern American Spiritualism* (1870)[79] by Emma Hardinge Britten, who was shortly to praise all three again in *Nineteenth Century Miracles* (1884),[80] penning sorrowful adjoining obituaries for Mansfield's wife and Newton.

Such connections may reveal only that Twain had come into contact at various times and places with the central structure of professional mediumship in America. But while no specific parallels need be urged at length, certainly Mansfield's name should be included in any list of what Walter Blair has called the "brazen cheats, diddlers, and confidence men"[81] in Twain's mind as he created the Duke and the Dauphin. Perhaps, too, his brief return to spiritualistic material in *Life on the Mississippi* had something to do with his burlesque of spiritual manifestations in the final section of *Huckleberry Finn*. For the moment, at least, his privately motivated attack on Mansfield repudiated his earlier professions of friendliness toward the spiritualists and publicly placed him in the camp of hostile skepticism.

III | Defenders and detractors of the Phelps farm episode of *Adventures of Huckleberry Finn* would agree that in these last twelve chapters of his greatest work Mark Twain returned, rightly or wrongly, to a kind of humor characteristic of his earlier writings. Walter Blair has shown that the efforts of Tom and Huck to liberate Jim constituted a burlesque of romantic escape literature punctuated by slapstick comedy of the Sut Lovingood sort.[82] What has escaped attention, however, is the less-obvious pattern of spiritualistic comedy in this controversial part of the novel. In fact, during their escapade at the Phelps farm Tom and Huck acted as unwitting poltergeists in a burlesque of spiritual manifestations reminiscent of sketches by Benjamin Shillaber and similar in many respects to the Stratford rappings of 1850.

---

[79] Britten, *Modern American Spiritualism*, pp. 150, 186, 198–201, 252, 456–57.
[80] Britten, *Nineteenth Century Miracles*, pp. 175–81, 241–45, 464–65, 469–72, 551.
[81] Blair, p. 269.
[82] Ibid., p. 350.

Blair has demonstrated that Shillaber's sharp-tongued but affectionate Mrs. Partington and her scapegrace nephew Ike served Twain as partial models for Aunt Polly and Tom in *The Adventures of Tom Sawyer* (1876).[83] One of the parallels between Ike and Tom mentioned in passing by Will D. Howe in *The Cambridge History of American Literature* (1918)[84] involved the spiritualistic mischief with which Ike had teased his aunt in Shillaber's sketches. Ike had posed as his Uncle Paul's apparition, had caused a teapot to float in the air next to Paul's portrait, and from inside a trunk had rapped out a disrespectful message in his uncle's name.[85] With these practical jokes and Mrs. Partington's credulous reactions, staple comic situations had taken on a spiritualistic slant; and Mrs. Partington's modulation from anger to forgiveness upon discovering the truth had appealed to sentiment. Similarly, Tom Sawyer tormented Aunt Polly by allowing her to think him dead, and she responded to his "materialization" at his own funeral, and to his subsequent explanation of the prank, with a Partingtonian mixture of love, anger, and hurt feelings. Thus the funeral section of *Tom Sawyer* resembled Shillaber's spiritualistic sketches in pattern, if not precisely in substance.

Twain used that pattern again, elaborating it at length, when he returned to the manner of *Tom Sawyer* for the Phelps farm episode of *Huckleberry Finn*. Attempting to liberate Jim according to the conventions of romantic escape, Tom and Huck harassed the Phelps family with thefts, warnings, and other mystifications resembling the pranks of the earlier Tom and of Ike Partington. With her malapropisms, her irritability, and her forgiveness for the scamps, Aunt Sally Phelps was traced from the models of Aunt Polly and Mrs. Partington.

This time, however, Twain made it clear that Tom and Huck were comic poltergeists. Arriving at the Phelps farm feeling the melancholy presence of "spirits,"[86] Huck was reborn as Tom Sawyer, and shortly thereafter the real Tom thought Huck a "ghost"[87] come back to haunt.

[83] Ibid., pp. 62–64.
[84] William Peterfield Trent, John Erskine, Stuart P. Sherman, and Carl Van Doren, eds., *The Cambridge History of American Literature* (New York, 1918), II, 155.
[85] Benjamin P. Shillaber, *Life and Sayings of Mrs. Partington and Others of the Family* (New York, 1854), pp. 51–53, 83, 347–48.
[86] Clemens, *Huckleberry Finn*, p. 277.
[87] Ibid., p. 284.

Boyish ghostlore and talk of "spirits" had figured throughout *Tom Sawyer* and the earlier chapters of *Huckleberry Finn*,[88] of course, and would not of themselves require a spiritualistic frame of reference. What explicitly defined the boys' roles as poltergeists, rather, was Aunt Sally's reaction to the hocus-pocus concocted by Tom to free Jim. In Twain's "Kearny Street Ghost Story," servant girls had been frightened by ghostly antics which San Francisco spiritualists had cited as evidence for their beliefs.[89] Now, as a result of the mysterious phenomena which afflicted them, the entire Phelps family became fearfully nervous. Huck noted that after Tom's first anonymous warnings of trouble the family "couldn't a been worse scared if the place had a been full of ghosts laying for them behind everything and under the beds and shivering through the air."[90] Aunt Sally jumped at noises and unexpected physical contact, felt a presence always at her back, "was afraid to go to bed," and yet "dasn't set up."[91] And when she summarized for her excited neighbors the strange happenings in her household—a shirt, spoons, flour, candles, candlesticks, a warming pan, a dress, and Jim himself had been stolen from under the family's watchful eyes—she knew who to blame: "Why, *sperits* couldn't a done better, and been no smarter. And I reckon they must a *been* sperits—because, *you* know our dogs, and ther' ain't no better; well, them dogs never even got on the *track* of 'm once! You explain *that* to me if you can!"[92] Neither Tom nor Huck, of course, had intended this ghostly effect; for the moment it was simply the only way in which Aunt Sally could interpret their complicated "evasion."[93] By thus explaining how she could have been taken in by so outlandish a scheme, Twain's bogus spiritual manifestations (like those of earlier humorists) satirized adult credulity at the same time that his burlesque of escape literature made sport of Tom's derring-do.

Just how pervasive the note of poltergeist farce was in these chapters may be illustrated by comparing the experiences of Silas Phelps and his family during the visit of Tom and Huck with the indignities in-

88 Blair, pp. 104–5.
89 Clemens, *The Washoe Giant*, pp. 120–21.
90 Clemens, *Huckleberry Finn*, p. 338.
91 Ibid.
92 Ibid., p. 351.
93 Ibid., p. 337.

flicted by a mischievous spirit on the household of the Reverend Eliakim Phelps during the Stratford rappings of 1850.

Real and fictional Phelpses had a good deal more than surname in common. Eliakim was a respected old minister of distinguished New England stock—a lineal descendant of one William Phelps, who had come to America in 1630. While Eliakim was easily convinced of the supramundane and probably demonic character of the rappings (as was his son Austin, a professor at Andover Seminary), the same phenomena were hailed by the spiritualists as dramatic confirmation of the Fox sisters' revelations at Rochester. More skeptical observers, however, quietly blamed the childish disturbances on two of the minister's recently acquired stepchildren, a boy of eleven and a girl of sixteen.[94] It is true that Mark Twain's Silas Phelps was a Mississippi Valley farmer without stepchildren. But he was a lay preacher with his own log church; he was proud that his ancestors had arrived "with William the Conqueror in the *Mayflower* or one of them early ships"; and he was extremely gullible—"the innocentest, best old soul"[95] Huck had ever known. With his family and eventually his neighbors, Silas was completely taken in by the strange events which began shortly after the arrival of his "nephews," Tom and Huck.

Although some of these happenings were not at all like those at Stratford, the two cases shared straw-stuffed dummies, irrepressible sheets and spoons, captious nails and candlesticks, anonymous letters, and mysterious writings in unknown tongues. The Stratford ghost constructed life-size dummies by stuffing Eliakim's clothing with cloth and straw. Among other things, he dashed a brass candlestick to pieces; he dropped a key and a nail out of the air at the minister's feet; he repeatedly removed Mrs. Phelps's spoons from under lock and key, placing them on the table or bending them double and straightening them out again; and he took laundry from a locked cupboard, espe-

---

[94] Oliver Seymour Phelps and Andrew T. Servin, *The Phelps Family of America* (Pittsfield, Mass., 1899), I, 537–38; Austin Phelps's memoir of the rappings in Charles Beecher, *Spiritual Manifestations*, pp. 18–24; Samuel W. Johnson, "Spiritualism Tested by Science," *New Englander* XVI (May 1858), 263; Frank Podmore, *Modern Spiritualism: A History and a Criticism* (London, 1902), I, 194–201.

[95] Clemens, *Huckleberry Finn*, pp. 322, 286.

cially one sheet which reappeared each time Eliakim shut it away.[96]

Events in *Huckleberry Finn* resembling this random mischief were calculated steps in Tom's plan for Jim's escape. Tom and Huck drove Uncle Silas and Aunt Sally to distraction by appropriating one of Silas's shirts on which Jim could keep a journal; tin plates on which he could scratch messages; a brass candlestick, a spoon, and some shingle-nails for his writing instruments; and one of Sally's sheets for his rope ladder. Like the Stratford ghost, the boys broke the candlestick into pieces. When they tried to smuggle writing tools to Jim by means of Silas, the bewildered old man found the missing spoon in his coat pocket, and the nail they hid in his hatband fell on the floor at his feet. They had better luck setting Aunt Sally to counting her spoons over and over, while Huck kept taking one and replacing it, until she gave up in frustration; it was an easy matter, then, to slip one into her pocket along with a nail for Jim to retrieve later. Similarly, after Sally became aware that one of her sheets was missing, they returned it to the clothesline and took another from the closet, and like the Stratford spirit "kept on putting it back and stealing it again . . . till she didn't know how many sheets she had. . . ."[97] Although the boys did not match the Stratford poltergeist's dramatic tableaux, Tom did make a straw-filled dummy out of Jim's clothes to mislead their pursuers.

Just as Eliakim Phelps could not recognize the "regular schoolboy's hand"[98] responsible for the puerile written communications which appeared from out of nowhere in his parsonage, so Twain's Silas and Sally failed to see through the warnings left under their door and on their sleeping watchman's neck by an "Unknown Friend."[99] Indeed, it was their reaction to the first of these messages which led Huck to say that they "couldn't a been worse scared if the place had a been full of ghosts. . . ."[100] Despite the triviality of the Stratford poltergeist's messages—he rapped out a demand for pumpkin pie and, in the words of

[96] Austin Phelps in Beecher, *Spiritual Manifestations*, pp. 18–24; Podmore, I, 194–201; Elizabeth Stuart Phelps, "The Day of My Death," *Men, Women, and Ghosts* (Boston, 1869), pp. 113–60.
[97] Clemens, *Huckleberry Finn*, p. 321.
[98] Podmore, I, 200.
[99] Clemens, *Huckleberry Finn*, pp. 337, 338.
[100] Ibid., p. 338.

Eliakim's son Austin, appeared "to be specially *down on* St. Paul"[101]— Eliakim's servants were terrified. Twain, of course, had already written about similarly frightened servants in "The Kearny Street Ghost Story." Now the slave who tended Jim, convinced from the start that "witches was pestering him awful, these nights, and making him see all kinds of strange things, and hear all kinds of strange words and noises," was easily led by Tom into letting the boys protect him with the "witch pie"[102] containing Jim's rope ladder and tin plates.

There were also what seemed to be unintelligible writings at Stratford. Turnips carved with mysterious characters dropped from the ceiling; a piece of shingle flew about, covered with strange symbols; sentences appeared on the walls; and the trousers of Eliakim's stepson Harry turned up bearing hieroglyphic scrawls. Some observers detected demonic spirits in the parsonage, and skeptical investigators decided that Harry was responsible. But Andrew Jackson Davis, the Poughkeepsie seer, reached a different conclusion. Going into trance, he read the exotic inscriptions on the turnips and Harry's trousers as indications that angelic beings were attempting to communicate with mortals.[103]

Equally mysterious writings were discovered in Twain's Pikesville. Jim inscribed meaningless symbols on tin plates, scratched marks on the wall of his cabin, and kept his bloody journal not on trousers but on Silas's shirt. Brother Marples, one of the neighbors who gathered to marvel at Jim's escape and to suggest various theories, thought that an entire houseful of slaves must have been at work, and he offered to pay two dollars for a translation of the "secret African writ'n" on the shirt. It was at this point that Aunt Sally, reviewing the events leading up to Jim's disappearance, decided that "*sperits* couldn't a done better. . . . And I reckon they must a *been* sperits. . . ."[104]

These parallels between *Huckleberry Finn* and the Stratford phenomena may have been accidental. Yet Twain probably knew some-

[101] Austin Phelps in Beecher, *Spiritual Manifestations*, p. 23.

[102] Clemens, *Huckleberry Finn*, p. 314.

[103] Austin Phelps in Beecher, *Spiritual Manifestations*, pp. 20, 22; Podmore, I, 195–97.

[104] Clemens, *Huckleberry Finn*, p. 351. After the boys' tricks were explained to the befuddled Silas, he preached an unintelligible sermon that gave him "a rattling ruputation" (ibid., p. 362).

thing of Eliakim Phelps and his celebrated rappings. During the early 1850's, after all, they had yielded precedence only to the Rochester rappings of the Fox sisters, which Twain had mentioned in an 1853 letter to his mother.[105] James Russell Lowell had spoken of the Stratford ghost in his comic poem about poltergeist pranks, "The Unhappy Lot of Mr. Knott" (1851). Benjamin Shillaber had devised similar tricks for Ike Partington to play on his aunt. As for the durability of their reputation, Eliakim's granddaughter Elizabeth Stuart Phelps was to say in 1891 that for almost four decades the Stratford disturbances had "haunted the columns of the American press,"[106] and Twain's friend Howells was to speak knowingly of them in a discussion of similar events as late as 1912.[107]

No such reach of memory may have been required of Twain as he hurried to finish *Huckleberry Finn* in the summer of 1883. We can only wonder whether talk of J. V. Mansfield's foolish victims during the previous year's Mississippi journey could have led Twain's stenographer, Roswell Phelps of Hartford, another lineal descendant of William Phelps, to mention Eliakim's gullibility.[108] We do know, however, that Eliakim's son Austin and his granddaughter Elizabeth Stuart Phelps had written relatively recent accounts of the Stratford rappings. And it is altogether possible that Twain's skeptical observations of spiritualism at Nook Farm, along with his admitted dislike of the sentimental depiction of immortality in Miss Phelps's *Gates Ajar*, could have led him to make sport of the rappings in his novel.

In 1879 (the same year that Twain had mentioned the fraudulent Mansfield séance in his notebook) Austin Phelps had recollected the Stratford rappings in a memoir which formed the second chapter of Charles Beecher's *Spiritual Manifestations*.[109] Among other things, the professor of sacred rhetoric and homiletics at Andover Seminary remembered stuffed dummies made of his father's clothing, spoons

[105] Brashear, p. 154.

[106] Elizabeth Stuart Phelps, *Austin Phelps: A Memoir* (New York, 1891), p. 5.

[107] William Dean Howells, "Editor's Easy Chair," *Harper's* CXXV (November 1912), 959.

[108] Phelps and Servin, *The Phelps Family in America*, II, 1251. Roswell Phelps had continued to work for Twain at least until May, 1883 (Clemens and Howells, *Mark Twain-Howells Letters*, I, 393, 432).

[109] Charles Beecher, *Spiritual Manifestations*, pp. 18–24.

manipulated by invisible agency, a key and nail mysteriously dropped at the minister's feet, and a spirit's request for pie. Despite such "consummate pettiness,"[110] he explicitly rejected the old accusations that it was all "a roguish trick of the boys"[111] (his stepbrothers), fixing responsibility instead on deceitful spirits.[112]

Phelps's contribution to Beecher's *Spiritual Manifestations* must have interested some of Twain's Nook Farm neighbors. Beecher's sister Mrs. Stowe had probably heard the story during her husband's tenure at Andover. And the very next chapter of Beecher's volume was given over to Mrs. Stowe's curious narrative of her own conversations in 1868 with the spirits of Charlotte Bronte and the Duchess of Sutherland.[113] As an increasingly devout spiritualist, moreover, Isabella Beecher Hooker was surely aware of her half-brother's book. The breach between Mrs. Hooker and the rest of Nook Farm had partially healed by the end of the 1870's, and the wife of Twain's friend and former collaborator Charles Dudley Warner may already have begun to seek ghostly advice through her occult neighbor.[114] Mrs. Hooker was a steady patron of professional mediums; early in 1885 she was to introduce one of her favorites to Florence Marryat, the English believer who found the American atmosphere conducive to materializations.[115] That Twain himself kept a skeptical eye on such goings-on was indicated by his 1880 reference to a "Gammer Hooker" who was possessed of a "legion"[116] of devils. Years later, in fact, while writing an episode of séance comedy for one of his Mysterious Stranger narratives, he was to note that Mrs. Hooker and her husband had been instructed by their spiritual guide "what to eat, drink, think, believe ... & what to wear & how to vote."[117] Might not his mordant glance have also taken in the comic potential of the events related by Austin Phelps?

A decade before her father's account of rappings, Elizabeth Stuart

---

[110] Ibid., p. 24.
[111] Ibid., p. 19.
[112] Ibid., p. 24.
[113] Ibid., pp. 25–36.
[114] Andrews, *Nook Farm*, pp. 59–63.
[115] Florence Marryat, *There Is No Death* (New York, 1891), p. 238.
[116] Andrews, pp. 191–92, 244; Blair, p. 407, n. 3.
[117] Clemens, *Mark Twain's Mysterious Stranger Manuscripts*, p. 444.

Phelps (another Andover resident and friend of Mrs. Stowe) had incorporated Eliakim's sufferings into a tale for *Harper's*, "The Day of My Death" (1868).[118] Replacing her grandfather with a whimsical lay narrator named Hotchkiss, she included the same dummies, spoons, falling key, and demand for pie later recalled by her father, along with an errant sheet and other laundry that refused to stay locked away. Hotchkiss told of his experiences with a good deal of humor (certainly with more geniality than Sally Phelps's shrewish neighbor, Sister Hotchkiss, displayed in discussing the Pikesville disturbances in Twain's novel). But although belittling the spiritualistic cult, he accepted the phenomena as authentic and inexplicable. Not surprisingly, so did the author. Collecting the story in *Men, Women, and Ghosts* (1869),[119] she said that the incidents had been given to her by "eyewitnesses whose testimony would command a verdict from any honest jury."[120]

Long before *Huckleberry Finn*, Twain had entered his own secret verdict against Elizabeth Stuart Phelps. His onetime friend Bret Harte had commended her story of the rappings in an 1869 review of both *Men, Women, and Ghosts* and her best-selling *Gates Ajar*.[121] But the latter work had so offended Twain with its "mean little ten cent heaven about the size of Rhode Island"[122] that by 1870 he had burlesqued it in the first draft of a narrative which was not to see daylight until 1909 as *Extracts from Captain Stormfield's Visit to Heaven*. Late in his life he was to remember that the burlesque character of this work-in-progress had kept him from accepting Howells's advice that he publish it in the early 1870's, and he had returned to it intermit-

---

[118] Elizabeth Stuart Phelps, "The Day of My Death," *Harpers* XXXVII (October 1868), 621–32.

[119] E. S. Phelps, *Men, Women, and Ghosts*, pp. 113–60.

[120] Ibid., p. 113. Miss Phelps had given essentially the same explanation to Kate Field, saying that the testimony was sufficient "to hang a regiment" (Whiting, *Kate Field: A Record*, p. 164). Kate Field had written *Planchette's Diary* (New York, 1868); Mrs. Stowe had planned an *Atlantic* article on the subject in 1868, long before contributing an account of her experiences with it to Charles Beecher's *Spiritual Manifestations*; and Elizabeth Stuart Phelps, who had known Mrs. Stowe at Andover, also wrote "Planchette," *Watchman and Reflector* XXXIX (September 3, 1868), 5.

[121] [Bret Harte,] "Current Literature," *Overland Monthly* III (September 1869), 292–93.

[122] Clemens, *Mark Twain in Eruption*, p. 247.

tently throughout that decade.[123] His Hartford crony Joseph Twichell may have been able to supply grist for this slow-grinding mill, for after mustering out as a Union Army chaplain Twichell had completed his ministerial studies at Andover while Miss Phelps was writing *The Gates Ajar* to assuage her grief over the death of a Union officer.[124] Whether or not Twain was also piqued by her next, more fanciful effort in the same vein, *Beyond the Gates* (1883),[125] he was still tinkering with *Captain Stormfield* in 1883.[126] Long reluctant to subject Miss Phelps's saccharine vision of the afterlife to public attack, perhaps he found irresistible the opportunity to make veiled sport of her grandfather's rappings in *Huckleberry Finn*.

Even if we grant Twain's knowlege of the Stratford rappings, that it manifested itself in *Huckleberry Finn* might be thought inconclusive. Yet the overall force of the parallels cannot easily be discounted. According to Walter Blair, as Twain rushed to finish his novel in a mood of "reckless improvisation,"[127] he took great pleasure in working out the tricks played by Tom and Huck on Uncle Silas and Aunt Sally. Given his long-suppressed contempt for Elizabeth Stuart Phelps, his impatience with Nook Farm's occultism and with spiritualistic sentimentality in general, and his barely disguised attack on J. V. Mansfield and Mansfield's foolish victims only a year earlier in *Life on the Mississippi*, it seems fair to conclude that on the basis of what he remembered of the Stratford rappings (from whatever sources) he improvised some remarkably similar disturbances for Tom and Huck to inflict on another gullible Phelps family.

To see in Huck's adventure at the Phelps farm a comic version of the ghostly absurdities tolerated at Stratford, Andover, and Nook Farm will not rectify the episode for readers who find it defective. Such a view is consistent, however, with Twain's treatment of tricksters and gulls throughout the novel, and it points up the contrast be-

---

[123] Ibid., pp. 246–47; Clemens and Howells, *Mark Twain-Howells Letters*, I, 236, 238, 250, 376.

[124] Andrews, *Nook Farm*, p. 14; Mary Angela Bennett, *Elizabeth Stuart Phelps* (Philadelphia, 1939), p. 45.

[125] Elizabeth Stuart Phelps, *Beyond the Gates* (Boston, 1883).

[126] Clemens, *Mark Twain's Notebook*, ed. Albert Bigelow Paine (New York, 1935), pp. 168–69.

[127] Blair, p. 350.

tween the trivial supernaturalism of riverbank society and the potent natural magic invoked by Jim and Huck on the river; the two fugitives, after all, shared neither Tom's romantic enthusiasms nor Aunt Sally's superstitious response. Would it not be richly ironic, moreover, if Aunt Sally, married to a slave-holding preacher of New England descent, feared slave-robbing "sperits" taken by Twain from the lore of spiritualism, that peculiarly Yankee and often (in prewar days) abolitionist form of occultism still practiced by some of his ex-abolitionist neighbors? (In writing one of his Mysterious Stranger narratives, Twain was to make note of Isabella Beecher Hooker's spiritualism, along with Orion Clemens's faddism, in sketching a slave-holder who was both a foolish believer in the Fox sisters and a theoretical abolitionist too innocuous for his fellow townsmen to lynch.)[128] Whatever its critical ramifications, the Phelps hypothesis does offer cogent personal reasons for Twain's tomfoolery in making these chapters a burlesque of spurious poltergeists in the tradition of Lowell, Shillaber, and his own "Kearny Street Ghost Story."

IV | Twain's later works showed an increasingly speculative interest in all sorts of psychical phenomena. Under the stress of his own or his wife's grief, moreover, he was even willing to accompany her to séances after the death of their daughter Susy in 1896. Yet it was still the amusing or vexing aspects of spiritualism which claimed his attention in *The American Claimant* (1892) and the unfinished Mysterious Stranger narrative, "Schoolhouse Hill" (1898).

Rather than Howells, it was probably Twain, with Huck Finn as poltergeist immediately behind him, who suggested the humorous possibilities of spirit materialization for "Colonel Sellers as a Scientist,"[129] the ill-fated stage comedy on which the pair collaborated in the fall of 1883. Sellers's nonsensical invention for raising the dead by means of electric batteries was only one of the farcical devices rather ineffectively assembled by the two writers. Twain was much taken with the notion, however, for in *The American Claimant* (1892),[130] the hastily

[128] Clemens, *Mark Twain's Mysterious Stranger Manuscripts*, pp. 206, 411, 444.
[129] Howells, *The Complete Plays of W. D. Howells*, ed. Walter J. Meserve (New York, 1960), pp. 205–41; Clemens and Howells, *Mark Twain-Howells Letters*, I, 447.
[130] Samuel Clemens, *The American Claimant* (New York, 1892).

written novel based on the play, he relied on materialization to characterize Sellers as a self-deluded entrepreneur of the occult. With invective reminiscent of his creator's earlier diatribe against J. V. Mansfield, Sellers was properly contemptuous of the ordinary séance in which "ignorant charlatans" titillated "sentimental gulls" by impersonating spirits ranging from dead relatives to John Milton and Siamese twins. As a "scientist," however, the Colonel hoped to mass produce materialized ghosts for mankind's benefit and his own profit: a cheap and indestructible police force for New York City; Greek and Roman legions to pursue Indians on "materialized horses"; and experienced statesmen for "a Congress that knows enough to come in out of the rain. . . ." A comic Frankenstein, he even thought of killing his talkative servants so as to render them "adjustable—with a screw or something."[131] Beneath these amusing echoes of the humorous rappings of an earlier day, there were chilling implications in a version of spiritualism governed by commercial and technological rather than religious or consolatory imperatives. Even at the level of farce, unfortunately, the Colonel's stubborn faith in his sketchily described invention marked him as a madman or fool rather than the loveable eccentric (originally inspired by Orion Clemens)[132] Twain evidently had in mind.

Materialization also supplied a Twainian mistaken identity which was important for the novel's romantic subplot and international theme. Like Tom and Huck, a young English nobleman unwittingly played a spirit's part when he was taken for the ghostly ancestor of a dead bank-robber whom the Colonel was trying to raise from the grave and turn in for repeated rewards. According to Sellers the materialization was simply incomplete: "*Every man is made up of heredities*, long-descended atoms and particles of his ancestors. We have only brought it down to perhaps the beginning of this century. . . . We've materialized this burglar's ancestor!"[133] Clyde L. Grimm has suggested that the descent from British aristocrat to American criminal implicit in Sellers's genetic explanation reflected Twain's serious concern about the possibility that English character had degenerated in democratic

131 Ibid., pp. 44, 45, 82.
132 Clemens and Howells, *Mark Twain-Howells Letters*, I, 246.
133 Clemens, *The American Claimant*, p. 193.

America over the course of the nineteenth century.[134] The Englishman, of course, was Viscount Berkeley, son of the Earl of Rossmore,
and he had come to America to investigate the Colonel's status as the
"American claimant" to the Rossmore title.

A series of comic shudders followed as the "materializee" displayed
a sickening appetite for food, embraced Sellers's daughter ("Oh, my
God, she's kissing it!"),[135] and eventually won her hand. Here Twain
was perhaps making sport of the morbid and potentially scandalous
séance-marriages which did occasionally take place between living persons and spirits supposedly returned in the flesh.[136] The Colonel's
daughter was saved from such a fate by the revelation of the "materializee's" identity. The Colonel's claim to the Rossmore title was vicar-
iously satisfied, and the best of American and British stock were united
in the wedding of the lovers—but nothing could rescue *The American
Claimant* from its just reputation as one of Twain's least-inspired
performances.

Characteristically, although he satirically identified Colonel Sellers
as a "Hypnotizer" and "Mind-Cure dabbler" as well as a "Materializer," Twain was dabbling in the mind cure himself, thinking it a kind
of hypnosis.[137] (He also still had hopes for the Paige typesetter, an invention which was eventually to prove no more reliable than Sellers's
materialization process.) From boyhood, of course, Twain had been
fascinated by a wide variety of psychical phenomena. Toward the end
of the century, as the study of hypnosis, telepathy, apparitions, and
dream states became respectable through the efforts of psychologists
and psychical researchers, he came like many other writers to make
increasingly unashamed literary use of such mysteries. He credited the

[134] Clyde L. Grimm, "*The American Claimant*: Reclamation of a Farce," *American Quarterly* XIX (Spring 1967), 101.

[135] Clemens, *The American Claimant*, p. 224.

[136] In 1879 J. V. Mansfield had officiated at the wedding of two materialized
spirits, one of whom was the son of Franklin Pierce (Earl Wesley Fornell, *The
Unhappy Medium: Spiritualism and the Life of Margaret Fox* [Austin, Tex., 1964],
pp. 150–51). An intensely imagined rather than fleshly ceremony between a young
man and a dead girl occurred, evidently in a séance, in Henry James's "Maude-
Evelyn" (1900). See *The Ghostly Tales of Henry James*, ed. Leon Edel (New
Brunswick, N.J., 1948), pp. 598–629.

[137] Clemens, *The American Claimant*, p. 28; Kaplan, pp. 326–27.

work of the Society for Psychical Research with having made possible the publication in "Mental Telegraphy" (1891) of a telepathic experience which he had left out of *A Tramp Abroad* (1880) for fear of public disbelief.[138] The long dream back into time which transported his Connecticut Yankee to Camelot was not too different a device from the trance which took the hero of Edward Bellamy's *Looking Backward: 2000–1887* (1888) into the utopian future. A growing obsession with his own dream life led Twain in the 1890's to write the chaotic psychical fantasies which have only recently been published in full; at the same time, his Mysterious Stranger narratives reflected his interest in apparitions and multiple personality.[139] And whereas in 1880 he had glanced cynically at "Gammer Hooker's" subjection to a "legion" of devils,[140] he now wrote a sympathetic account of a young heroine governed by what she thought were angelic voices in *Personal Recollections of Joan of Arc* (1896).[141] Joan's auditory mediumship was merely reported by Twain's unanalytic narrator; it remained for Henry James to dramatize the consciousness of another young woman of high mission in touch with allegedly supernatural beings—the governess of "The Turn of the Screw" (1898).[142]

Joan of Arc turned out to be a memorial for Susy Clemens, who died in the summer of 1896. Twain's suspicion of mediumistic impostures like J. V. Mansfield's impersonation of Henry Clemens must have softened somewhat after the loss of his favorite daughter, for during the following winter he and his wife consulted a pair of London seeresses recommended by Henry James's friends F. W. H. Myers and Andrew Lang, both of whom were leading figures in the field of psychical research. How seriously Twain sought such consolation for himself is not clear; certainly he found none, though, for in a letter of 1901 he more humorously than bitterly recalled one of the mediums as deceit-

[138] Samuel Clemens, *In Defense of Harriet Shelley and Other Essays* (New York, 1929), p. 111.
[139] Samuel Clemens, *Mark Twain's Which Was the Dream?*, ed. John S. Tuckey (Berkeley, 1967); Clemens, *Mark Twain's Notebook*, pp. 348–52; John S. Tuckey, *Mark Twain and Little Satan: The Writing of "The Mysterious Stranger"* (West Lafayette, Ind., 1963), pp. 26–28; William M. Gibson, "Introduction," in Clemens, *Mark Twain's Mysterious Stranger Manuscripts*, pp. 26–33.
[140] Andrews, *Nook Farm*, pp. 191–92, 244.
[141] Samuel Clemens, *Personal Recollections of Joan of Arc* (New York, 1896).
[142] James, *The Ghostly Tales of Henry James*, pp. 425–550.

ful, the other as inane, and he described Myers as an uncritical spiritualist. Politely expressing a willingness to investigate further, he said
that neither he nor his wife had ever received a convincing spirit-
communication.[143]

Whatever Twain's motive in attending them, the séances which followed Susy's death did nothing to inhibit his sense of spiritualistic
comedy. Only two years later he returned with obvious enjoyment to
old patterns of poltergeist and séance burlesque in the never-finished
"Schoolhouse Hill" (1898).[144] In this attempt to tell the story of the
Mysterious Stranger, he nostalgically re-created the Hannibal of his
youth once again, placing a young Satan named Forty-four in Tom
Sawyer's St. Petersburg at about the year 1850. In the second half of the
narrative, Forty-four utterly mystified Oliver Hotchkiss, his St. Petersburg host, by changing costumes at will although he had arrived without baggage; by replacing a tallow candlestick with a wax taper of a
purity unknown in the village; by seeing in the dark, charming the
watchdog, and talking to the ferocious housecat. Terrifying Hotchkiss's house-slaves, who believed in "bewitchments,"[145] the boy's innocent behavior resembled the ghostly tricks played by Tom and Huck
on the Phelpses in *Huckleberry Finn*. Aunt Sally, for instance, had
noted that the slave-robbing "sperits" had escaped the notice of her
watchdogs, and Jim's guard had complained of being pestered by
witches. The difference was that Forty-four was a genuinely supernatural being rather than a spurious poltergeist, and that he appeared
in an explicitly spiritualistic household. For his host, Hotchkiss, was
not simply a fearful believer in "sperits." He was a chronic enthusiast
whose latest religion was "the Fox-girl Rochester rappings."[146] (For
once Twain explicitly linked spiritualism with reform, identifying
Hotchkiss also as an ineffectual abolitionist.)[147] And when Forty-four
was thought dead in a blizzard, Hotchkiss attempted to call up the
boy's spirit in a séance.

[143] Samuel Clemens, *Mark Twain's Letters*, ed. Albert Bigelow Paine (New York,
1917), II, 706–7; Clara Clemens, *My Father: Mark Twain* (New York, 1931),
p. 184.
[144] Clemens, *Mark Twain's Mysterious Stranger Manuscripts*, pp. 175–220.
[145] Ibid., p. 196.
[146] Ibid., p. 191.
[147] Ibid., pp. 206, 411.

It is clear from Twain's working notes for "Schoolhouse Hill" that his brother Orion served as the chief model for the faddistic Hotchkiss. It may be that the mercurial Orion had passed through a spirit-rapping phase; notes of what evidently were Hannibal memories included the mediumistic rope trick of the Davenport brothers. But probably more pertinent to Hotchkiss's rapt faith in séance revelations (and an indication, perhaps, that Nook Farm's occultism could have found its way into *Huckleberry Finn*) was a note on the absolute dependence of Isabella Beecher Hooker and her husband on their spirit guide, who had instructed them "what to eat, drink, think, believe . . . & what to wear & how to vote." As Twain remarked of both Orion and the Hookers, Hotchkiss had begun as a Presbyterian.[148]

In composing the "Schoolhouse Hill" séance, however, Twain was guided more by well-remembered burlesque conventions than by memories of enthusiasts like Orion and the Hookers, or mediums like the Davenports, Mansfield, and the recent London seeresses. The first rappings elicited by Hotchkiss consisted of interminable poetry from the spirit of Byron, who was plausibly identified as "the most active poet on the other side of the grave in those days," but whose jingling verses showed that "his mind had decayed since he died."[149] Byron's effusions were followed by ill-informed excuses for Waterloo from Napoleon (who, like the spirit uncle of the Manchester séance, had a bad memory for dates), negligible offerings from Shakespeare, and messages from ancient Romans who curiously were able to rap in English. These comic shades of the 1850's were entirely appropriate, of course, to the narrative's mid-century setting.

Finally Forty-four himself rapped thunderously on the table. Unlike the ghostly "Smiths" of San Francisco, who had complained about their infernal abode, the boyish Satan shattered spiritualistic precedent and startled his auditors by saying that he was quite happy in hell. He quickly brought the séance to the familiar chaotic climax by obliging Hotchkiss's request that he materialize. The superstitious house-slaves forced by Hotchkiss to clasp hands with him around the table were thrown into shrieking consternation by the boy's sudden

[148] Ibid., pp. 411, 432, 436, 444, 190–91.
[149] Ibid., p. 206.

appearance in their midst. But their master, in the manner of Howells's Dr. Boynton or Twain's own Colonel Sellers, ecstatically hailed Forty-four's return as a triumph for his cause: *"Now* let the doubter doubt and the scoffer scoff if they want to—but they've had their day!"[150] As usual, however, the spiritual hypothesis failed, for the underworld "spirit" announced that he was very much alive. Soon Hotchkiss was overwhelmed with revelations far beyond the scope of the inane rapping ghosts; burlesque gave way to the satiric theological and cosmological fantasy at the heart of the Mysterious Stranger narratives as the boy disclosed at length that he was Satan's child, come to mitigate the curse his father had brought down on mankind. The story broke off with a glimpse of an efficient little red devil summoned by Forty-four to wait on Hotchkiss.

The juxtaposition of foolish rappings with Forty-four's astonishing story and marvelous powers may have owed something to Twain's recent encounters with spiritualism and psychical research in London. John S. Tuckey has shown that the figure of Satan in the Mysterious Stranger tales, with his ability to transcend space and time, his apparitional entrances and exits (one might add his amiable disdain of human limitations), was in part a projection of what Twain described as his "dream self" or "spiritualized self"—an autonomous and irresponsible second self, free to wander at will in the writer's dreams.[151] Twain's concept of dual consciousness took shape as he studied his own dream life in light of contemporary investigations of dream psychology, apparitions, and secondary personality revealed under hypnosis. Tuckey has noted that at the end of 1896 Twain was reading one such study, the Society for Psychical Research's *Phantasms of the Living* (1886),[152] just a few days before he traced in his notebook the evolution of his notion of the "spiritualized self."[153] One of the authors of *Phantasms* was Twain's new acquaintance F. W. H. Myers. And it should be remembered that Twain was examining this book during the very winter in which, still grief-stricken over Susy's death, he and his

---

150 Ibid., p. 207.
151 Tuckey, pp. 26–28; Clemens, *Mark Twain's Notebook*, pp. 349–50.
152 Edmund Gurney, F. W. H. Myers, and Frank Podmore, *Phantasms of the Living*, 2 vols. (London, 1886).
153 Tuckey, p. 26.

wife consulted two mediums recommended to them by Myers—and that he was later to recall both mediums with good-natured contempt and to characterize Myers not only as a psychical researcher but also as a gullible spiritualist.[154] In short, the same psychical milieu which encouraged the writer's projection of his "spiritualized self" as the all-powerful Satan was also the locus of the bereaved if skeptical father's visits to séances which in retrospect seemed foolish.

Whether the "Schoolhouse Hill" séance comically reflected the London séances (and thus indicated that the writer, at least, had assimilated the trauma of Susy's death), or whether as an echo of the humorous rappings of Doesticks and Artemus Ward the episode was an exercise in sheer literary nostalgia, it typified Twain's literary response to spiritualism. William M. Gibson has observed that toward psychical mattters Twain alternated between "a rational and satiric view and a speculative and psychological view."[155] About spiritualism itself, however, from first to last he wrote almost entirely from the "rational and satiric" viewpoint implicit in the humorous tradition he inherited, alternating only between vexation and amusement at the fraudulent and inane mediums, vapid spirits, and credulous believers he encountered over the years. Although drawn several times to the séance-table for reasons of speculative curiosity or private grief, he left the religious and psychological significance of such experiences to be explored in fiction by Howells and James; nor did he ever use spiritualism for serious occult effect, unless we are to take the procession of clacking skeletons preceded by a stir of cold air in the penultimate chapter of the "Printshop" version of the Mysterious Stranger as a vast, macabre séance, with Forty-four himself as mediumistic illusionist.[156] It was as a literary comedian that Twain had reported Ada Hoyt Foye's baffling séances and the ghostly cat of Kearny Street; it was as a literary comedian that he had denounced J. V. Mansfield in *Life on the Mississippi* and burlesqued the Stratford rappings, perhaps as a thrust at Elizabeth Stuart Phelps or Nook Farm's occultists, in

---

[154] Clemens, *Mark Twain's Letters*, II, 706–7.
[155] William Gibson, "Introduction," in Clemens, *Mark Twain's Mysterious Stranger Manuscripts*, p. 27.
[156] Clemens, *Mark Twain's Mysterious Stranger Manuscripts*, pp. 400–403.

Adventures of Huckleberry Finn; he had ridiculed speculation itself in Colonel Sellers's antics as a pseudoscientific "Materializer" in *The American Claimant*. It was fitting, then, that for "Schoolhouse Hill" Twain summoned the psychical young Satan to confound a foolish disciple of the Fox sisters in one of the funniest and surely the last of the comic séances of the nineteenth century.

VIII: "THE YOUNG PROPHETESS" [1]

Memories of Spiritualism and Intimations of Occult Consciousness in Henry James's *The Bostonians*

I | Mark Twain could have and William Dean Howells must
have taken close personal interest in Henry James's handling
of spiritualistic and related matters in *The Bostonians* (1886). If
Twain read far enough (despite his dislike of the novel's analytic method), its delineation of the partnership between a patrician feminist
and a beautiful trance-speaker might very well have reminded him of
Isabella Hooker's alliance with Victoria Woodhull in behalf of wom-
en's rights and spirtualism; surely he would have recognized James's
debt to Ada Hoyt Foye for the name of "Mrs. Ada T. P. Foat,"[2] a
spiritualistic lecturer. As for Howells, he can hardly have escaped noticing similarities to his own *Undiscovered Country* (1880) in James's
presentation of the struggle between Basil Ransom, the skeptical conservative, and Olive Chancellor, the compulsive feminist, for control
of Verena Tarrant, the "young prophetess" whose father was a mesmeric healer.

1 Henry James, *The Bostonians* (London, 1886), p. 59.
2 James, *The Bostonians*, p. 72; Clemens and Howells, *Mark Twain-Howells Letters:
The Correspondence of Samuel L. Clemens and William Dean Howells, 1872–
1910*, ed. Henry Nash Smith and William M. Gibson (Cambridge, Mass., 1960),
I, 534.

James naturally touched on the American spiritualistic experience at different points and with different intentions than had Twain or Howells, both of whose contacts with the movement were much closer than his. Amused yet incisively critical, he was animated neither by the outright laughter nor by the personal antipathy which ludicrous séances, fraudulent mediums, and credulous believers had aroused in Twain, nor by the compassion which Robert Dale Owen had inspired in Howells. Nor was he at all concerned about the movement's role in the struggle between faith and science. His Swedenborgian father, after all, had long ago dismissed rapping spirits as "so many vermin revealing themselves in the tumbledown walls of our old theological hostelry."[3]

Rather, as a social satirist whose specific target was the women's rights agitation of the early 1870's, James regarded spiritualism, along with temperance, vegetarianism, communal utopianism, and free love, as raveled strands in the tattered fabric of antebellum reform-enthusiasm from which, as he saw it, the feminist movement took its example. At the same time, as a psychological novelist exploring sinister "magnetic" relationships similar to those already traced by Hawthorne and Howells, he took a deep interest in the puzzle of mediumistic personality posed by his heroine, Verena Tarrant. The result of this combination of social and psychological interests was that in several respects *The Bostonians* resembled both the anti-spiritualistic, anti-reform satires and the magnetic romances of the 1850's, while also anticipating the studies of psychical consciousness which lay ahead in James's supernatural fiction.[4]

[3] Henry James, Sr., "Spiritual Rappings," *Lectures and Miscellanies* (New York, 1852), p. 418.
[4] Alfred Habegger has recently reached somewhat similar conclusions in "The Disunity of *The Bostonians*," *Nineteenth Century Fiction* XXIV (September 1969), 193–209. Analyzing the work's narrative technique, Habegger has found James the omniscient satirist of the first part of the novel giving way to James the psychologist in the second part: "*The Bostonians* is unique among James's novels, for it brings together, though without reconciling, the two extremes of his fiction. Book First is the fullest expression of one side of James—the Balzacian realist who surfaced throughout his life and flourished from 1878 to 1888. . . . Book Second is a less successful example of the second and major side of James—the psychological realist. . . . The former James looks down upon entire cultures from a detached point of vantage, and . . . his own ethos of good taste and broad experience forms the basis for a satire of national types and provincial mentalities.

The novel began in the satiric vein. In an early scene, Basil Ransom ironically noted spiritualists among the reformers gathered at the home of the aging transcendentalist, Miss Birdseye. Warned to expect a meeting of "witches and wizards, mediums, and spirit-rappers, and roaring radicals," Ransom found a group of tired eccentrics. Miss Birdseye seemed redolent of a lifetime of futile "conventions" and "phalansteries" and "*séances.*" The guests whom he playfully imagined to be "mediums, communists, vegetarians," were down at the heels. Only Verena Tarrant's feminist trance-oration sounded a youthful and vital note.[5]

But Verena herself was the daughter of parents in the summary of whose career James brilliantly evoked the decline of the old reform spirit. Long ago Selah Tarrant, Verena's father, had participated in a free-love experiment at "Cayuga" (an obvious allusion to the Oneida Community), where he had been "associated" with Mrs. Ada T. P. Foat, herself later a spiritualistic lecturer. After marrying the daughter of a prominent old-line abolitionist, Selah had taken part in any number of social, religious, and dietary experiments in "humanitary Bohemia." For a time he had flourished as a medium, relying on his wife to move furniture and to counterfeit the soft touches of the departed in the darkened séance-room. A committee of investigators had brought this phase of his career to an end by exposing him, in "the fierce light of the scientific method," as a fraud. Recently, however, he had established a successful Cambridge practice as a mesmeric physician whose magnetic hands ministered to middle-aged ladies. And with an eye to publicity and profit he was promoting the trance-

---

The latter James uses a self-effacing narrator, a point of view restricted to the conscious mind of a flexible and growing character, a detailed recording of the character's passing impressions . . . for the purpose of exploring the conscious mind—the conscious growing mind. In *The Bostonians*, just as in the full span of James's career, the second of these two Jameses, the psychologist, supplants the satirist and social realist" (ibid., p. 209). I would only add that the "realist" and "satirist" was almost anachronistic in observing the conventions of American anti-reform and anti-spiritualistic satire; that the shift from social realism to psychological exploration was paralleled in the occult world by the growth of psychical research out of spiritualism; and that in dealing with Verena Tarrant's mediumistic possession, James was showing a concern, albeit from an external point of view, with the "unconscious" mind.

[5] James, *The Bostonians*, pp. 5, 27, 31.

speaking career of his daughter, supplying the magnetic stimulation he thought necessary to call forth "the spirit" within her.[6]

With the introduction of Verena Tarrant, the novel's psychological themes emerged from its satirically presented social background. Although Verena had been "suckled in the midst of manifestations. . . . and had been passed from hand to hand by trance-speakers," James did not explicitly label her as a medium. Yet her speech on the "woman question" to the reformers assembled at Miss Birdseye's followed the pattern of spiritualistic trance-oratory. First Selah asked for silence while his daughter "listened for the voice." As he stroked her head he murmured, "The spirit, you know; you've got to let the spirit come out when it will." After waiting with her eyes closed Verena began to speak as if "in a dream"; when her father explained that she was "trying to get in report," Ransom understood that he meant *"en rapport"* (a conventional designation for the medium's sensitive attunement to vibrations emanating from the unseen world).[7] Finally she began to speak coherently:

> She proceeded slowly, cautiously, as if she were listening for the prompter, catching, one by one, certain phrases that were whispered to her a great distance off, behind the scenes of the world. Then memory, or inspiration, returned to her, and presently she was in possession of her part. She played it with extraordinary simplicity and grace; at the end of ten minutes Ransom became aware that the whole audience . . . were under the charm. . . . The effect was not in what she said . . . but in the picture and figure of the half-bedizened damsel. . . . It was full of schoolgirl phrases, of patches of remembered eloquence, of childish lapses of logic. . . . It was simply an intense personal exhibition, and the person making it happened to be fascinating.[8]

It was her charisma as a medium, the oracular and sexual mystery beneath the trivial language, which made Verena the subject of struggle between Ransom and Olive Chancellor.

James gave his heroine no real supernatural power, of course. He

[6] Ibid., pp. 72, 73, 134, 59.
[7] Ibid., pp. 83, 59–60.
[8] Ibid., pp. 60–61.

seems rather to have conceived of Verena's "inspirational" gift as the emergence in trance of an ordinarily subdued histrionic impulse which was unconsciously susceptible to the influence of others. Although she thought that the origin of her vision of woman's tribulations was as mysterious as the source of Joan of Arc's "idea of the suffering of France," it derived in fact from the latest stir in the atmosphere of reform which she had breathed from birth, and it answered to her father's encouragement. Now Olive gradually displaced Selah, buying him off and weaving her own "fine web of authority, of dependence ... as dense as a suit of golden mail" about the girl, who became more and more the voice of Olive's own feminism. Before long the trappings of magnetic trance dropped away, and Verena reinforced inspiration with deliberate study of the woman question. Even as a student, however, like other trance-mediums "she read quickly and remembered infallibly; could repeat, days afterward, passages that she appeared only to have glanced at." Always she looked beyond herself for the source of her power; after her triumphal address to a "Female Convention" she told Ransom, "It's Miss Chancellor as much as me!"[9]

Thoroughly charmed from the beginning, Ransom fell in love with Verena. His hatred of reformers, whether they came like Selah from "humanitary Bohemia," or like Olive from patrician Charles Street, led him to think rather melodramatically of rescuing the girl from "the pernicious forces which were hurrying her to her ruin." So forcefully did he press his courtship that he undermined Olive's influence and cast his own "spell" over Verena.[10] She fled from him out of loyalty to her patroness and their cause, but when he turned up backstage at Boston's Music Hall while an impatient crowd awaited her appearance, she was helpless to resist his demand that she elope with him at once, leaving Olive to the mercy of the audience. The "young prophetess" had simply responded to a more explicitly personal and sexual "magnetism" than either her father or Olive Chancellor possessed.

Set in "187–,"[11] the satiric narrative of Verena's career as a feminist orator must have owed much of its data to James's memories of the

---

[9] Ibid., pp. 85, 167, 176, 202, 225.
[10] Ibid., pp. 247, 385.
[11] Ibid., p. 158.

"séances, demonstrations of mesmerism, speeches by ardent young reformers or discourses by lady-editors," which he had witnessed, according to Leon Edel,[12] early in the 1870's in Boston. Surely the novelist could hardly have avoided noticing the rise and fall of Victoria Woodhull, during those years the most visible and audible of lady editors, inspired lecturers, and women's rights reformers. Early in 1871 she had sprung to prominence as a feminist when she captivated Isabella Beecher Hooker and an entire suffragist convention by petitioning Congress for the vote. Suspicious of Mrs. Woodhull's reputation as an adventuress and her advocacy of "passional freedom," the conservative leaders of the movement in Boston had been unwilling to accept her as an ally; doubtless they had felt vindicated by the protracted furor which followed her charge, first publicly delivered in 1872 at a national convention of spiritualists in Boston, that Henry Ward Beecher was guilty of hypocritical adultery. Later James had resided in New York during the Beecher-Tilton trial which eventually grew out of that accusation (and which more than once drew Mark Twain as a spectator).[13] And in *The Terrible Siren: Victoria Woodhull* (1928),[14] Emanie Sachs argued convincingly that Mrs. Woodhull's astonishing subsequent marriage to a respectable English banker was reflected in James's story of the conquest of a baronet by Mrs. Headway, an American divorcée, in "The Siege of London" (1883),[15] a tale which appeared while *The Bostonians* was taking shape in his mind.[16]

Against this background it seems clear that the problems raised for the feminist movement by Victoria Woodhull's American career were evidenced in *The Bostonians* by Verena Tarrant's sudden celebrity as the result of her appearance before a "Female Convention"; by Olive

[12] Leon Edel, *Henry James: The Conquest of London, 1870-1881* (Philadelphia, 1962), p. 26.
[13] *Woodhull and Claflin's Weekly* III (June 3, 1871), 4–5; VI (November 2, 1872), 8–13; Emanie Sachs, *The Terrible Siren: Victoria Woodhull* (New York, 1928), pp. 75–78, 168–77; Kenneth R. Andrews, *Nook Farm: Mark Twain's Hartford Circle* (Cambridge, Mass., 1950), pp. 35, 40.
[14] Sachs, pp. 312–16.
[15] Henry James, "The Seige of London," *Cornhill Magazine* XLVII (January–February 1883), 1–34, 225–56.
[16] Henry James, *The Notebooks of Henry James*, ed. F. O. Matthiessen and Kenneth B. Murdock (New York, 1947), pp. 46–47.

Chancellor's concern about her naïve protégée's chaste preference for "free unions" over "the marriage-tie";[17] and by Olive's failure to secure for Verena the endorsement of a hardheaded and respectably married veteran of the cause:

> Mrs. Farrinder had behaved in the strangest way about Verena. First she had been struck with her, and then she hadn't; first she had seemed to want to take her in, then she had shied at her unmistakably—intimating to Olive that there were enough of that kind already. Of "that kind" indeed!—the phrase reverberated in Miss Chancellor's resentful soul. Was it possible she didn't know the kind Verena was of, and with what vulgar aspirants to notoriety did she confound her?[18]

Among the "scenes of the feminist agitation"[19] which James planned for the novel, then, some were ironic glimpses of the turbulence caused in the early 1870's by Victoria Woodhull's occult radicalism and aspiration to notoriety. More generally, the feminist efflorescence of those years provided the focus for the novelist's concern with social and sexual confusion in American life, functioning as had the spiritualistic excitement of the same period in Howells's treatment of religious malaise, *The Undiscovered Country* (1880).

In satiric tone and atmosphere, however, *The Bostonians* harked back to an earlier time. In its attitude toward reform it differed from the satires of mid-century chiefly in being more ironic and less fearfully melodramatic; its use of the language of reform would have made sense to readers of Hawthorne's *Blithedale Romance* (1852), of course, but even more sense to readers of Orestes Brownson's *Spirit-Rapper* (1854), or the pseudonymous Fred Folio's *Lucy Boston; or, Women's Rights and Spiritualism, Illustrating the Follies and Delusions of the Nineteenth Century* (1855), or Bayard Taylor's *Hannah Thurston: A Story of American Life* (1863). And its portrait of Verena Tarrant, "the young prophetess," resembled Victoria Woodhull less than it did

---

[17] James, *The Bostonians*, pp. 202–3, 84.
[18] Ibid., p. 162.
[19] James, *Notebooks*, p. 47.

Cora L. V. Hatch, a spiritualistic celebrity of that earlier day whom James himself, as a young man, had once heard speak.

II | On a Sunday evening in November, 1863, James and his cousin Bob Temple had paid ten cents each to hear Cora Hatch hold forth under spirit control in Clinton Hall, a basement lecture room in New York City. Shepherded by Cora's manager, a committee chosen from the audience proposed the topic of spirit survival— doubtless a familiar one to the twenty-three-year-old medium after a decade of such appearances. Following a period of motionless silence (later duplicated by Verena Tarrant as she tried to get "in report" at Miss Birdseye's), Cora began to give voice to a torrent of spiritual clichés which was still flowing as James and his cousin departed an hour later. Apparently unimpressed, James described the occasion to Thomas Sergeant Perry in a tone of exasperated amusement, comparing Cora's audience to the early Christians, labeling her manager "Chorus V. L. [*sic*] Hatch," and characterizing her utterances as "a string of . . . arrant platitudes."[20] Still, as Leon Edel has observed, "we recognize the type of female oratory we will encounter . . . in *The Bostonians*."[21] And in spite of the flippancy of James's letter to Perry, we can also recognize in Cora Hatch an enigma of mediumistic personality something like that dramatized in Verena Tarrant.

Cora Hatch had emerged from a background of occult and reform enthusiasm quite similar to that sketched by James in his history of the Tarrant family. She first appeared on the "spiritual rostrum" in the early 1850's as a "child medium." Managed by her father, she voiced the support of spirits for his vision of a communal utopia modeled on Adin Ballou's Hopedale Community. After her father's death she married Benjamin Hatch, a mesmeric physician, and under his guidance appeared before large crowds in Boston and New York in 1857 and 1858, pleasing even such skeptical listeners as Cornelius Felton, Henry Wadsworth Longfellow, and N. P. Willis with her innocent

[20] James to Perry [November 1863], in Virginia Harlow, *Thomas Sergeant Perry: A Biography* (Durham, N.C., 1950), pp. 269–71.
[21] Leon Edel, *Henry James: The Untried Years, 1843–1870* (Philadelphia, 1953), p. 110.

good looks and never-failing gift of spirit-dictated eloquence on religious, historical, and scientific subjects. The first of several collections of her discourses appeared in Boston in 1858.[22]

At the height of her youthful career Cora had attracted unpleasant publicity by divorcing Hatch amidst charges of sexual irregularity and magnetic imposition. She accused him of holding her in thrall, misappropriating her earnings, and abusing her sexually; Hatch replied publicly, in letters to the press and in *Spiritualists' Iniquities Unmasked* (1859), that his innocent but magnetically susceptible wife had fallen under the control of demonically possessed spiritualists bent on making her the spokeswoman for their free-love doctrines.[23] The official spiritualistic version offered by Emma Hardinge Britten was that the easily entranced Cora had been inveigled into marriage at the age of sixteen by "the old crafty and experienced magnetizer," and had finally fled him in terror.[24] Although Cora won her case in court, Hatch's revelations added fuel to the popular revulsion against spiritualism at the end of the 1850's; they were soon echoed, for instance, in Bayard Taylor's "Confessions of a Medium" (1860).[25] And as reported by both sides, the episode was as melodramatic an illustration of the trance maiden's precarious state as either the struggle for control of Verena Tarrant in *The Bostonians* or the fate of the deaf and dumb girl spellbound by the "spiritual magnetism" of a charlatan eager to exhibit her for profit in James's earlier tale on similar themes, "Professor Fargo" (1874).

After Cora's divorce the spirits had controlled her to warn of the impending civil conflict and to urge that slavery be abolished. In 1861 the ghost of Andrew Jackson expressed through her the opinion that

---

[22] Harrison D. Barrett, *Life Work of Mrs. Cora L. V. Richmond* (Chicago, 1895), pp. 5–31, 51–62, 83, 104, 144–63, 169–70; Benjamin Hatch, *Spiritualists' Iniquities Unmasked, and the Hatch Divorce Case* (New York, 1859), pp. 24–43; *New York Times*, October 14, 1858, p. 4; November 29, 1858, p. 3; *New York Tribune*, November 25, 1858, p. 3; November 29, 1858, p. 7; December 2, 1858, p. 7; January 4, 1859, pp. 4, 5; January 8, 1859, p. 5; January 19, 1859, p. 6; *New York Weekly Tribune*, July 3, 1858, pp. 2–3; October 2, 1858, pp. 2, 7.

[23] Hatch, pp. 24–43.

[24] Emma Hardinge Britten, *Autobiography*, ed. Margaret Wilkinson (Manchester, 1900), pp. 227–31.

[25] [Bayard Taylor,] "Confessions of a Medium," *Atlantic Monthly* VI (December 1860), 699–715.

"Jim Buchanan" was "a coward, a traitor, a fool."[26] She helped bind up old political wounds on a swing through Illinois by serving as the voice for "Spirit Douglas's" endorsement of Lincoln's conduct of the war.[27] Never regaining the popular favor she had enjoyed before her divorce, Cora nonetheless continued to play a prominent role in the spiritualistic movement, meanwhile remarrying at least twice. Politicians ignored the advice she passed along from "Spirit Lincoln" during the early years of Reconstruction.[28] But as Mrs. Cora L. V. Tappan she dedicated appropriate sections of *Hesperia* (1871),[29] an allegorical trance-poem about American history, to Lucretia Mott ("Fraternia"), Wendell Phillips ("Athenia"), Walt Whitman ("Laus Natura"), and President Grant ("The Benediction"), thereby eliciting from each a note of thanks (and from Whitman the promise of a personal visit).[30] Carrying letters of introduction from Robert Dale Owen to Alfred Russel Wallace and William Crookes, she was warmly received by audiences in England from 1873 to 1875.[31] By that year, according to the spirit-dictated biographical preface to a London edition of her discourses, she had delivered over 3,000 trance lectures.[32] Even by the time that James heard her speak in 1863, the pretty young

26 Cora L. V. Richmond, *A Lecture on Secession, by Gen. Andrew Jackson, Delivered at Dodsworth's Hall, on the Evening of Sunday, Jan. 19, 1861. Mrs. Cora L. V. Hatch, Medium* (New York, 1861), p. 12.

27 Barrett, pp. 195–99.

28 Ibid., p. 245.

29 Cora L. V. Richmond, *Hesperia* (New York, 1871).

30 Barrett, pp. 529–45. But in a letter of July 20, 1857, written at the height of Cora's popularity and later printed by Rollo Silver in "Seven Letters of Walt Whitman," *American Literature* VII (March 1935), 77, Whitman had expressed less enthusiasm: "I got into quite a talk with Mr. Arnold about Mrs. Hatch,—He says the pervading thought of her speeches is that *first* exists the spirituality of any thing and *that* gives existence to things, the earth, plants, animals, men, women.— But that Andrew Jackson Davis puts *matter* as the subject of his homilies, and the primary source of all results—I suppose the soul among the rest.—Both are quite determined in their theories.—Perhaps when they know . . . more, both of them will be less determined." As a poet, of course, Whitman himself played the role of prophetic clairvoyant.

31 Barrett, pp. 248–59. Cora had returned to England in 1880, 1884, and 1885 (ibid., pp. 365, 405, 413).

32 Cora L. V. Richmond, "A Narrative of Mrs. Cora L. V. Tappan's Experiences as a Medium, Given by Her Spirit-Guides, at St. George's Hall, London, December 29th, 1873," *Discourses through the Mediumship of Mrs. Cora L. V. Tappan* (London, 1875), American ed. (Boston, 1876), p. xvii.

medium had been a celebrity within and occasionally without the spiritualistic movement for a decade.

As a satirist, James drew on his memory of the young Cora, and evidently on knowledge of her subsequent career, for details of the shabby occult milieu in which Verena Tarrant had grown up. The Tarrant family had gone to lectures on "the Summer-land" (the spiritualists' heaven) given by Mrs. Ada T. P. Foat, Selah's former "associate" in the free-love community at Cayuga. Basil Ransom, moreover, was disgusted to find in the Tarrants' parlor a biography of this "celebrated trance lecturer," whose portrait exhibited "a surprised expression and innumerable ringlets."[33] Obviously James derived Mrs. Foat's name from that of Ada Hoyt Foye, whose San Francisco séances had attracted amused yet respectful attention from Mark Twain. Ada Foye, however, was noted neither for trance oratory nor for ringlets.[34] But Cora L. V. Hatch was a well-known trance-speaker (with two middle initials); she had advertised a speech on "the Summer Land" during her Clinton Hall appearances in November, 1863, one of which the novelist had witnessed;[35] her first husband had pictured her as the pawn of free-love advocates (he had also attacked Mrs. Foye, then known as "Mrs. Ada Coan," for deserting her husband);[36] a biographical sketch had accompanied published collections of Cora's utterances;[37] and her crowning glory as a young woman had been the profusion of curls admired by observers and evidenced by her portrait in Emma Hardinge Britten's *Modern American Spiritualism* (1870),[38] a volume which James might easily have noticed in his prowls among occultists and reformers during the early 1870's.

As for Verena Tarrant's own feminist afflatus, Cora Hatch had often

---

[33] James, *The Bostonians*, pp. 72, 222.

[34] Emma Hardinge Britten, *Modern American Spiritualism: A Twenty Years' Record of the Communion between Earth and the World of Spirits* (New York, 1870), pp. 135–37, 148–50; Britten, *Nineteenth Century Miracles; or, Spirits and Their Work in Every Country of the Earth* (New York, 1884), pp. 241–45, and portraits of Mrs. Foye and J. V. Mansfield facing pp. 284, 509.

[35] "Religious Notices," *New York Tribune*, November 14, 1863, p. 11.

[36] Hatch, p. 15; Britten, *Modern American Spiritualism*, pp. 135–37.

[37] Richmond, *Discourses through the Mediumship of Mrs. Cora L. V. Tappan*, pp. ix–xxii.

[38] Facing p. 156. This portrait represented the young Cora of 1857 and had probably been used in editions of her discourses.

been controlled by the spirits to speak out for the emancipation of women;[39] indeed, in the early 1870's she had been on friendly terms with the radical suffragists led by Victoria Woodhull, who was then president of the American Association of Spiritualists.[40] Basil Ransom need not have wondered whether the biography of Ada T. P. Foat "was the sort of thing Miss Tarrant had been brought up on," for it epitomized her upbringing. She had been "suckled in the midst of manifestations; she had begun to 'attend lectures' . . . when she was quite an infant. . . . She had sat on the knees of somnambulists, and had been passed from hand to hand by trance-speakers. . . ." As demonstrated by her address to the reformers at Miss Birdseye's, she had begun as a trance speaker herself, assisted (like Cora Hatch) by her father. And just as the young James had dismissed Cora's speech as "a string of . . . arrant platitudes," so Basil Ransom thought Verena's message "vague, thin, rambling, a tissue of generalities."[41]

Although Verena's occult and feminist milieu drew the satirist's irony, as a novelist increasingly devoted to psychological analysis James paid a great deal of attention to her charismatic effect on her audiences and to her peculiar mode of consciousness. Despite Ransom's contempt for Mrs. Foat, for the Tarrants, and for Verena's own oratorical "moonshine," he found the girl utterly fascinating. On first hearing her perform at Miss Birdseye's, he thought it her function "not to make converts to a ridiculous cause, but to emit those charming notes of her voice . . . to please everyone who came near her, and to be happy that she pleased."[42] A year later, as she entered the room in which he was pondering the effect of Mrs. Foat's biography on her, Ransom saw that Verena was even more pleasing than before:

> Her splendid hair seemed to shine. . . . She had appeared to him before as a creature of brightness, but now she lighted up the place. . . . with the native sweetness of her voice forcing him to listen till she spoke again. . . . her glance was as pure as it was direct, and that fan-

[39] Barrett, pp. 508–9, 536.
[40] *Woodhull and Claflin's Weekly* II (November 19, 1870), 16; (December 17, 1870), 1, 16; (March 18, 1871), 6; (May 6, 1871), 16; III (June 10, 1871), 11; V (June 22, 1872), 11.
[41] James, *The Bostonians*, pp. 222, 83, 268.
[42] Ibid., pp. 264, 61.

tastic fairness hung about her which had made an impression on him of old, and which reminded him of unworldly places—he didn't know where—convent-cloisters or vales of Arcady.[43]

Cora Hatch, at least in her youth, had possessed for believers and some skeptics alike the same intense personal charm, the same exotic yet innocent air of mystery, as that with which James endowed his heroine. Long afterward a spiritualist remembered Cora as

> a bright young woman, 'divinely fair' . . . radiant with beauty, purity, and intelligence from a righteous indwelling soul, crowned by a rich profusion of pretty blonde hair . . . in graceful ringlets upon her shoulders with countenance benign and voice of melody orating in sweetest tones of deep religious fervor on the love of the Infinite, the glories of the universe, and the kingdom of the soul.[44]

Longfellow, after hearing her speak in 1857, had described her as "a pretty young woman, with long sunny locks and a musical voice." Like Ransom listening to Verena among the reformers, the poet had received little edification from what the seeress had to say, "but thought her very superior to her audience."[45] A year later N. P. Willis had told his readers of Cora's "ringlets falling over her shoulders, movements deliberate and self-possessed, voice calm and deep, and eyes and fingers no way nervous." A confirmed skeptic about the Fox sisters and the rappings he had once helped to publicize, the journalist had nonetheless declared Cora's oratory "as nearly supernatural eloquence as the most hesitating faith could reasonably require." For Willis, "*how to explain it*, with her age, habits and education," had been the great question[46]—exactly the problem which in *The Bostonians* faced Basil Ransom and Olive Chancellor as to the mechanism of Verena's inspiration and the contrast between her innocent glamour and the corruption from which she sprang.

That Verena and Cora attracted similar compliments should perhaps be expected. Admiration for the nineteenth-century's oracular

[43] Ibid., pp. 223–24.
[44] Barrett, p. 182.
[45] Samuel Longfellow, *Life of Henry Wadsworth Longfellow* (Boston, 1891), II, 347.
[46] N. P. Willis, *The Convalescent* (New York, 1859), pp. 303–6.

sibyls, from Fanny Wright and the Fox sisters to Victoria Woodhull and even Madame Blavatsky, took conventional form; the occult or inspirational life, at least as described by believers and publicists, seems often to have imitated art. It is also true that after hearing Cora at Clinton Hall, the young novelist-to-be had shown no awareness that she could appeal to intelligent listeners, or that she had ever been the center of a magnetic melodrama. Since then, however, he had taken professional notice of the type of the trance maiden, re-reading Hawthorne's romances with their sensitive, passive clairvoyants, and finding Howells's medium, Egeria Boynton, without distinct personality.[47] That James had seen the ethical and sexual implications of the vulnerability exhibited by Hawthorne's seeresses had been evidenced in the deaf and dumb heroine of his own "Professor Fargo" (1874),[48] the climax of which tale in a basement lecture room may have reflected his visit to Clinton Hall. And the likenesses in the histories and performances of Verena Tarrant and Cora Hatch, along with echoes of a spiritualistic account of Cora's career in references to Ada T. P. Foat, suggest that James enlivened his study of the trance maiden ("the kind Verena was of") and her background of occult reform, with what he knew about the ostensibly innocent, magnetically susceptible, platitudinous, and (by many accounts) charming medium he had once seen and heard in the flesh.

III | With Verena, James revealed a curiosity about the mediumistic mind which resembled, less clinically to be sure, the attention which his brother William was beginning to give the same subject as a psychologist and psychical researcher. In Basil Ransom's eyes the trance maiden's "gift" was simply a willingness to please which led her to utter the sentiments of others, mixing their idiom and her own schoolgirl language, without compromising her innocence (or naïveté). The nature of those sentiments depended on the person to whom she stood closest, at the given moment, in a relation of dependency—hence her suitability as the focal point of the sexual and ideological warfare waged by Ransom and Olive Chancellor. Through

---

47 Henry James, *Hawthorne* (London, 1879); James to Howells, July 2, 1880. MS at Houghton Library.
48 Henry James, "Professor Fargo," *Galaxy* XVIII (August 1874), 233–53.

Ransom's exasperated fascination with Verena the novelist indicated his own interest in her malleability:

> . . . she didn't mean it, she didn't know what she meant, she had been stuffed with this trash by her father, and she was neither more nor less willing to say it than to say anything else; for the necessity of her nature was . . . to please every one who came near her, and to be happy that she pleased. I know not whether Ransom was aware of the bearings of this interpretation, which attributed to Miss Tarrant a singular hollowness of character; he contented himself with believing that she was as innocent as she was lovely, and with regarding her as a vocalist of exquisite faculty, condemned to sing bad music.[49]

Ransom's analysis was sound to the extent that the old concept of an external mesmeric force had given way to the notion of suggestibility within the medium herself. Thus Selah's supposedly magnetic hands were easily dispensed with as Verena responded in turn to the more powerful egoisms of Olive and Ransom. Thus, too, the locus of evil was shifted to the psychological plane, from the once-demonic villainy now made trivial in Selah to the misunderstood sexual compulsions which drove Olive Chancellor.

As indicated by James's caveat about her "hollowness of character," however, Verena was more complex than Ransom realized (more complex, too, than the novelist was consistently able to show). Certainly Olive, no fool, was puzzled by her protégée's talent, and for want of a better answer was forced to conclude that it "was literally inspiration." Selah, the old spiritualist, identified the mysterious power as "the spirit," and Verena herself could only say, "Oh, it isn't me, you know; it's something outside!"[50] She was, in fact, "possessed"—not by a spirit, but by an ordinarily quiescent second self which emerged in trance.

Thus she spoke sightlessly and incoherently at first, as if "in a dream"; then "as if she were listening for the prompter, catching . . .

49 James, *The Bostonians*, p. 61.
50 Ibid., p. 79.

phrases that were whispered to her a great distance off";[51] until the latent impulse, fully liberated, dictated its message to her in coherent form. Susceptible below the level of her waking mind to the influence of others, this second self gave her the ability (said to be characteristic of trance mediums) to absorb what she heard and read without apparent effort or even awareness, later to weave it into her inspired discourse. Although her first speech struck Ransom as including "patches of remembered eloquence," she was clearly innocent of plagiarism.[52] Similar tribute was later paid Cora Hatch, "the supreme example in this line," by the skeptical psychical researcher Frank Podmore. According to Podmore, Cora's trance poetry contained many echoes of better-known poets, yet showed no evidence of deliberate plagiarism. As for Cora's spirit-dictated oratory in general, there was "little doubt that her utterances were in large measure unpremeditated, and that she was not herself a wholly conscious or voluntary agent in their production."[53]

In short, the performances of Verena and Cora were examples of a kind of behavior which was claiming attention from psychologists: the manifestation of "alternate personality" in mediumistic trance. William James, who in 1885 began to study the Boston medium Mrs. Piper, was shortly to include Verena's sort of "inspirational speaking" in his description of the mediumistic varieties of "Mutations of Self" in *Principles of Psychology* (1890):[54]

Mediumistic possession in all its grades seems to form a perfectly natural special type of alternate personality, and the susceptibility to it in some form is by no means an uncommon gift, in persons who have no other obvious nervous anomaly. . . . The lowest phase of mediumship is automatic writing . . . where the Subject knows what words are coming, but feels impelled to write them as if from with-

[51] Ibid., p. 60.
[52] Ibid.; Frank Podmore, *Modern Spiritualism: A History and a Criticism* (London, 1902), I, 165–68.
[53] Podmore, II, 139, 134. According to her biographer, however, Cora had been able as a schoolgirl to do her lessons without opening her books—with the aid of spirits (Barrett, pp. 27–28).
[54] William James, *Principles of Psychology* (London, 1901), I, 393–400.

out. . . . Inspirational speaking, playing on musical instruments, etc., also belong to the relatively lower phases of possession, in which the normal self is not excluded from conscious participation in the performance, though their initiative seems to come from elsewhere. In the highest phase the trance is complete, the voice, language, and everything are changed. . . . The subject assumes the role of a medium simply because opinion expects it of him under the conditions which are present, and carries it out with a feebleness or a vivacity proportionate to his histrionic gifts.[55]

Set in a feminist rather than spiritualistic context, Verena's vivacious oratory belonged among the "lower phases of possession." Her "normal self" played a conscious part in the performance, for, like the automatic-writing "Subject," she knew what she was saying yet felt her words dictated "from without." More fully possessed was Cora Hatch, who regularly if not always assumed the specific identities of the departed in her speeches; Mrs. Piper, whose trances belonged to "the highest phase," impersonated even the different voices of the dead in the séances witnessed by William James. Given the nature of their "nervous anomaly" and the "conditions" under which they were raised, it was "perfectly natural" for James's heroine and Cora to take "the role of a medium" speaking for reform. (Spiritualism itself may be said to have provided an institutional outlet for a variety of such anomalies during the last century.) In Verena's case, however, a change in "conditions" effected something like a cure, for her "gift" disappeared as she was taken from her occult environment, exposed to Olive Chancellor's ardent tutelage, and eventually forced to acknowledge the strength of her feeling for Ransom. Indeed, to the extent that Verena's "alternate self" was a buried or displaced capacity for passion, James implied as sexual a basis for her inspiration as he did for Olive's compulsive behavior.

Verena's "mediumistic possession," though studied by James largely from without, anticipated the similar states of occult consciousness dramatized from a subjective point of view in his "ghostly tales" of the 1890's. Except for "Maude-Evelyn" (1900),[56] where " 'mediums,' don't

[55] Ibid., pp. 393–94.
[56] Henry James, *The Ghostly Tales of Henry James*, ed. Leon Edel (New Brunswick, N.J., 1948), pp. 598–629.

you know, and raps, and sittings"[57] provided a vulgar contrast, off-stage, for a young man's sensitive if morbid cultivation of a girlish spirit within his own mind, none of these stories touched explicitly on spiritualism. Yet like Mark Twain's Mysterious Stranger narratives, some of them reflected their author's familiarity with the Society for Psychical Research, the intellectually and socially respectable offshoot of spiritualism which was investigating not only the case for immortality but also the psychology of ghost-seeing and mediumistic trance. That familiarity has long been a matter of record: James was friendly with Henry and Eleanor Sidgwick, Edmund Gurney, and F. W. H. Myers, the leaders of the British S.P.R.; his brother William was the moving spirit of the American branch and eventually served as president of the transatlantic organization; and shortly after reading his brother's report on Mrs. Piper, the Boston trance medium, to a meeting of the London group late in 1890, James began to publish his ambiguously "supernatural" and "psychological" occult tales.[58]

It is also a matter of record, of course, that James later denied any narrative inspiration in the "psychical record" of "attested 'ghosts.' "[59] Yet in "The Friends of the Friends" (1896),[60] his ambiguous handling of a man's vision of a woman who was dying elsewhere—"one of those inexplicable occurrences that are chronicled in thrilling books and disputed about at learned meetings"[61]—showed an awareness of the evidential problems that led psychical researchers to discount most accounts of such "crisis apparitions" as inadequate proof of spirit survival.[62] As for "The Turn of the Screw" (1898),[63] that "thrilling" tale itself the subject of much "learned" dispute, Francis X. Roellinger demonstrated years ago that some of its narrative details and spectral

---

[57] Ibid., p. 612.
[58] Leon Edel, "Introduction," in James, *The Ghostly Tales of Henry James*, pp. xi–xii; Gay Wilson Allen, *William James: A Biography* (New York, 1967), pp. 282–85, 326–27.
[59] Henry James, *The Art of the Novel: Critical Prefaces of Henry James*, ed. Richard P. Blackmur (New York, 1934), p. 174.
[60] James, *The Ghostly Tales of Henry James*, pp. 395–424.
[61] Ibid., p. 419.
[62] Alan Gauld, *The Founders of Psychical Research* (New York, 1968), pp. 160–71. This book is by far the best history of psychical research through the end of the last century.
[63] James, *The Ghostly Tales of Henry James*, pp. 425–550.

images could have been suggested by such S.P.R. publications as Mrs. Sidgwick's "Phantasms of the Dead" (1885).[64]

Like many other commentators, Roellinger insisted that James's governess was to be trusted, that Peter Quint and Miss Jessel were real apparitions rather than, as Edmund Wilson argued, Freudian hallucinations on the part of the governess. Perhaps because the presence of Freud long tended to dominate psychological analysis of the story, perhaps because James artfully denied any interest in psychical "ghosts" without mentioning the states of mind in which they might be seen, it has generally been overlooked that the S.P.R.'s writers—whether skeptics like Mrs. Sidgwick and Frank Podmore or believers like Edmund Gurney and F. W. H. Myers—were applying sophisticated theories of trance, hysteria, alternate personality, and hallucination to the *perception* of spirits by the living.[65] Even the apparitions which they thought genuine, agreed Gurney and Myers, were not ghosts themselves, but hallucinatory images telepathically or clairvoyantly received from the spectral agents.[66] (Thus, as an S.P.R. "percipient," James's governess would have been hallucinating whether or not Peter Quint and Miss Jessel were "real.") And although Myers sent Mark Twain to unreliable mediums and sought word from a lost love in countless séances, between 1885 and 1900 he developed in the S.P.R.'s *Proceedings* a comprehensive hypothesis of "subliminal consciousness" to account for behavior ranging from dreams, through physical tics, trance, and hysteria, to (he hoped) communication with the dead; in so doing, he was evidently the first Englishman to call public attention to Freud's work with hysteria.[67] Of course, as Leon Edel and

---

[64] "Psychical Research and 'The Turn of the Screw,' " in Henry James, *The Turn of the Screw*, ed. Robert Kimbrough (New York, 1966), pp. 132–42.

[65] Ibid., p. 137; Edel, "Introduction," in James, *The Ghostly Tales of Henry James*, p. xii.

[66] Gauld, pp. 162, 167, 171.

[67] Samuel Clemens, *Mark Twain's Letters*, ed. Albert Bigelow Paine (New York, 1917), II, 706–7; Podmore, II, 357; Gauld, pp. 322–25, 275–93. In "The Subliminal Consciousness: The Mechanism of Hysteria," *Proceedings of the Society for Psychical Research* IX (1893), 3–128, Myers saluted an early paper of Freud and Josef Breuer as confirming his own theory that hysteria is the eruption of subliminal "hypnoid" conditions into waking life (ibid., pp. 12–15). The fullest exposition of Myers's occult psychological theories was his posthumously published *Human Personality and Its Survival of Bodily Death* (London, 1903). Myers has been called "one of the great systematizers of the notion of the unconscious mind"

Oscar Cargill have pointed out, James's interest in depth psychology was nourished from a variety of sources, including the writings of his brother and perhaps the Frenchman Charcot, and his own attempt to understand the nervous disorder of his dying sister Alice (who, curiously enough, was visited more than once in her last years by the S.P.R.'s Eleanor Sidgwick).[68] But for ghosts who could be taken as either supernatural or psychological, or ambiguously both, he needed to look no further than the hallucinatory presences and their "percipients" studied by his and his brother's friends of the S.P.R.

Viewed in this light, the governess—who first saw Peter Quint and Miss Jessel in moments of deep revery—was a study, like Verena Tarrant, in altered consciousness. As such, she combined the neurotic complexity of an Olive Chancellor (the high-minded, near-hysteric spinster) with a "nervous anomaly" of spectral hallucination which was quite as appropriate to the "conditions" of her upbringing and situation as Verena's trance oratory (dictated to her from "outside" as if by an auditory hallucination) was to the milieu of occult reform. The detached narrator of "Professor Fargo" had been unable to penetrate the veil of the deaf and dumb trance-maiden; in *The Bostonians,*

---

by Henri F. Ellenberger in *The Discovery of the Unconscious: The History and Evolution of Dynamic Psychiatry* (New York, 1970), p. 314.

[68] Edel, "Introduction," in James, *The Ghostly Tales of Henry James*, pp. xii-xiv; Oscar Cargill, *The Novels of Henry James* (New York, 1961), pp. 127–29; Alice James, *The Diary of Alice James*, ed. Leon Edel (New York, 1964), pp. 25–26, 49–50, 152. In suggesting that Myers could have called James's attention to Freud and Breuer's *Studien über Hysterie* (1895), with its account of the conversion-hysteria of a governess infatuated with her employer ("The Case of Miss Lucy R."), Oscar Cargill has identified Myers's 1893 discussion of Freud and Breuer's earlier paper—which did not deal with "Lucy R."—as a notice of the 1895 book (Cargill, "The Turn of the Screw and Alice James," in James, *The Turn of the Screw*, ed. Robert Kimbrough, p. 161). In fact, Myers did not write about *Studien über Hysterie* until over two years after James had recorded the anecdotal germ of "The Turn of the Screw" in his notebook (Myers, "Hysteria and Genius," *Journal of the Society for Psychical Research* VIII (April 1897), 50–59; James, *The Notebooks of Henry James*, pp. 178–79). This would not of itself invalidate Cargill's argument that James was indebted to Freud; William James's profession and Alice James's hysteria, as Cargill noted, could have led the novelist to Freud's work. But in his eagerness to prove the Freudian origin of "The Turn of the Screw," Cargill (like Francis X. Roellinger in his demonstration of the ghostly essence of the tale) ignored the psychological potential of James's familiarity with both the ghosts and the "percipients" of the S.P.R.

James examined a more articulate version of the same figure through the keen if aggrandizing regard of Basil Ransom and Olive Chancellor, and toward the end of the novel he even peered directly into the mind of the no longer "inspired" girl; by 1898, in "The Turn of the Screw," he was able to step altogether within the hysterical consciousness and allow it to represent itself to the reader for better or worse, qualified only by the intricate framework of the tale.

Most of the ghostly tales, of course, were by no means so pathological in their ambience; their apparitions, whether doubles of the living or spectres of the dead, were often instruments of new insight on the part of the beholders. Indeed, for a writer who described his obligation as "carrying the field of consciousness further and further, making it lose itself in the ineffable,"[69] ghost-seeing could also serve as one mode of the subtilized, almost preternatural sensitivity which distinguished the major characters of his later works generally. And the ghosts, perhaps, were but occult personifications of the metaphorical illuminations through which those characters, as if trance mediums themselves, sometimes perceived reality.[70]

Late in his life, in giving an affirmative answer to the question, "Is There a Life After Death?" (1910),[71] James indicated his abiding interest in the personality of "the trance medium," even while rejecting her intimations of immortality:

I can only treat here as absolutely not established the value of those personal signs that ostensibly come to us through the trance medium. These often make, I grant, for attention and wonder and interest—but for interest above all in the medium and the trance. Whether or no they may in the given case seem to savor of another state of being on the part of those from whom they profess to come, they savor intensely, to my sense, of the medium and the trance, and, with their remarkable felicities and fitnesses, their immense call for

---

[69] "Is There a Life after Death?" in William Dean Howells, Henry James, John Bigelow, Thomas Wentworth Higginson and others, *In After Days: Thoughts on the Future Life* (New York, 1910), p. 223.
[70] For the fullest discussion to date of the "psychical" element in James's fiction, see two studies by Martha Banta: "Henry James and 'The Others,' " *New England Quarterly* XXXVII (June 1964), 171–84; "The Two Worlds of Henry James: A Study in the Fiction of the Supernatural" (Ph.D. diss.: Indiana University, 1964).
[71] Howells et al., *In After Days*, pp. 199–233.

explanation, invest that personage, in that state, with an almost ir-resistible attraction.[72]

Modeled in part on Cora Hatch, and emerging as psychological enigma from the satiric context of shabby American spiritualism rather than from the occult context of respectable English psychism, Verena Tar-rant was a relatively early instance of the "attraction" which "the medium and the trance" possessed for Henry James.

IV | James had his eye on the work of other writers when he deliberately set out to show in *The Bostonians* that he could write a lively "American" novel. Spiritualism was by no means his major interest in the work. But as both social and occult experience it was not only among the personal memories which went into the book; it was also a recurrent topic in the kind of native fiction James was trying to write. The result of this union of personal and literary retrospection was that *The Bostonians* recapitulated the patterns of magnetic romance and anti-reform satire which had characterized much of the American literary response to spiritualism since the early 1850's.

In many ways, of course, the novel reworked the feminist, utopian, and magnetic materials which Hawthorne had dealt with in *The Blithedale Romance* (1852) at the very time spiritualism was replacing mesmerism as a subject of occult interest. In *The Complex Fate* (1952), Marius Bewley traced the transformation of Hawthorne's Priscilla and Zenobia into Verena Tarrant and Olive Chancellor, and suggested that James made over the vaguely Gothic Westervelt into the equally corrupt but recognizably American Selah Tarrant.[73] As for the satiric treatment of reform, Bewley implied that James simply brought Hawthorne's version of "the idiom of the reformers" up to date:

This idiom as used by Hawthorne and James, and a little later by W. D. Howells in *The Undiscovered Country*—an unsatisfactory

[72] Ibid., p. 211. Another contributor to this symposium on immortality was Eliza-beth Stuart Phelps.
[73] Marius Bewley, *The Complex Fate: Hawthorne, Henry James and Some Other American Writers* (London, 1952), pp. 13–28.

novel that is, at least in its first part, deeply indebted to both its distinguished predecessors—is undoubtedly in touch with the facts as they were—but the line of influence should not, on that account, be underestimated.[74]

On this basis it would be reasonable to assume that James supplemented Hawthorne's mesmeric materials with his own observations of spiritualism and reform. Thus the names of Mrs. Ada T. P. Foat and her "Summer-land" lecture, both singled out by Bewley as expert satiric touches,[75] originated in James's knowledge of the spiritualistic milieu.

But the American literary background of *The Bostonians* consisted less of a single romance by Hawthorne than it did of a relatively coherent tradition. And by mistakenly placing *The Undiscovered Country* (1880)[76] after *The Bostonians* (1886) in time, Bewley overlooked a very important point on "the line of influence" stretching from Hawthorne to James.[77]

The exemplary force of *The Blithedale Romance* cannot be gainsaid. In a context combining mesmerism and spiritualism, it had manifested itself a decade earlier in the figures of the evil medium (Fargo), the helpless trance-maiden (Miss Gifford), and her eccentric father (Colonel Gifford), in James's own "Professor Fargo" (1874). The narrator of that tale, moreover, had possessed an ironic detachment like that with which Hawthorne's Miles Coverdale had distanced himself from the world. And the theme—the magnetic violation of

[74] Ibid., p. 14.
[75] Ibid., p. 17.
[76] William Dean Howells, *The Undiscovered Country* (Boston, 1880).
[77] Oscar Cargill protested against what he termed Bewley's claim of "almost complete indebtedness on James's part" to Hawthorne, noting that Verena Tarrant also looked like George Eliot's Dinah Morris and pointing out the further debt (almost admitted by James) to Daudet's *L'Evangeliste* and to *Antigone*. He also demonstrated the novel's likeness in some aspects of theme and character to Howells's *Doctor Breen's Practice* (Boston, 1881). But no more than Bewley did Cargill notice any native "line" of descent (*The Novels of Henry James*, pp. 125–29). A thematic interpretation of "Psychic Vampirism" in *The Bostonians* with comparisons to other treatments of the same theme by Hawthorne, Howells, and James himself (in "Professor Fargo") will be found in Banta, "The Two Worlds of Henry James," pp. 158–72.

vulnerable innocence—was a legacy of Hawthorne and popular fiction claimed by both James and Howells.

In adapting this theme to a serious study of spiritualism in *The Undiscovered Country*, Howells had reduced the sexual and ideological tangle of *The Blithedale Romance* to the struggle between a forceful skeptic (Ford) and an idealistic but eccentric and jealous father (Boynton) for the latter's magnetically susceptible daughter (Egeria). James had done the same thing in "Professor Fargo." But Howells had simplified further by making the father a magnetic physician, by making the daughter his spiritualistic medium, and by dispensing with the first-person narrator of Hawthorne and James. The ironic tone of that narrator had become more sardonic when given by Howells to Ford, the journalist-scientist in love with the medium but (like James's Colonel Gifford, whose last name he bore in manuscript)[78] hostile toward spiritualism.

When James developed similar relationships once again in *The Bostonians*, he must have been aware of Howells's way with his own and Hawthorne's examples. To be sure, that awareness was fundamentally critical: he had told Howells that *The Undiscovered Country* was relatively uninteresting.[79] Yet, as in Howells's novel, the father of James's trance maiden was now a magnetist; the girl herself was a trance speaker; the detached narrator of "Professor Fargo" had disappeared; and the point of view receiving most attention was that of Ransom, the skeptical and ironical would-be journalist in love with the medium. There were also satiric glimpses of the same kind of shabby occult milieu as that which Howells had sketched in the first part of *The Undiscovered Country*—a setting which James had criticized his friend for abandoning in favor of the blander one of the Shaker village.[80] (Of course, the introduction of Shakerism, with its doctrine of celibacy, had allowed Howells to treat the questions of marriage and the condition of women.)

Verena Tarrant and Basil Ransom may have benefited in particular

---

[78] Kermit Vanderbilt, *The Achievement of William Dean Howells: A Reinterpretation* (Princeton, 1968), p. 47.
[79] James to Howells, July 2, 1880.
[80] Ibid.

from James's reading of Howells. The latter's readers had witnessed the partial transformation of the trance medium, so pallid and pensive in Hawthorne and literally deaf and dumb in "Professor Fargo," from a sickly medium at the opening of *The Undiscovered Country* to a healthy and happily married suburban matron at its end. But Howells's attempt to resuscitate the type had not been altogether successful. Egeria's trances had been confusingly attributed not only to nervous disorder and paternal dominance, but also to mesmerism and static electricity; nor had her appeal as a young woman awakening to life been adequately demonstrated—she had remained a rather passive Gothic residue. Thomas Wentworth Higginson's generally enthusiastic review had found her lifeless,[81] and James himself had told Howells that she was the least distinctive of his heroines.[82]

James attempted to bring Verena to life by emphasizing the intensity of her charm while treating her (through the eyes of Ransom and Olive) with a good deal of irony, and by dramatizing her mediumistic possession as a purely psychological process in which her father's spurious "magnetism" had no part. Defined in large measure by the satiric context in which she functioned, and less complex even in trance than Ransom or Olive Chancellor, Verena was in some respects an occult version of Daisy Miller. But as a trance maiden she was far more lively than any of her predecessors in Hawthorne or Howells, and unlike them she was capable, at least in Ransom's eyes, of "an intensely personal exhibition."[83]

Ransom himself was perhaps a more deliberate attempt to improve on Howells. Oscar Cargill has suggested that in *Dr. Breen's Practice* (1881), with the character of Mulbridge, a male chauvinist whose father had supported the Confederacy, Howells had provided the literary inspiration for Ransom's assertive masculinity, his contempt for feminism, and his Southern background.[84] But Ransom had as much if not more in common with Ford. Both were outlanders, Ford from a depressed country village and Ransom from war-impoverished

---

[81] T. W. Higginson, "Howells' 'Undiscovered Country,' " *Scribner's* XX (September 1880), 794.
[82] James to Howells, July 2, 1880.
[83] James, *The Bostonians*, p. 61.
[84] Cargill, *The Novels of Henry James*, pp. 125–26.

Mississippi; both were scornful of polite society; and both led boarding-house existences. More pertinently, Ransom resembled Ford in being a free-lance journalist of independent and skeptical turn of mind, and in successfully courting the hand of a trance maiden enlisted in a cause he despised. In pursuing her with a display of self-conscious mascu-linity, he was (like Mulbridge) an example of what Higginson, in describing Ford, had called "the ungracious . . . type of wooer now most in vogue with our novelists."[85]

Brooks Adams had assailed Howells on the latter score for allowing Ford at one point to fail to propose to Egeria because of fears of an imagined rival. Adams had thought this failure of nerve incongruous in a character "represented as an intensely 'masculine man'. . . . Such men have the animalistic side pretty strongly developed, and they are usually more likely to fight their rivals than to surrender the woman they love."[86] James, whose own remarks about Ford had been unen-thusiastic, came close to burlesquing the vogue of the rough young wooer with Basil Ransom. Certainly Brooks Adams could have found little fault with the way Ransom invaded Verena's Music Hall dressing room in the novel's last scene, consigned her waiting audience and the "city of Boston" to damnation, and carried her off despite the agonized pleas of his "rival," Olive Chancellor. James had also ex-pressed his dislike for the happy Cambridge marriage which ended Howells's novel, and now he closed *The Bostonians* with the ironic fear that the tears which Verena wept as she fled with Ransom "were not the last she was destined to shed."[87]

In rediscovering Boston, then, James seems to have glanced at How-ells's map of New England, *The Undiscovered Country*. He may have seen unfulfilled possibilities in that novel's satiric opening sketch of Boston spiritualism, which was part of the patchwork of enthusiasms to have caught his own eye in the early 1870's. Probably equally useful was Howells's adaptation of the pattern of magnetic romance. That pattern had often given form to melodramatic attacks on mesmerism and spiritualism in such works as Fitz-James O'Brien's "Bohemian"

[85] Higginson, pp. 793–94.
[86] Brooks Adams, "The Undiscovered Country," *International Review* IX (August 1880), 151–52.
[87] James, *The Bostonians*, pp. 445, 449.

(1853), or T. S. Arthur's potboiler, *The Angel and the Demon* (1858). Also available for serious fiction, the magnetic pattern had already proved useful to Hawthorne, Howells, and James himself (in "Professor Fargo") in a sequence of closely related works dealing with major social, religious, and psychological issues. It remained for James to strike a more clinical note in *The Bostonians* by allowing Verena's "mediumistic possession" to originate in her own consciousness rather than in external "magnetism."

At the same time, however, James's satiric attitude toward reform in *The Bostonians* was more reminiscent of such writers as Orestes Brownson and Bayard Taylor than of Hawthorne or Howells. He had faulted Hawthorne for failing to realize the satiric potential of the early Brook Farm scenes of *The Blithedale Romance*,[88] and he had criticized Howells for abandoning the grotesque spiritualistic setting of the first part of *The Undiscovered Country*.[89] Now his own ironic treatment of occult and reform movements as absurd legacies of an earlier era put the finishing touches to Orestes Brownson and Bayard Taylor's satiric histories of the radical impulse of the 1850's. Selah Tarrant and the collection of anachronistic "witches and wizards, mediums, and spirit-rappers, and roaring radicals" presided over by Miss Birdseye were but the aging remnants of the demonically inspired band of "enthusiasts and fanatics, socialists and communists, abolitionists and anti-hangmen, radicals and women's-rights men of both sexes"[90] against whom Orestes Brownson's spirit-rapper had warned the public in 1854. Bayard Taylor, looking back to 1853 as the high point of radical enthusiasm, had held up to retrospective ridicule the same kinds of reformers, without their demonic ambience, in *Hannah Thurston* (1863).

Thus *The Bostonians* had a double historical focus. Written in the 1880's it was set in the previous decade. But its image of the early 1870's reflected the 1850's as well. Just as its feminist orator was modeled in part on Cora Hatch as she had been a generation earlier, so its study of reform and occultism included the same enthusiasms and attitudes caught at apogee by Brownson and Taylor. And its use

[88] James, *Hawthorne*, pp. 88, 137.
[89] James to Howells, July 2, 1880.
[90] Orestes Brownson, *The Spirit-Rapper* (Detroit, 1884), p. 29.

of the reform "idiom," described by Marius Bewley as "undoubtedly in touch with the facts as they were,"[91] was perhaps equally in touch with the facts as they had been according to the satirists of an earlier day. By 1886, after all, "spirit-rapping" was a memory for most people, even for spiritualists.[92]

Indeed, James's general attitude toward reform was strikingly similar to Bayard Taylor's. In *Hannah Thurston* Taylor had characterized women's rights, spiritualism, and other enthusiasms as typical "peculiarities" of an American villatic culture which placed more value on intellectual "activity" than on intellectual "development."[93] In the first part of his novel, James placed the same provincial eccentricities in Boston. And he had the temerity to identify them with the revered Elizabeth Peabody ("Miss Birdseye"), implying with his title that his seedy enthusiasts were representative or quintessential Bostonians. (Three decades earlier, the pseudonymous author of *Lucy Boston; or, Women's Rights and Spiritualism, Illustrating the Follies and Delusions of the Nineteenth Century*, had struck at Boston's reformers and the suffragette Lucy Stone through *his* title.)

Despite the difference in setting, in fact, readers of *The Bostonians* who could remember *Hannah Thurston* might have noticed some surprising similarities. In both works a strong-minded man, disgusted by women's rights, spiritualism, and temperance, and distrustful of reformers in general, successfully won a musically voiced feminist orator away from her silly and sinister associates. Taylor had made sincere Quakerism rather than irresponsible trance the basis of his heroine's personality. Nonetheless, Ransom's belittlement of women's capacity for public life and his appreciation of their domestic functions was only a more aggressive and ironic version of the views of Taylor's gentlemanly and wooden Max Woodbury. (James, of course, treated Ransom himself with irony, while Taylor meant everything that

[91] Bewley, *The Complex Fate*, p. 14.
[92] Oscar Cargill pointed out that "Van Wyck Brooks was the first to emphasize the fact that *The Bostonians* is not a report on the reform movement but on the late stragglers and queer continuators of the movement" (*The Novels of Henry James*, p. 131). But the anachronistic quality of the report itself has gone unnoticed. Spiritualism had always been a "queer" companion of reform, ever since 1850, and had been so satirized.
[93] Bayard Taylor, *Hannah Thurston*, I, vi, 192.

Woodbury said.) And though Selah Tarrant has been shown by Marius Bewley to have descended from Hawthorne's Westervelt, it is a curious fact that Tarrant's career resembled more closely that of Dyce, Taylor's itinerant magnetic medium. Both were or had been associated with a communal free-love society ("Aqueanda" and "Cayuga")[94] suggestive of the Oneida Community. Both were veterans of fraudulent dark séances in which furniture moved, music played, and invisible hands touched the living. Through such séances Dyce had recruited for Aqueanda the foolish Mrs. Merryfield, who had gone from respectable abolitionism to such panaceas as graham flour, the water cure, and spiritualism; Tarrant had married the daughter of an old-time abolitionist, had reduced her to participation in the fugitive religious, social, and dietary experiments of "humanitary Bohemia," and had relied on her to assist him in his séances by moving furniture and touching sitters in the dark.

James had probably read *Hannah Thurston* during his apprentice years—it was exactly the sort of novel to strike the attention of a young writer who hoped to become an American Balzac. (He did allow Olive Chancellor to quote from Taylor's translation of *Faust*.)[95] On the other hand, the figure of the sinister magnetic medium had long existed as a stereotype in the popular as well as the literary imagination, nourished from such diverse sources as Benjamin Hatch's unmasking of *Spiritualists' Iniquities* (1859) and Hawthorne's romances. Also conventional in anti-reform satire was the rescue of the innocent maiden from the clutches of radicals of one sort or another. And to the extent that Taylor's novel and his earlier "Confessions of a Medium" (1860) had reflected the image of spiritualism projected by Benjamin Hatch's depiction of his ex-wife Cora in the grasp of demonically possessed mediums and believers, they had shared a source closely related to the background of *The Bostonians*.

Whether or not memories of *Hannah Thurston: A Story of Ameri-*

---

[94] Ibid., II, 52; James, *The Bostonians*, p. 72. In reviewing Charles Nordhoff's *Communistic Societies of the United States* (New York, 1875), James had noted that the Oneida Community, led by the "very skilful and (as we suppose it would say) 'magnetic'" John Humphrey Noyes, was "prosperous" but "morally and socially . . . hideous" (Henry James, *Literary Reviews and Essays on American, English and French Literature*, ed. Albert Mordell [New York, 1957], p. 266).
[95] James, *The Bostonians*, p. 85.

can Life lurked at or below the level of James's consciousness as he wrote his "American" story, these similarities in plot, character, and satiric theme provide further evidence of the extent to which *The Bostonians*, despite its insight into sexual politics and trance psychology, was essentially a backward look at one phase of American life along lines already established by other writers. As such it shaped its spiritualistic materials according to the traditional patterns of magnetic romance and anti-reform satire. Only the comic séance and the humorous poltergeist of the literary comedians, recently revived by Mark Twain in *Life on the Mississippi* and *Adventures of Huckleberry Finn* and still to be apotheosized in his "Schoolhouse Hill" (1898) manuscript, were absent from James's synthesis of the ways in which American writers had responded to the spiritualistic movement since its beginning.

Though oriented toward the past, James's ironic sense of spiritualism as a decaying institution accurately reflected the low estate to which the movement had fallen by 1886. Selah Tarrant's wife could fondly remember "the darkened room, the waiting circle, the little taps on the table and wall, the little touches on cheek and foot, the music in the air. . . ."[96] Selah, of course, had been forced out of professional mediumship by "a committee of gentlemen who had investigated the phenomena of the 'materialization' of spirits, some ten years before, and had bent the fierce light of the scientific method upon him."[97] Here James the omniscient satiric narrator, evidently failing to distinguish between his own restrospection and that of his characters, anachronistically revealed his awareness of the Katie King controversy: materialization séances had not yet been devised "ten years before" the unspecified year of "187-" from which the Tarrants were looking back; but the disastrous exposure of Katie's materializations as a fraud perpetrated by a mediumistic married couple—the very scandal which had undone Robert Dale Owen and led to Howells's *Undiscovered Country* and Edward Bellamy's *Miss Ludington's Sister* (1884)[98]—had occured in the winter of 1874–75, just a decade before *The Bostonians* was composed. Since Katie's downfall, spiritualism

[96] Ibid., p. 73.
[97] Ibid., p. 154.
[98] Edward Bellamy, *Miss Ludington's Sister* (Boston, 1884).

had become a risky way of life for professional mediums ever more likely to be identified by press and police as conjurors and swindlers, and a way of undoctrinal consolation for the bereaved. Societies of believers continued to hold meetings, picnics, and summer camps, but with the years the crowds grew older and smaller.

To be sure, individual figures here and there kept alive the old millennial enthusiasm. Isabella Beecher Hooker was still expecting to rule a spiritual matriarchy,[99] and in 1887, a year after *The Bostonians* appeared, Cora Hatch (now Mrs. Richmond) petitioned the governor of Illinois for clemency in the case of the Haymarket anarchists.[100] In the 1890's Benjamin Orange Flower, editor of the reformist *Arena*, published a good deal of spiritualistic and psychical material as one phase of the reform effort. Disturbed by what he thought was the overly skeptical approach of the Society for Psychical Research, Flower organized a shortlived rival organization, the American Psychical Society. Saying that mediums had received harsh treatment at the hands of writers like Howells and James, Flower persuaded Hamlin Garland to undertake the séance investigations which continued to fascinate him (unprofitably for his fiction) long after his populist zeal had atrophied.[101] As for the radical spiritualist in fiction, John Hay characterized a labor unionist as a fraudulent materializing medium and free-loving libertine in *The Bread-Winners* (1883);[102] Hay's skeptical account of a séance was in the realistic vein, but his attempt to attach spiritualism to the labor movement merely indicated the persistence of the old pattern of anti-reform satire.[103] Generally speaking, with the defeats of Victoria Woodhull and Robert Dale Owen, spiritualism's radical social millenarianism and intermittent public excitement over new manifestations promising empirical proof of immortality had declined to the level of tired reminiscence suggested in 1886 by *The Bostonians*. Two years later, when Margaret Fox brought four decades of spiritualism to a close by announcing to a capacity audience at the Academy of Music in New York that in her own and

[99] Andrews, pp. 61–62.
[100] Barrett, pp. 478–79.
[101] Hamlin Garland, *Forty Years of Psychic Research* (New York, 1936), pp. 1–6.
[102] John Hay, *The Bread-Winners* (New York, 1883).
[103] John Hay, *The Bread-Winners*, Biographical edition (New York, 1899), pp. 99–114.

her sister Kate's toe joints had resided the mysterious intelligence responsible for ushering in the era of rapping spirits at mid-century, it was widely if erroneously claimed that spiritualism had suffered its "Death-Blow."[104]

In those forty years, however, its mediums, manifestations, believers, and doctrines had caught the attention of a good many American writers, providing some of them with memorable personal experience and significant literary material. Only Orestes Brownson, Herman Melville, and William Dean Howells had dealt with the problem of spiritualism as an unorthodox response to increasing religious doubt. More typically it had been seen as a social phenomenon—by humorists as a ludicrous departure from common sense, by serious satirists as evidence of foolish or sinister tendencies in American life. Even at the height of skeptical literary realism, though, the subject of spiritualism had retained a sense of occult mystery as it impelled Howells and James prophetically to explore new psychological dimensions, for if the puzzle of mediumistic personality could be explained neither by spiritual agency, nor by externally imposed "magnetism," nor by simple fraud, the answer lay somewhere in the unconscious mind of the medium herself.

Most American writers, whatever their particular responses to the movement, had been critical to some degree. And from James Russell Lowell's spoof of the Fox sisters to Mark Twain's burlesques of spurious séances and poltergeists, from Hawthorne's late romances and Fitz-James O'Brien's ghostly science-fiction to the anti-reform satires of Bayard Taylor and Henry James, they had shaped their criticisms through well-defined humorous, occult, and satiric patterns. As striking as this formal and thematic continuity, moreover, was the topical coherence of these works as a group. To a surprising extent, these literary manifestations of spiritualism had been elicited under the mediumship of writers inspired by a few (and for the most part closely related) figures of importance in the movement's history— the Fox sisters, Eliakim Phelps, Andrew Jackson Davis, Judge John

[104] Reuben Briggs Davenport, *The Death-Blow to Spiritualism, Being the True Story of the Fox Sisters as Revealed by Authority of Margaret Fox Kane and Catherine Fox Jencken* (New York, 1888); Earl Wesley Fornell, *The Unhappy Medium: Spiritualism and the Life of Margaret Fox* (Austin, Tex., 1964), pp. 174–81.

Edmonds, Thomas Lake Harris, Robert Dale Owen, Ada Hoyt Foye, J. V. Mansfield, Victoria Woodhull, and Cora L. V. Hatch.

By the time Margaret Fox's confession had threatened to lay it to rest, the spiritualistic movement had already been given a kind of immortality by some of the major writers of two literary generations in America.

SOURCES CITED

Adams, Brooks. "The Undiscovered Country." *International Review* IX (August 1880), 149–54.

Alcott, Amos Bronson. *The Letters of A. Bronson Alcott.* Edited by Richard L. Herrnstadt. Ames, Iowa, 1969.

Allen, Gay Wilson. *William James: A Biography.* New York, 1967.

American Whig Review XIV (December 1851), 491–93.

"Among the Materializers." *Nation* XXXVIII (January 3, 1884), 9–10.

Andrews, Kenneth R. *Nook Farm: Mark Twain's Hartford Circle.* Cambridge, Mass., 1950.

"An Apology for Vagrant Spirits." *Knickerbocker* XL (November 1852), 385.

Appleton, Thomas Gold. Letter to William Dean Howells, February 23, 1880. Houghton Library.

————. *A Sheaf of Papers.* Boston, 1875.

Arthur, Timothy Shay. *The Angel and the Demon: A Tale of Modern Spiritualism.* Philadelphia, 1858.

Arvin, Newton. *Herman Melville.* New York, 1950.

B., E. L. "To the Rapping Spirits." *Knickerbocker* XXXVII (April 1851), 311.

Bacon, Henry. "The Mysterious Bell Ringing." *Gleason's Pictorial Magazine* IV (June 25, 1853), 403.

Ballou, Adin. *An Exposition of Views Regarding the Principal Facts,*

Causes, and Peculiarities Involved in Spirit Manifestations. Boston, 1852.

Banta, Martha. "Henry James and 'The Others.'" *New England Quarterly* XXXVII (June 1964), 171–84.

———. "The Two Worlds of Henry James: A Study in the Fiction of the Supernatural." Ph.D. dissertation: Indiana University, 1964.

Barnum, Phineas Taylor. *The Humbugs of the World.* London, 1866.

Barrett, Harrison D. *Life Work of Mrs. Cora L. V. Richmond.* Chicago, 1895.

Beecher, Charles. A *Review of the "Spiritual Manifestations."* New York, 1853.

———. *Spiritual Manifestations.* Boston, 1879.

Bellamy, Edward. Letters to William Dean Howells, August 21, 1881; March 18, 1884; March 22, 1884; April 10, 1884. Houghton Library.

[———.] "Literary Notices." *Springfield Union,* August 21, 1875, p. 6.

———. *Miss Ludington's Sister: A Romance of Immortality.* Boston, 1884.

[———.] "Recent Miracles." *Springfield Union,* August 11, 1874, p. 4.

Bennett, George N. *William Dean Howells: The Development of a Novelist.* Norman, Okla., 1959.

Bennett, Mary Angela. *Elizabeth Stuart Phelps.* Philadelphia, 1939.

Benson, Ivan. *Mark Twain's Western Years.* Stanford, Calif., 1938.

Bewley, Marius. *The Complex Fate: Hawthorne, Henry James and Some Other American Writers.* London, 1952.

Bierce, Ambrose. *Tales of Soldiers and Civilians.* New York, 1891.

Bigelow, Jacob. *Eolopoesis: American Rejected Addresses. Now First Published from the Original Manuscripts.* New York, 1855.

Blair, Walter. *Mark Twain and Huck Finn.* Berkeley, 1960.

Blunsdon, Norman. A *Popular Dictionary of Spiritualism.* New York, 1962.

Boston Public Library. *The Tosti Engravings: The Gift of Mr. Thomas G. Appleton, Esq.* Boston, 1873.

Bowman, Sylvia E. *The Year 2000: A Critical Biography of Edward Bellamy.* New York, 1958.

Branch, E. Douglas. *The Sentimental Years: 1836–1860*. New York, 1934.

Brashear, Minnie M. *Mark Twain, Son of Missouri*. Chapel Hill, N.C., 1934.

Britten, Emma Hardinge. *Autobiography*. Edited by Margaret Wilkinson. Manchester, 1900.

———. *Modern American Spiritualism: A Twenty Years' Record of the Communion between Earth and the World of Spirits*. New York, 1870.

———. *Nineteenth Century Miracles; or, Spirits and Their Work in Every Country of the Earth*. New York, 1884.

Brooks, Van Wyck. *The Dream of Arcadia: American Writers and Artists in Italy, 1760–1915*. New York, 1958.

———. *Howells: His Life and World*. New York, 1959.

Brougham, John. *A Basket of Chips*. New York, 1855.

Brown, Herbert Ross. *The Sentimental Novel in America 1789–1860*. Durham, N.C., 1940.

Browne, Charles Farrar [Artemus Ward]. *The Complete Works of Artemus Ward*. London, 1884.

[Brownson, Orestes A.] *Brownson's Quarterly Review*, 3rd series, II (October 1854), 531.

[———.] *Brownson's Quarterly Review*, 5th series, I (April 1860), 265.

———. *The Spirit-Rapper: An Autobiography*. Detroit, 1884.

———. *The Works of Orestes A. Brownson*. Edited by Henry F. Brownson. Vol. XIX. Detroit, 1884.

Burgess, Gelett. *The Heart-Line: A Drama of San Francisco*. Indianapolis, 1907.

Cady, Edwin Harrison. *The Road to Realism: The Early Years, 1837–1885, of William Dean Howells*. Syracuse, 1956.

Capron, Eliab Wilkinson. *Modern Spiritualism: Its Facts and Fanaticisms, Its Consistencies and Contradictions*. Boston, 1855.

Capron, Eliab Wilkinson, and Barron, Henry D. *Singular Revelations: Explanation and History of the Mysterious Communion with Spirits*. 2nd ed. Auburn, N.Y., 1850.

Cargill, Oscar. *The Novels of Henry James*. New York, 1961.

————. "*The Turn of the Screw* and Alice James." In *The Turn of the Screw*, by Henry James. Edited by Robert Kimbrough. New York, 1966.

Carter, Everett. *Howells and the Age of Realism*. Philadelphia, 1954.

Chase, Emma Lester, and Parks, Lora Ferry, eds. *The Correspondence of Thomas Holley Chivers, 1838–58*. Providence, R.I., 1957.

Cheesebrough, Caroline. "Magnetic Influences." *Knickerbocker* XXXVII (May 1851), 430–41.

[Clark, Lewis Gaylord.] "Editor's Drawer." *Harper's* VI (March 1853), 562–68; (May 1853), 850–56; VII (June 1853), 133–37; (July 1853), 273–79; (October 1853), 707–13; VIII (December, 1853), 134–37.

[————.] "Letter from the Late Editor of the 'Bunkum Flag Staff.'" *Knickerbocker* XLIV (August 1854), 190–92.

[————.] "A Visit from the Mysterious Knockers." *Knickerbocker* XL (August 1852), 176–78.

Clemens, Clara. *My Father: Mark Twain*. New York, 1931.

Clemens, Samuel Langhorne [Mark Twain]. *Adventures of Huckleberry Finn*. New York, 1885.

————. *The American Claimant*. New York, 1892.

————. *Extracts from Captain Stormfield's Visit to Heaven*. New York, 1909.

————. *The Forgotten Writings of Mark Twain*. Edited by Henry Duskis. New York, 1963.

————. *In Defense of Harriet Shelley and Other Essays*. New York, 1929.

————. *Life on the Mississippi*. Boston, 1883.

————. *Life on the Mississippi*. Illustrated by Thomas Hart Benton, with an introduction by Edward Wagenknecht, and a number of previously suppressed passages, now printed for the first time, and edited with a note by Willis Wager. New York, 1944.

————. *Mark Twain in Eruption: Hitherto Unpublished Pages about Men and Events*. Edited by Bernard DeVoto. New York, 1940.

————. *Mark Twain's Autobiography*. Edited by Albert Bigelow Paine. 2 vols. New York, 1924.

————. *Mark Twain's Letters*. Edited by Albert Bigelow Paine. 2 vols. New York, 1917.

———. *Mark Twain's Mysterious Stranger Manuscripts*. Edited by William M. Gibson. Berkeley, 1969.

———. *Mark Twain's Notebook*. Edited by Albert Bigelow Paine. New York, 1935.

———. *Mark Twain's Which Was the Dream?* Edited by John S. Tuckey. Berkeley, 1967.

———. "Old Times on the Mississippi." *Atlantic Monthly* XXXV (January 1875), 69–73.

———. *Personal Recollections of Joan of Arc*. New York, 1896.

———. *Report from Paradise*. Edited by Dixon Wecter. New York, 1952.

———. "A True Story." *Atlantic Monthly* XXXIV (November 1874), 591–94.

———. *The Washoe Giant in San Francisco*. Edited by Franklin Walker. San Francisco, 1938.

Clemens, Samuel Langhorne, and Howells, William Dean. *Mark Twain-Howells Letters: The Correspondence of Samuel L. Clemens and William Dean Howells, 1872–1910*. Edited by Henry Nash Smith and William M. Gibson. 2 vols. Cambridge, Mass., 1960.

Cooke, Delmar Gross. *William Dean Howells: A Critical Study*. New York, 1922.

Cust, Lionel Henry. "Kirkup, Seymour Stocker (1788–1880)." *DNB*.

Damon, S. Foster. *Thomas Holley Chivers, Friend of Poe*. New York, 1930.

Davenport, Reuben Briggs. *The Death-Blow to Spiritualism, Being the True Story of the Fox Sisters as Revealed by Authority of Margaret Fox Kane and Catherine Fox Jencken*. New York, 1897.

Davidson, Edward Hutchins. *Hawthorne's Last Phase*. New Haven, 1949.

Davidson, Frank. "Melville, Thoreau, and 'The Apple-Tree Table.'" *American Literature* XXV (January 1954), 479–88.

Davis, Andrew Jackson. *The Philosophy of Spiritual Intercourse: Being an Explanation of Modern Mysteries*. New York, 1851.

———. *The Principles of Nature, Her Divine Revelations, and a Voice to Mankind*. 3rd ed. New York, 1847.

Davis, Richard Harding. *Vera, the Medium*. New York, 1908.

"The Debatable Land." *Nation* XV (October 24, 1872), 269–70.

Dods, John Bovee. *Spirit Manifestations Examined and Explained: Judge Edmonds Refuted.* New York, 1854.

Dorson, Richard M. *Jonathan Draws the Long Bow.* Cambridge, Mass., 1946.

Doten, Elizabeth. *Poems from the Inner Life.* 7th ed. Boston, 1869.

Doyle, Arthur Conan. *The History of Spiritualism.* 2 vols. New York, 1926.

————. *Our American Adventure.* New York, 1923.

Edel, Leon. *Henry James: The Conquest of London, 1870–1881.* Philadelphia, 1962.

————. *Henry James: The Untried Years, 1843–1870.* Philadelphia, 1953.

————. "Introduction." *The Ghostly Tales of Henry James.* New Brunswick, N.J., 1948.

"Editorial Notes." *Putnam's* II (November 1853), 563; (December 1853), 680–81; VII (January 1856), 103–4.

Edmonds, John Worth, and Dexter, George T. *Spiritualism.* 2 vols. New York, 1853, 1855.

Ellenberger, Henri F. *The Discovery of the Unconscious: The History and Evolution of Dynamic Psychiatry.* New York, 1970.

Elliott, Charles Wyllys. *Mysteries; or, Glimpses of the Supernatural.* New York, 1852.

Ellis, John B. *Free Love and Its Votaries; or, American Socialism Unmasked.* New York, 1870.

"The End of a Notable Humbug." *Springfield Union,* December 18, 1874, p. 2.

Ewer, Ferdinand C. *The Eventful Nights of August 20th and 21st, 1854; and How Judge Edmonds Was Hocussed; or, Fallibility of "Spiritualism" Exposed.* New York, 1855.

Ferris, William H. "Review of Modern Spiritualism." *Ladies Repository* XVI (January–June 1856), 46–52, 88–92, 139–44, 229–33, 297–304, 364–70.

Field, Kate. *Planchette's Diary.* New York, 1868.

Fiske, John. *Outlines of Cosmic Philosophy.* Boston, 1874.

Folio, Fred [pseud.]. *Lucy Boston; or, Women's Rights and Spiritualism, Illustrating the Follies and Delusions of the Nineteenth Century.* Auburn, N.Y., 1855.

Fornell, Earl Wesley. *The Unhappy Medium: Spiritualism and the Life of Margaret Fox.* Austin, Tex., 1964.

[Fox, Margaret.] *Memoir and the Love-Life of Doctor Kane: Containing the Correspondence, and a History of the Acquaintance, Engagement and Secret Marriage between Elisha K. Kane and Margaret Fox.* New York, 1866.

Franklin, H. Bruce, ed. *Future Perfect: American Science Fiction of the Nineteenth Century.* New York, 1966.

Fryckstedt, Olov W. *In Quest of America: A Study of Howells' Early Development as a Novelist.* Cambridge, Mass., 1958.

[Furness, Horace Howard.] *Preliminary Report of the Commission Appointed by the University of Pennsylvania to Investigate Modern Spiritualism in Accordance with the Request of the Late Henry Seybert.* Philadelphia, 1887.

Garland, Hamlin. *Forty Years of Psychic Research.* New York, 1936.

————. *The Shadow World.* New York, 1908.

————. *The Tyranny of the Dark.* New York, 1905.

Garrison, Wendell Phillips, and Garrison, Francis Jackson. *William Lloyd Garrison, 1805–1879: The Story of His Life.* 4 vols. New York, 1885–89.

Gauld, Alan. *The Founders of Psychical Research.* New York, 1968.

Gibson, William M. "Introduction." *Mark Twain's Mysterious Stranger Manuscripts.* Edited by William M. Gibson. Berkeley, 1969.

Graham's Magazine XLVI (May 1855), 472.

[Greeley, Horace.] "Modern 'Spiritualism.' " *Putnam's* I (January 1853), 59–64.

————. *Recollections of a Busy Life.* New York, 1868.

Grimm, Clyde L. "*The American Claimant*: Reclamation of a Farce." *American Quarterly* XIX (Spring 1967), 86–103.

[Griswold, Rufus Wilmot.] "Authors and Books." *International Monthly Magazine of Literature, Science, and Art* I (July 29, 1850), 138; II (February 1, 1851), 309.

Gurney, Edmund; Myers, F. W. H.; and Podmore, Frank. *Phantasms of the Living.* 2 vols. London, 1886.

Habegger, Alfred. "The Disunity of *The Bostonians.*" *Nineteenth Century Fiction* XXIV (September 1969), 193–209.

Hale, Susan, ed. *Life and Letters of Thomas Gold Appleton.* New York, 1885.

Hall, Trevor H. *The Spiritualists: The Story of Florence Cook and William Crookes.* London, 1962.

Hammond, Charles. *Light from the Spirit World: Comprising a Series of Articles on the Condition of Spirits and the Development of Mind in the Rudimental and Second Spheres.* Rochester, 1852.

————. *Light from the Spirit World: The Pilgrimage of Thomas Paine and Others to the Seventh Circle in the Spirit World.* Rochester, 1852.

Hansen-Taylor, Marie, and Scudder, Horace E., eds. *Life and Letters of Bayard Taylor.* 2 vols. Boston, 1884.

Hare, Robert. *Experimental Investigation of the Spirit Manifestations: Demonstrating the Existence of Spirits and Their Communion with Mortals.* New York, 1856.

Harlow, Virginia. *Thomas Sergeant Perry: A Biography.* Durham, N.C., 1950.

Harris, Thomas Lake. *An Epic of the Starry Heaven.* New York, 1854.

————. *A Lyric of the Golden Age.* New York, 1856.

————. *A Lyric of the Morning Land.* New York, 1856.

————. *Modern Spiritualism and the Power and the Glory of the Church of Christ.* London, 1860.

————. *The Wisdom of Angels.* New York, 1857.

[Harte, Francis Bret.] "Current Literature." *Overland Monthly* III (September 1869), 292–96.

[Hastings, Arthur.] "Birchknoll: A New Ghost Story of Old Virginia." *Harper's* XII (February 1856), 336–40.

Hatch, Benjamin. *Spiritualists' Iniquities Unmasked, and the Hatch Divorce Case.* New York, 1859.

Hawthorne, Julian. *Hawthorne and His Circle.* New York, 1903.

————. *A Messenger from the Unknown.* New York, 1892.

Hawthorne, Nathaniel. *The Blithedale Romance and Fanshawe.* Centenary edition of the works of Nathaniel Hawthorne. Edited by William Charvat et al. Columbus, Ohio, 1964.

————. *Dr. Grimshawe's Secret.* Edited by Julian Hawthorne. Boston, 1882.

————. *The Dolliver Romance.* Boston, 1876.

———. *The English Notebooks*. Edited by Randall Stewart. New York, 1941.

———. *The House of the Seven Gables*. Centenary edition of the works of Nathaniel Hawthorne. Edited by William Charvat et al. Columbus, Ohio, 1965.

———. *The Marble Faun*. 2 vols. Boston, 1860.

———. *Passages from the American Note-Books*. Boston, 1891.

———. *Passages from the French and Italian Note-Books*. Boston, 1893.

Hay, John. *The Bread-Winners*. Biographical edition. New York, 1899.

———. *A Poet in Exile: Early Letters of John Hay*. Edited by Caroline Ticknor, Boston, 1910.

[Hearn, Lafcadio.] "Among the Spirits." *Cincinnati Enquirer*, January 25, 1874, p. 8.

[———.] "Artful Ambidexterity: The Mysterious Manifestations of Spiritualism Exposed." *Cincinnati Enquirer*, July 4, 1874, p. 8.

[———.] "Spirit Photography." *Cincinnati Commercial*, November 14, 1875, pp. 1, 3.

Hequembourg, C. L. "The Necromancy of the Nineteenth Century." *New Englander* XII (February 1854), 33–44.

Higginson, Thomas Wentworth. "Howells' 'Undiscovered Country.'" *Scribner's* XX (September 1880), 793–95.

[Hill, T.] "Were They Crickets?" *Atlantic Monthly* XVII (April 1866), 397–406.

Hingston, Edward. *The Genial Showman, Being Reminiscences of the Life of Artemus Ward, and Pictures of a Showman's Career in the Western World*. New York, 1870.

Hoffman, Daniel G. *Form and Fable in American Fiction*. New York, 1961.

[Holmes, Oliver Wendell.] "The Professor at the Breakfast-Table." *Atlantic Monthly* III (January 1859), 85–96; (May 1859), 609–20.

———. "Thomas Gold Appleton." *Atlantic Monthly* LIII (June 1884), 848–50.

Hosmer, Elizabeth Ruth. "Science and Pseudo-Science in the Writings of Nathaniel Hawthorne." Ph.D. dissertation: University of Illinois, 1948.

"An Hour with 'the Spirits.'" *New York Tribune,* June 5, 1850, p. 1.

Howard, Leon. *Victorian Knight-Errant: A Study of the Early Literary Career of James Russell Lowell.* Berkeley, 1952.

Howells, William Dean. *Between the Dark and the Daylight: Romances.* New York, 1907.

————. *Dr. Breen's Practice.* Boston, 1881.

————. "Editor's Easy Chair." *Harper's* CIX (October 1904), 803–6; CXXV (November 1912), 958–61; CXXX (February 1915), 472–75; CXXXV (November 1917), 882–85; CXXXIX (August 1919), 445–48.

————. *Impressions and Experiences.* New York, 1896.

————. *The Landlord at Lion's Head.* New York, 1897.

————. Letter to Charles Dudley Warner, December 27, 1879. Watkinson Library.

————. Letters to Francis Jackson Garrison, May 21, 1874; December 28, 1874. Princeton University Library.

————. *Life in Letters of William Dean Howells.* Edited by Mildred Howells. 2 vols. New York, 1928.

————. *Literary Friends and Acquaintance.* New York, 1901.

————. *A Modern Instance.* Edited by William M. Gibson. New York, 1959.

————. *Questionable Shapes.* New York, 1903.

[————.] "Recent Literature." *Atlantic Monthly* XXXIII (February 1874), 230–43.

[————.] "*The Story of Kennett,* by Bayard Taylor." *Atlantic Monthly* XVII (June 1866), 775–78.

————. "Two Notable Novels." *Century* XXVIII (August 1884), 632–34.

————. *The Undiscovered Country.* Boston, 1880.

————. *Years of My Youth.* New York, 1916.

Howells, William Dean, and Clemens, Samuel Langhorne. "Colonel Sellers as a Scientist." In *The Complete Plays of W. D. Howells.* Edited by Walter J. Meserve. New York, 1960.

Howells, William Dean; James, Henry; Bigelow, John; Higginson, Thomas Wentworth; and others. *In After Days: Thoughts on the Future Life.* New York, 1910.

Huntington, Jedediah Vincent. *Alban: A Tale of the New World.* New York, 1851.

James, Alice. *The Diary of Alice James.* Edited by Leon Edel. New York, 1964.

James, Henry. *The Art of the Novel: Critical Prefaces of Henry James.* Edited by Richard P. Blackmur. New York, 1934.

————. *The Bostonians.* London, 1886.

————. *The Ghostly Tales of Henry James.* Edited by Leon Edel. New Brunswick, N.J., 1948.

————. *Hawthorne.* London, 1879.

————. "Is There a Life after Death?" In *In After Days: Thoughts on the Future Life,* by William Dean Howells, Henry James, John Bigelow, Thomas Wentworth Higginson, and others. New York, 1910.

————. Letter to William Dean Howells, July 2, 1880. Houghton Library.

————. *Literary Reviews and Essays on American, English, and French Literature.* Edited by Albert Mordell. New York, 1957.

————. *The Notebooks of Henry James.* Edited by F. O. Matthiessen and Kenneth B. Murdock. New York, 1947.

————. "Professor Fargo." *Galaxy* XVIII (August 1874), 233–53.

————. "The Siege of London." *Cornhill Magazine* XLVII (January–February 1883), 1–34, 225–56.

————. *The Turn of the Screw.* Edited by Robert Kimbrough. New York, 1966.

James, Henry, Sr. *Lectures and Miscellanies.* New York, 1852.

————. "Spiritualism New and Old." *Atlantic Monthly* XXIX (March 1872), 358–62.

James, William. *Principles of Psychology.* 2 vols. London, 1901.

Johnson, Samuel W. "Spiritualism Tested by Science." *New Englander* XVI (May 1858), 225–70.

Jones, John B. *Life and Adventures of a Country Merchant.* Philadelphia, 1875.

Jung-Stilling, Heinrich. *Theory of Pneumatology.* Translated by George Bush. New York, 1851.

Kaplan, Justin. Letter to the author, October 9, 1966.

————. *Mr. Clemens and Mark Twain: A Biography.* New York, 1966.
Knickerbocker XLV (March 1855), 301–2.
"Last Phases of the Philadelphia Sensation." *Springfield Union,* December 22, 1874, p. 4.
Lathrop, George Parsons. *A Study of Hawthorne.* Boston, 1876.
Lathrop, Rose Hawthorne. *Memories of Hawthorne.* Boston, 1897.
Lawton, George. *The Drama of Life after Death: A Study of the Spiritualist Religion.* New York, 1932.
Leopold, Richard W. *Robert Dale Owen: A Biography.* Cambridge, Mass., 1940.
Levin, Harry. *The Power of Blackness.* New York, 1958.
Lewis, E. E. *A Report of the Mysterious Noises Heard in the House of Mr. John D. Fox.* Canandaigua, N.Y., 1848.
[Lewis, Tayler.] "Editor's Table." *Harper's* VI (April 1853), 699–703.
Leyda, Jay, ed. *The Melville Log: A Documentary Life of Herman Melville.* 2 vols. New York, 1951.
"Literature and Logic of 'The Interior.'" *National Magazine* I (October 1852), 349–58.
Lively, Bob [pseud.]. "Mysterious Rappings Explained; or, An Artful Dodge." In *Dodge's Sketches,* issued with Robert Morris, *The Faithful Slave.* Boston, 1853.
Locke, David Ross [Petroleum V. Nasby]. *The Struggles (Social, Financial and Political) of Petroleum V. Nasby.* Boston, 1872.
Longfellow, Samuel. *Life of Henry Wadsworth Longfellow.* 3 vols. Boston, 1891.
Lowell, James Russell. *The Biglow Papers, Second Series.* Boston, 1867.
————. *The Complete Poetical Works of James Russell Lowell.* Boston, 1897.
————. *The Function of the Poet and Other Essays.* Edited by Albert Mordell. Boston, 1920.
————. *Letters of James Russell Lowell.* Edited by Charles Eliot Norton. 2 vols. New York, 1894.
————. *New Letters of James Russell Lowell.* Edited by M. A. DeWolfe Howe. New York, 1932.
————. *The Poetical Works of James Russell Lowell.* 2 vols. Boston, 1858.

[————.] "Witchcraft." *North American Review* CVI (June 1868), 176–232.

Lynn, Edith Willis, and Bazin, Henry, eds. *Alcott Memoirs, Posthumously Compiled from Papers, Journals, and Memoranda of the Late Dr. Frederick L. H. Willis.* Boston, 1915.

McCabe, Joseph. *Spiritualism: A Popular History from 1847.* London, 1920.

Mahan, Asa. *Modern Mysteries Explained and Exposed.* Boston, 1855.

Marryat, Florence. *Open! Sesame!* 3 vols. London, 1875.

————. *There Is No Death.* New York, 1891.

"Materializations in Philadelphia." *Religio-Philosophical Journal* XVI (July 25, 1874), 5.

Maynard, Theodore. *Orestes Brownson: Yankee, Radical, Catholic.* New York, 1943.

[Melville, Herman.] "The Apple-Tree Table." *Putnam's* VII (May 1856), 465–75.

————. *The Complete Stories of Herman Melville.* Edited by Jay Leyda. New York, 1949.

————. *Pierre; or, The Ambiguities.* New York, 1963.

Miller, Tobias [Uncle Toby]. "Spiritual Knockings." *Gleason's Pictorial Magazine* I (October 18, 1851), 247.

Mirville, Jules Eudes de. *Pneumatologie: Des Esprits et de leurs manifestations fluidiques.* Paris, 1853.

Mitchell, S. Weir. *The Autobiography of a Quack and the Case of George Dedlow.* New York, 1900.

[————.] "The Case of George Dedlow." *Atlantic Monthly* XVIII (July 1866), 1–11.

[————.] "Was He Dead?" *Atlantic Monthly* XXV (January 1870), 86–102.

"Modern Sorcerers." *Knickerbocker* XLIII (February 1854), 171.

"More about the 'Rapping.' " *New York Tribune,* April 27, 1850, p. 6.

"More 'Rappings'—in Connecticut." *New York Tribune,* April 22, 1850, p. 4.

Myers, F. W. H. *Human Personality and Its Survival of Bodily Death.* 2 vols. London, 1903.

————. "Hysteria and Genius." *Journal of the Society for Psychical Research* VIII (April 1897), 50–59.

———. "The Subliminal Consciousness: The Mechanism of Hysteria." *Proceedings of the Society for Psychical Research* IX (1893), 3–128.

Nadal, E. S. A *Virginian Village and Other Papers*. New York, 1917.

New York Times, October 14, 1858, p. 4; November 29, 1858, p. 4.

New York Tribune, November 25, 1858, p. 3; November 29, 1858, p. 7; December 2, 1858, p. 7; December 6, 1858, p. 5; January 4, 1859, pp. 4, 5; January 5, 1859, p. 3; January 8, 1859, p. 5; January 19, 1859, p. 6.

New York Weekly Tribune, July 3, 1858, pp. 2–3; October 2, 1858, pp. 2, 7.

Nordhoff, Charles. *Communistic Societies of the United States*. New York, 1875.

[North, William.] "The Living Corpse." *Putnam's* I (January 1853), 32–39.

Norton, Charles Eliot. Letter to William Dean Howells, June 24, 1880. Houghton Library.

———. *Letters of Charles Eliot Norton*. Edited by Sarah Norton and M. A. DeWolfe Howe. 2 vols. Boston, 1913.

Noyes, John Humphrey. *History of American Socialisms*. Philadelphia, 1870.

[O'Brien, Fitz-James.] "The Bohemian." *Harper's* XI (July 1855), 233–42.

[———.] "The Diamond Lens." *Atlantic Monthly* I (January 1858), 354–67.

[———.] "Fragments from an Unpublished Magazine." *American Whig Review* XVI (September 1852), 269.

———. *The Poems and Stories of Fitz-James O'Brien*. Edited by William Winter. Boston, 1881.

Owen, Robert Dale. *Beyond the Breakers: A Story of the Present Day*. Philadelphia, 1870.

———. *The Debatable Land between This World and the Next*. Philadelphia, 1871.

———. "An Earnest Sowing of Wild Oats." *Atlantic Monthly* XXXIV (July 1874), 67–78.

———. *Footfalls on the Boundary of Another World*. Philadelphia, 1860.

———. "How I Came to Study Spiritual Phenomena. A Chapter of

Autobiography." *Atlantic Monthly* XXXIV (November 1874), 578–90.

———. "Lecture." *Religio-Philosophical Journal* XVI (July 11, 1874), 5.

———. Letters to William Dean Howells, September 14, 1874; September 18, 1874; November 24, 1874; December 4, 1874; December 7, 1874; December 12, 1874; December 29, 1874; November 4, 1876. Houghton Library.

———. *Neurology: An Account of Some Experiments in Cerebral Physiology, by Dr. Buchanan*. London, 1842.

———. "Political Results from the Varioloid." *Atlantic Monthly* XXXV (June 1875), 660–70.

———. "Some Results from My Spiritual Studies. A Chapter of Autobiography." *Atlantic Monthly* XXXIV (December 1874), 719–31.

———. *Threading My Way: Twenty-seven Years of Autobiography*. New York, 1874.

———. "Touching Spiritual Visitants from a Higher Life. A Chapter of Autobiography." *Atlantic Monthly* XXXV (January 1875), 57–69.

Owen, Rosamond Dale. *My Perilous Life in Palestine*. London, 1928.

Paltsits, Victor, ed. *Family Correspondence of Herman Melville, 1830–1904, in the Gansevoort-Lansing Collection*. New York, 1929.

Pattee, Fred Lewis. *The Feminine Fifties*. New York, 1940.

[Peabody, A. P.] "Modern Necromancy." *North American Review* LXXX (April 1855), 512–27.

Peebles, James Martin. *What Is Spiritualism? Who Are the Spiritualists? And What Can Spiritualism Do for the World?* 5th ed. Battle Creek, Mich., 1910.

Perry, Thomas Sergeant. Letter to William Dean Howells, February 6, 1878. Houghton Library.

Phelps, Elizabeth Stuart. *Austin Phelps: A Memoir*. New York, 1891.

———. *Beyond the Gates*. Boston, 1883.

———. *The Gates Ajar*. Boston, 1869.

———. *Men, Women, and Ghosts*. Boston, 1869.

———. "Planchette." *Watchman and Reflector* XXXIX (September 3, 1868), 5.

Phelps, Oliver Seymour, and Servin, Andrew T. *The Phelps Family of America*. 2 vols. Pittsfield, Mass., 1899.

Pinkerton, Allan. *The Spiritualists and the Detectives*. New York, 1876.

Podmore, Frank. *Modern Spiritualism: A History and a Criticism*. 2 vols. London, 1902.

Porter, Katherine H. *Through a Glass Darkly: Spiritualism in the Browning Circle*. Lawrence, Kans., 1958.

Price, Harry, and Dingwall, Eric J., eds. *Revelations of a Spirit Medium*. Facsimile edition. London, 1922.

[Ripley, George.] "An Evening with the Spirits." *New York Tribune*, June 8, 1850, p. 4.

Richmond, Cora L. V. [Cora L. V. Tappan]. *Discourses through the Mediumship of Mrs. Cora L. V. Tappan*. Boston, 1876.

———— [Cora L. V. Tappan]. *Hesperia*. New York, 1871.

———— [Cora L. V. Hatch]. *A Lecture on Secession, by Gen. Andrew Jackson, Delivered at Dodsworth's Hall, on the Evening of Sunday, Jan. 19, 1861. Mrs. Cora L. V. Hatch, Medium*. New York, 1861.

Robbins, Rossell Hope. "The Rochester Rappings." *Dalhousie Review* XLV (Summer 1965), 153–64.

"The Rochester 'Rappings.' " *New York Tribune*, April 10, 1850, p. 3.

"The Rochester Rappings—Letter from Mr. Munn." *New York Tribune*, April 26, 1850, p. 6.

Roellinger, Francis X. "Psychical Research and 'The Turn of the Screw.' " In *The Turn of the Screw*, by Henry James. Edited by Robert Kimbrough. New York, 1966.

Sachs, Emanie. *The Terrible Siren: Victoria Woodhull*. New York, 1928.

Schiffman, Joseph. "Mutual Indebtedness: Unpublished Letters of Edward Bellamy to William Dean Howells." *Harvard Library Bulletin* XII (Autumn 1958), 363–74.

Schlesinger, Arthur M., Jr. *The Age of Jackson*. Boston, 1946.

————. *Orestes A. Brownson: A Pilgrim's Progress*. Boston, 1939.

Schneider, Herbert Wallace, and Lawton, George. *A Prophet and a Pilgrim: Being the Incredible History of Thomas Lake Harris and Laurence Oliphant; Their Sexual Mysticisms and Utopian Communities*. New York, 1942.

Seitz, Don C. *Artemus Ward (Charles Farrar Browne): A Biography and Bibliography.* New York, 1919.

Shillaber, Benjamin P. *Life and Sayings of Mrs. Partington and Others of the Family.* New York, 1854.

————. *Rhymes, with Reason and Without.* Boston, 1853.

Silver, Rollo. "Seven Letters of Walt Whitman." *American Literature* VII (March 1935), 76–81.

Southworth, E. D. E. N. *The Haunted Homestead and Other Nouvellettes, with an Autobiography of the Author.* Philadelphia, 1860.

"The Spirits in 1692 and What They Did at Salem." *Putnam's* VII (May 1856), 505–11.

"Spiritual Manifestations." *Southern Literary Messenger* XIX (July 1853), 385–95.

"Spiritual Materialism." *Putnam's* IV (August 1854), 158–72.

"Spiritualism in New York." *Religio-Philosophical Journal* XVI (July 11, 1874), 4–5.

"The Spiritualists Checkmated." *Harper's Weekly* I (July 11, 1857), 438.

Springfield Union, December 15, 1874, p. 4; December 16, 1874, p. 4; December 24, 1874, p. 4.

Stewart, Randall. "Introduction." *American Notebooks,* by Nathaniel Hawthorne. Edited by Randall Stewart. New Haven, 1932.

Stowe, Harriet Beecher. *My Wife and I.* New York, 1871.

————. "Spiritualism." *Christian Union,* n.s., II (September 3, 1870), 129–30; (September 10, 1870), 145–46; (September 24, 1870), 177–78.

Strong, George Templeton. *The Diary of George Templeton Strong.* Edited by Allan Nevins and Milton Halsey Thomas. 4 vols. New York, 1952.

"Table-Turning in France." *Harper's* XIV (May 1857), 767–72.

[Taylor, Bayard.] "Confessions of a Medium." *Atlantic Monthly* VI (December 1860), 699–715.

[————.] "The Experiences of the A. C." *Atlantic Monthly* IX (February 1862), 170–88.

————. *Hannah Thurston: A Story of American Life.* 3 vols. London, 1863.

[————.] "The Haunted Shanty." *Atlantic Monthly* VIII (July 1861), 57–72.

Taylor, William G. Langworthy. *Katie Fox, Epochmaking Medium, and the Making of the Fox-Taylor Record.* New York, 1933.

Thomson, Mortimer Neal [Q. K. Philander Doesticks, P.B.]. *Doesticks What He Says.* New York, 1855.

————. *Plu-ri-bus-tah: A Song That's by-No-Author.* New York, 1856.

————. *The Witches of New York.* New York, 1859.

Thoreau, Henry David. *Letters to Various Persons.* Boston, 1865.

————. *The Variorum Walden.* Edited by Walter Harding. New York, 1962.

"Those Rochester 'Rappings.'" *New York Tribune,* March 6, 1850, p. 1.

Ticknor, Caroline. *Poe's Helen.* New York, 1916.

Tilton, Eleanor M., and Currier, Thomas Franklyn, eds. *A Bibliography of Oliver Wendell Holmes.* New York, 1953.

"To All Our Readers and Correspondents." *Holden's Dollar Magazine* VI (September 1850), 573–74.

"Tolliwotte's Ghost." *Putnam's* V (April 1855), 421–26.

Trent, William Peterfield; Erskine, John; Sherman, Stuart P.; and Van Doren, Carl, eds. *The Cambridge History of American Literature.* Vol. II. New York, 1918.

Tuckey, John S. *Mark Twain and Little Satan: The Writing of "The Mysterious Stranger."* West Lafayette, Ind., 1963.

Underhill, A. Leah. *The Missing Link in Modern Spiritualism.* New York, 1885.

Vanderbilt, Kermit. *The Achievement of William Dean Howells: A Reinterpretation.* Princeton, 1968.

Walker, Franklin. *San Francisco's Literary Frontier.* New York, 1939.

Wallace, Alfred Russel. *Edgar Allan Poe: A Series of Seventeen Letters Concerning Poe's Scientific Erudition in Eureka and the Authorship of Leonainie.* New York, n.d.

"Want of Confidence." *Religio-Philosophical Journal* XIII (October 5, 1872), 8.

Watts, Charles Henry, II. *Thomas Holley Chivers: His Literary Career and His Poetry.* Athens, Ga., 1956.

Wecter, Dixon. *Sam Clemens of Hannibal*. Edited by Elizabeth Wecter. Boston, 1952.

Wells, Anna Mary. *Dear Preceptor: The Life and Times of Thomas Wentworth Higginson*. Boston, 1963.

[Whelpley, J. D.] "The Atoms of Chladni." *Harper's* XX (January 1860), 195–206.

Whiting, Lilian. *Kate Field: A Record*. Boston, 1899.

Whitman, Sarah Helen. *Edgar Poe and His Critics*. New York, 1860.

———. *Hours of Life and Other Poems*. Providence, R.I., 1853.

Whitman, Walt. *Leaves of Grass*. Edited by Harold E. Blodgett and Sculley Bradley. New York, 1968.

Whittier, John Greenleaf. "New England Supernaturalism." *United States Magazine and Democratic Review* XIII (November 1843), 515–20.

———. *The Supernaturalism of New England*. Boston, 1847.

Willis, Nathaniel Parker. *The Convalescent*. New York, 1859.

———. *The Rag-Bag*. New York, 1855.

Wilson, Edmund. *Patriotic Gore: Studies in the Literature of the American Civil War*. New York, 1962.

Wilson, Forrest. *Crusader in Crinoline: The Life of Harriet Beecher Stowe*. Philadelphia, 1941.

Wolle, Francis. *Fitz-James O'Brien: A Literary Bohemian of the Eighteen-Fifties*. Boulder, Colo., 1944.

Woodhull and Claflin's Weekly, II (November 19, 1870), 16; (December 17, 1870), 1, 16; (March 18, 1871), 6; (May 6, 1871), 16; III (June 3, 1871), 4–5; (June 10, 1871), 11; (July–November 1871); V (May 18, 1872), 13; (June 22, 1872), 11; VI (November 2, 1872), 8–13.

Zillah, the Child Medium: A Tale of Spiritualism. New York, 1857.

INDEX

Abolitionists: and spiritualism, 11, 23, 181; in fiction of Taylor, 100–101; of Twain, 185; of James, 218

Academy of Music: Margaret Fox confesses at, 119, 220

Adams, Brooks: on Howells's *The Undiscovered Country*, 127, 215; on male hero in fiction, 215

Afterlife: described by clairvoyants, 6; by spiritualists, 10, 12; by Doten, 17–18; by Edmonds, 66; by Phelps, 108–9, 180–81

—BURLESQUED: by Clark, 34; by Thomson, 36; by Browne, 38; by Twain, 157, 158–59, 166, 168–69, 179–80

Agassiz, Louis: and Boston test séances, 80, 98, 166; and Appleton, 130

Alcott, Amos Bronson: satirized by Brownson, 86; praises Davis, 105n

Aldrich, Thomas Bailey, 115

Alternate personality: revealed in trance, 117; Mark Twain and, 187–88; in James's *The Bostonians*, 204–6, 209–10; W. James on, 205–6; Society for Psychical Research and, 208. *See also* Mediumistic trance

American Association of Spiritualists: led by Woodhull, 108, 201

American Psychical Society: Garland and, 111n, 220

Andover Seminary, 109, 174–80 passim

Anti-spiritualistic satire: patterns of, 82, 84, 90, 99, 104–7, 140–42, 191–92; and reform, 84, 90, 99, 191–92; demonism and, 84, 99–100, 105–6; Howells and, 140–42, 147; Twain and, 185; James and, 191–92, 211, 212, 215, 216–19; and magnetic romance, 218. *See also* Afterlife; Comic séance

Appleton, Thomas Gold: as spiritualist, 62n, 129–31, 141; praises Howells's *The Undiscovered Country*, 126, 129, 131, 152; and Owen, 129, 130, 131, 144; Holmes on, 129; describes séance in "At the Medium's," 130, 141; Longfellow on, 130; Howells on, 130; in Howells's *The Rise of Silas Lapham*, 130; in Howells's *The Undiscovered Country*, 130–31

Arnold, Benedict: spirit of, 35, 36

Arthur, Timothy Shay: attacks spiritualism in *The Angel and the Demon*, 91–94, 95, 103, 104, 106, 216; and Hatch divorce case, 93; on child mediums, 93–94; and magnetic romance, 215; mentioned, 98